McGRAW-HILL'S ESSENTIAL

English
Irregular
Verbs

McGRAW-HILL'S ESSENTIAL

English Irregular Verbs

MARK LESTER, PH.D. • DANIEL FRANKLIN • TERRY YOKOTA

New York Chicago San Francisco Lisbon London Madrid Mexico City
Milan New Delhi San Juan Seoul Singapore Sydney Toronto

The *McGraw-Hill* Companies

Library of Congress Cataloging-in-Publication Data

Lester, Mark.
    McGraw-Hill's essential English irregular verbs / Mark Lester, Daniel Franklin,
Terry Yokota.
        p.   cm.
    Includes index.
    ISBN-10: 0-07-160286-0 (alk. paper)
    ISBN-13: 978-0-07-160286-0
    1. English language—Verb.   I. Franklin, Daniel.   II. Yokota, Terry.
III. Title.
    PE1271.L47   2010
    428.2—dc22
                          2009052291

1 2 3 4 5 6 7 8 9 10 11 12 13 14 15   WFR/WFR   1 9 8 7 6 5 4 3 2 1 0

ISBN   978-0-07-160286-0
MHID   0-07-160286-0

Interior design by Village Bookworks, Inc.

Contents

Preface

McGraw-Hill's Essential English Irregular Verbs contains basic conjugations and comprehensive usage patterns for 188 irregular verbs—all the irregular verbs that you are likely to encounter in even the most extensive reading. We have excluded only archaic and rarely used verbs, like *shrive* ("offer the religious rite of confession to") and *smite* ("to attack and kill/defeat," usually encountered only in the King James Bible of 1611).

In addition to the basic conjugation of each verb, *McGraw-Hill's Essential English Irregular Verbs* provides two unique features:

• A complete listing of the complements for each verb

Verb complements are grammatical structures that verbs use to make correct, meaningful sentences. Irregular verbs in English have 16 basic complements, plus dozens of combinations of these. For instance, the verb *make,* when it means "force, cause," uses two complements together: an object and an infinitive. The infinitive, however, must be in its base form, that is, used without the *to* that normally accompanies an infinitive.

OBJECT + BASE-FORM INFINITIVE   The teacher made **the students *sit quietly*.**

Most English learners, even advanced ones, make the mistake of using *to* with the infinitive, because that is the more common complement. *McGraw-Hill's Essential English Irregular Verbs* and its companion, *The Big Book of English Verbs,* are the only books that provide the correct complement in a useful format.

• A listing of the important phrasal verb constructions for each verb

Phrasal verbs are idiomatic combinations of verbs plus adverbs or prepositions. For example, the phrasal verb *show up* can mean "to arrive," even though nothing in the meaning of *show* or *up* would lead you to expect this meaning.

Moreover, there are important grammatical differences between phrasal verbs that consist of a verb + an adverb (separable phrasal verbs) and those that consist of a verb + a preposition (inseparable phrasal verbs). If the second element in a phrasal verb is an adverb, the adverb can (and in some cases MUST) be placed after the object. If the second element is a preposition, however, it can NEVER be moved away from the verb. *McGraw-Hill's Essential English Irregular Verbs* not only gives the meaning of every phrasal verb, but also indicates which combinations are separable and which are inseparable.

A 2007 study by Harvard scientists revealed that, over the centuries, English irregular verbs have been slowly becoming regular. *Help* and *work* were once irregular verbs! The scientists predict that *wed* will probably be the next irregular verb to become completely regular: *Wed ~ wed ~ have wed* will become *wed ~ wedded ~ have wedded.* The more common irregular verbs, like *be* and *come,* will take thousands of years to become regular. In the meantime, you have *McGraw-Hill's Essential English Irregular Verbs* to help you use all of these important verbs correctly.

Mark Lester
Daniel Franklin
Terry Yokota

The English Irregular Verb

REGULAR VS. IRREGULAR VERBS

A **regular verb** forms its past tense and past participle by adding *-d* or *-ed* to its base form. This ending may be pronounced /d/ (*cared, happened, viewed*), /ud/ (*committed, needed, listed*), or /t/ (*mixed, searched, slipped*). See pages 3–4 for details.

An **irregular verb** forms its past tense or past participle, or both, in an unpredictable way: by adding no ending at all, by changing the vowel of the base form, by adding a different ending, or by using a combination of these methods (*let ~ let ~ have let, meet ~ met ~ have met, swim ~ swam ~ swum, blow ~ blew ~ have blown*).

A verb is irregular based on its pronunciation, not on its spelling; for example, *lay* (*laid ~ have laid*) and *pay* (*paid ~ have paid*) are regular, because they add /d/ to their base forms for their past tense and past participle—like *stay* (*stayed ~ have stayed*)—even though the *ayed* is spelled *aid*.

Compound verbs, like *overeat* (< *eat*), *outsell* (< *sell*), and *withhold* (< *hold*), form their past tenses and past participles like their root verbs; for example, *overeat ~ overate ~ have overeaten*. A few high-frequency compound verbs, like *broadcast, overcome,* and *understand,* are included in the 188 irregular verbs presented here.

VERB FORMS AND TENSE USAGE

The Six Basic Verb Forms

Six basic verb forms are used to create the entire tense system of English: base form, present, past, infinitive, present participle, and past participle. These forms are illustrated in the following chart by the regular verb *walk* and the irregular verb *fly*.

BASE FORM	walk	fly
PRESENT	walk | walks	fly | flies
PAST	walked	flew
INFINITIVE	to walk	to fly
PRESENT PARTICIPLE	walking	flying
PAST PARTICIPLE	walked	flown

See "Guide to Conjugations" on page 18.

Base Form

The base form of a verb is its form in a dictionary entry. For example, if you looked up *sang,* the dictionary would refer you to the base form *sing.*

The base form is also the source (or base) for the present (with a few exceptions), infinitive, and present participle of the verb, whether the verb is regular or irregular.

The base form is used as a verb in three ways.

(1) It follows certain helping verbs, the most important being the **modal auxiliary verbs,** or **modals** for short: *can/could, may/might, will/would, shall/should,* and *must.* (Modal verbs themselves have no base form, infinitive, present participle, or past participle; they have only present and past forms.) Note the base form of the verb *be* in the following sentences.

I may **be** a little late.
He will **be** in New York all week.
You must **be** more careful.

Other verbs followed by the base form of a verb include *dare* (with *not*), *need* (with *not*), and *help*.

We need not **be** silent on the issue.

(2) The base form is used in imperatives (commands).

Be good!
Come here, please.
Ring the bell.

(3) Less commonly, the base form is used as a complement of certain verbs.

OBJECT + BASE-FORM INFINITIVE   The queen made **the guests** *wait* in the hall.

A base-form infinitive is an infinitive minus the *to*. If an infinitive including the word *to* were substituted for the base-form infinitive in the example above, the resulting sentence would be ungrammatical.

X The queen made **the guests** *to wait* in the hall.

Present

With the sole exception of the verb *be*, the present form of all verbs, including irregular verbs, is derived directly from the base form. The main difference between the present and base forms is that the third-person singular present form adds *-s* or *-es* to the base form of the verb; all other present forms are identical to the base form.

The base form of *be* is different from all of its present tense forms.

	SINGULAR	PLURAL
FIRST PERSON	I **am**	we **are**
SECOND PERSON	you **are**	you **are**
THIRD PERSON	he/she/it **is**	they **are**

Both the pronunciation and the spelling of the third-person singular present ending are predictable. If the base form ends in a sibilant sound (*s, z, x, sh, ch, tch,* or *j* (as in *judge*)), the ending is pronounced as a separate syllable rhyming with *buzz*. The ending is spelled *-es,* unless the base form already ends in *-e,* in which case only *-s* is added.

BASE FORM	THIRD-PERSON SINGULAR PRESENT FORM
lose	lose**s**
freeze	freeze**s**
beseech	beseech**es**
catch	catch**es**

If the base form ends in a voiceless consonant sound other than a sibilant, the ending is pronounced /s/ and is spelled *-es.* The voiceless consonants are usually spelled with a *p, t, ck, k, f,* or *gh* (when pronounced /f/).

keep	keep**s**
beat	beat**s**
seek	seek**s**
take	take**s**

If the base form ends in a voiced consonant other than a sibilant or in a pronounced vowel (as opposed to a silent final -*e*), the ending is pronounced /z/ and is spelled -*s*.

forbid	forbids
bend	bends
dig	digs
feel	feels
swim	swims
mean	means
prove	proves
pay	pays
flee	flees
fly	flies
throw	throws
strew	strews

Note that if the base form ends in -*y* without a preceding vowel, the -*y* changes to -*ie* before the -*s* ending (see *fly* above).

A few verbs have irregular third-person singular present forms.

be	**is**
have	**has**

Two verbs have irregular pronunciations in the third-person singular present form.

do	**does** (rhymes with *buzz*)
say	**says** (rhymes with *fez*)

Past

There are two types of past forms: regular and irregular.

Regular verbs form the past tense by adding -*ed* to the base form (or simply -*d* if the base form already ends in -*e*).

BASE FORM	REGULAR PAST FORM
open	open**ed**
place	place**d**

The regular past ending has three different, but completely predictable, pronunciations. If the base form ends in a /t/ or /d/ sound, the -*ed* is pronounced as a separate syllable rhyming with *bud*.

BASE FORM	PAST FORM PRONOUNCED AS A SEPARATE SYLLABLE
vote	vot**ed**
decide	decid**ed**

If the base form ends in a voiceless consonant sound other than /t/, the -*ed* is pronounced /t/. The final voiceless consonants are usually spelled with a *p, ck, k, s, sh, ch, tch, x, f,* or *gh* (when pronounced /f/).

BASE FORM	PAST FORM PRONOUNCED AS /t/
tap	tapp**ed**
attack	attack**ed**
miss	miss**ed**
match	match**ed**
cough	cough**ed**

Note that if the base form ends in a single consonant preceded by a stressed short vowel, the consonant is usually doubled to form the past: *permit ~ permitted, stop ~ stopped*.

If the base form ends in a pronounced vowel or in a voiced consonant sound other than /d/, the *-ed* is pronounced /d/. The voiced consonants are usually spelled with a *b, g, z, j, m, n, l,* or *r*.

BASE FORM	PAST FORM PRONOUNCED AS /d/
tie	tie**d**
enjoy	enjoy**ed**
kill	kill**ed**
care	care**d**

Note that if the base form ends in *-y* without a preceding vowel, the *-y* changes to *-ie* before the *-d* ending (*cry ~ cried*). Also note the spellings of the past forms of *lay* and *pay*: *laid* and *paid,* respectively.

The past forms of irregular verbs reflect older patterns of forming the past tense. These patterns have merged to such an extent that it is not practical to learn the past forms of irregular verbs on the basis of their historical patterns. Similarities exist, however, in how some irregular verbs form the past tense.

VOWEL CHANGE	ring	**rang**	sing	**sang**		
VOWEL CHANGE + **-d**	sell	**sold**	tell	**told**		
VOWEL CHANGE + **-t**	feel	**felt**	kneel	**knelt**		
	keep	**kept**	sleep	**slept**	sweep	**swept**
NO CHANGE	bet	**bet**	put	**put**	rid	**rid**

Following are the past forms of the 13 most common verbs in English, all irregular.

BASE FORM	PAST FORM
be	**was | were**
have	**had**
do	**did**
say	**said** (rhymes with *fed*)
make	**made**
go	**went**
take	**took**
come	**came**
see	**saw**
know	**knew**
give	**gave**
get	**got**
find	**found**

Infinitive

The infinitive of a verb consists of *to* + its base form. There are no exceptions—even the verb *be* is regular: *to be*.

BASE FORM	INFINITIVE
be	**to be**
fly	**to fly**
spend	**to spend**

Infinitives are used as complements of certain verbs.

I would like **to meet** your friend.
They invited us **to spend** the night.

Present Participle

The present participle is formed by adding *-ing* to the base form.

BASE FORM	PRESENT PARTICIPLE
be	be**ing**
do	do**ing**
fly	fly**ing**
spend	spend**ing**

Note that if a verb ends in a single consonant preceded by a stressed short vowel, the consonant is usually doubled: *bet ~ betting, dig ~ digging, forbid ~ forbidding*. If a verb ends in silent *-e*, the *-e* is dropped before the *-ing* ending: *come ~ coming, have ~ having, write ~ writing*.

The present participle is used in two ways. By far the more common is after a form of the verb *be* in the progressive tenses.

> The kids were **going** to the beach.
> I am **flying** to Chicago tomorrow.

Less common is the present participle's use as a complement of certain verbs.

> I hate **doing** the dishes every night.
> I saw Holly **speaking** with Christopher.

Past Participle

There are two types of past participles: regular and irregular.

Regular past participles are formed in exactly the same way as the regular past, that is, by adding *-ed* to the base form. To distinguish the two forms, remember that the past form can occur by itself, but the past participle almost always occurs after a form of *be* or *have*.

Like irregular past forms, irregular past participle forms are unpredictable. There is one generalization, however, that we can make about them. In older periods of English, most irregular past participles ended in *-en*. Today, about one third of irregular past participles still retain this *-en* ending. Thus, if an irregular verb form has an *-en* (or *-n*) ending, we know it is a past participle.

BASE FORM	PAST PARTICIPLE
choose	chos**en**
eat	eat**en**
fly	flow**n**
see	se**en**
speak	spok**en**

Past participles are used in three ways in English.

(1) They are used in the perfect tenses after the helping verb *have*.

> They have **flown** in from Pittsburgh for the wedding.
> We had **shut** the window earlier.
> He will have **broken** every record.

(2) Past participles are used in passive sentences after the helping verb *be*.

> Skirmishes are being **fought** at the border.
> Her play was **seen** by thousands of people.

(3) Much less common is the past participle's use as a complement of certain verbs.

> We need the car **taken** to the garage for an oil change.

Tense Formation and Usage

The term **tense** can have several different meanings, but we use **tense** to refer to any of the nine different verb constructions that result when the three logical time divisions (present, past, and future) are integrated with the three aspect categories of verbs (simple, perfect, and progressive—*simple* here means that it is not perfect or progressive). These nine tenses are illustrated in the following chart, with the first-person singular form of *fly*.

	SIMPLE	PERFECT	PROGRESSIVE
PRESENT	I fly	I have flown	I am flying
PAST	I flew	I had flown	I was flying
FUTURE	I will fly	I will have flown	I will be flying

The Three Simple Tenses

PRESENT TENSE

The most confusing feature of the present tense for English learners is that the simple present tense does not actually signify present time. Its three main uses are the following: (1) making factual statements and generalizations, (2) describing habitual actions, and (3) describing predictable future events or actions.

(1) The simple present tense is used to state objective facts that are not restricted by time.

> A mile **is** 5,280 feet.
> The sun **rises** in the east and **sets** in the west.

Similarly, the simple present tense is used to state facts that are true for the foreseeable future.

> She **teaches** algebra.

This sentence means, "She hasn't always taught algebra, and at some point in the future, she may teach another subject. Nevertheless, it is likely that she will continue teaching algebra indefinitely." Contrast this sentence with the following one, which uses the present progressive tense.

> She **is teaching** algebra.

This sentence means, "She is only teaching algebra temporarily, and she expects to teach another subject eventually."

The simple present tense is also used to make generalizations that are considered valid for the foreseeable future.

> I **know** Latin and Greek.
> Sneezing **spreads** germs.

(2) The simple present tense is used to describe habitual actions.

> Bob **reads** his e-mail first thing in the morning.

This sentence describes what Bob normally does first thing in the morning. It does not mean that Bob is reading his e-mail now, at this very moment. The sentence would still be valid if Bob were on vacation and hadn't read his e-mail in a week.

(3) The simple present tense is often used for near-future events or actions that one expects to happen.

> Our flight **leaves** at nine.
> I **go** home on Sunday.

Note that the simple present tense is not used for uncertain future events. For example, it is not used to describe future weather.

✗ It **freezes** tonight.

PAST TENSE

The simple past tense describes an event or action that was completed before the present moment in time; that is, the event or action has already taken place. The past tense can refer to a single point in past time.

I **mowed** the lawn yesterday afternoon.

The past tense can also refer to a span of time in the past, as long as it was completed before the present.

Ira **sang** in the choir for nearly 30 years.

This sentence means that Ira is no longer singing in the choir at this time.

In addition, the simple past tense has inherited one of the functions of the subjunctive from older periods of English: indicating that the speaker is talking hypothetically or even contrary to fact. This hypothetical use of the past tense does NOT indicate past time. Its most common use is in IF-CLAUSES.

If I **were** you, I **would** be sure that I **was** finished on time.

The use of *were* rather than the expected *was* survives from an old subjunctive form. Notice also that the other two verbs in the sentence are in the past tense, even though the sentence does not refer to past time.

FUTURE TENSE

The simple future tense consists of the helping verb *will* followed by the base form of the main verb.

I **will take** a taxi to the airport.
They **will meet** us at the restaurant.

The helping verb *will* is one of the nine modal auxiliary verbs: *can/could, may/might, will/ would, shall/should,* and *must.* Although *will* is used to form the future tense, any of the other eight modals can refer to future time.

I **can take** a taxi to the airport.
I **could take** a taxi to the airport.
I **may take** a taxi to the airport.
I **must take** a taxi to the airport.

Each of the nine modals has its own range of meanings, allowing English speakers to make a number of subtly different statements about the possibility, certainty, desirability, or necessity of a future action.

The Three Perfect Tenses

The three perfect tenses consist of a form of the helping verb *have* followed by the past participle of the main verb. The present tense form of *have* is used for the present perfect, the past tense form for the past perfect, and the future tense form for the future perfect.

PRESENT PERFECT TENSE

The present perfect tense consists of *have* or *has* followed by the past participle of the main verb. This tense is used to describe an action that began in the past and has continued up to the present time, with the implication that it will continue into the future. The best way to understand the present perfect tense is to compare it to the past tense.

PAST TENSE   John **took** a bus to work for five years.
PRESENT PERFECT TENSE   John **has taken** a bus to work for five years.

According to the past tense sentence, John no longer takes a bus to work; he is retired or he uses another means of transportation to get to work. According to the present perfect tense sentence, John still takes a bus to work and is expected to continue doing so into the foreseeable future.

PAST PERFECT TENSE

The past perfect tense consists of *had* followed by the past participle of the main verb. The most common use of this tense is to emphasize that an event in the past was completed before a more recent event took place.

> My parents **had left** for the airport before my plane landed.

This sentence describes two past-time events. The first event is the parents' leaving for the airport, and the second event is the plane landing. The use of the past perfect tense makes it clear that the first event was completed before the second one occurred. Note that the events can also be stated in reverse order.

> Before my plane landed, my parents **had left** for the airport.

FUTURE PERFECT TENSE

The future perfect tense consists of *will have* followed by the past participle of the main verb. This tense, which is rarely used, describes a future action or event that will be completed BEFORE a second future action, event, or time. The following sentence uses the future perfect tense to describe an event completed before a second event.

> The game **will have begun** before we get to the stadium.

Note that the two events can also be stated in reverse order.

> Before we get to the stadium, the game **will have begun**.

The following sentence uses the future perfect tense to describe an action completed before a specific time in the future.

> They **will have left** the deli by one o'clock.

The Three Progressive Tenses

The progressive tenses consist of a form of the helping verb *be* followed by the present participle of the main verb. The present progressive uses the present tense of *be*, the past progressive uses the past tense of *be*, and the future progressive uses the future tense of *be*.

The progressive tenses are used to describe an action in progress (hence the name **progressive**) at some present, past, or future time.

PRESENT PROGRESSIVE TENSE

The present progressive tense consists of *am, are,* or *is* followed by the present participle of the main verb. This tense can describe an action at the precise moment that the sentence is spoken.

> Turn the music down! I **am reading** a book.

The present progressive tense can also refer to a span of time that includes the present.

>The Cardinals **are winning** 4–1.

In addition, the tense is often used to describe future plans or events.

>We **are going** to Paris this June.
>Hurry, the taxi **is coming** in ten minutes.

PAST PROGRESSIVE TENSE

The past progressive tense consists of *was* or *were* followed by the present participle of the main verb. This tense refers to an action that took place at or during some time in the past, whether it occurred at a specific moment or during a span of time in the past.

>I **was sitting** at my desk by 9 o'clock.
>During the game, she **was knitting** a scarf.

The time in the past can be defined by another event.

>We **were eating** dinner when we heard the news.

The past progressive tense can also be used in an adverbial clause.

>We heard the news while we **were eating** dinner.

FUTURE PROGRESSIVE TENSE

The future progressive tense consists of *will be* followed by the present participle of the main verb. This tense describes an activity that will occur at some time in the future, whether it will occur at a specific moment or, more commonly, during a span of time in the future.

>Their plane **will be leaving** at 6:35.
>During the school year, I **will be spending** every weekend studying.

Often, the future time is defined by a present tense adverbial clause.

>Dad **will be sitting** on a bench while we are shopping.

The Intensive Tenses

The so-called intensive tenses consist of a form of the helping verb *do* followed by the base form of the main verb. The present intensive tense is formed with *do* or *does,* and the past intensive tense is formed with *did.* There is no future intensive tense, nor is the intensive used in the progressive tenses.

The intensive tenses are used in three ways.

(1) They emphasize the fact that the action of the verb is or was actually performed.

>She **does swim** for an hour every morning.
>I **did read** the novel.

(2) The intensive tenses are used with *not* to form the negative of the simple present and past tenses.

>They **do** not **go** to the library anymore.
>We **did** not **see** Larry at the mall.

(3) The intensive tenses are used to ask simple yes/no questions.

>**Does** the teacher **speak** loudly enough?
>**Did** all the children **write** about their summer vacation?

The Passive Voice

In traditional grammar, verbs have **voice**. Voice is determined by whether the subject is the performer of the action of the verb (**active voice**) or the receiver of the action (**passive voice**). Compare the following sentences.

ACTIVE VOICE	The dog **bit** the man.
PASSIVE VOICE	The man **was bitten** by the dog.

In the active voice sentence, the subject (the dog) performs the action of biting. In the passive voice sentence, the subject (the man) does not perform the action of biting; instead, he is the receiver of the action. The *by* phrase is not necessary and is, in fact, usually not used.

The passive voice is easily recognized, because it uses a form of the helping verb *be* immediately followed by the past participle form of the main verb—a combination found only in passive voice sentences.

PRESENT TENSE PASSIVE	My elbow **is hurt**.
PAST TENSE PASSIVE	My elbow **was hurt**.
FUTURE TENSE PASSIVE	My elbow **will be hurt**.

The progressive tenses may be used in the passive voice, although the future progressive tense usually sounds awkward.

PRESENT PROGRESSIVE TENSE PASSIVE	A movie **is being shown**.
PAST PROGRESSIVE TENSE PASSIVE	A movie **was being shown**.
FUTURE PROGRESSIVE TENSE PASSIVE	*?* A movie **will be being shown**.

The passive voice has two primary uses.

(1) It is used to switch attention from the subject of an active voice sentence to another part of the sentence (usually, but not always, the direct object).

ACTIVE VOICE	**The authors** sent the manuscript to Marisa.
PASSIVE VOICE	**The manuscript** was sent to Marisa.
PASSIVE VOICE	**Marisa** was sent the manuscript.

(2) The passive voice is used when the performer of the verb's action is not known.

This wool was spun in Italy.
The car was stolen yesterday afternoon.

VERB COMPLEMENTS

We use the term **complement** as a collective word for all the different grammatical structures required by verbs to make a grammatical sentence. **Complement** is much broader than the term **transitive**. In traditional grammar, a transitive verb must be followed by a direct or indirect object. The term **complement**, however, includes not only objects, but predicate adjectives, predicate nouns, infinitives, several types of clauses, and several types of adverbs. A verb may require one complement or more than one complement to make a grammatical sentence. Many intransitive verbs require no complement at all, for example, the intransitive verb *wept* in *John wept*.

The verb *put* with the sense "place, set" takes the double complement OBJECT + ADVERB OF PLACE, illustrated by the following sentence.

I put **my keys** *on the dresser*.

If either complement is deleted, the sentence is ungrammatical.

> ✗ I put *on the dresser.*
> ✗ I put **my keys.**

When you use the verb *put* to mean "place, set," you must put SOMETHING (an object) SOMEWHERE (an adverb of place).

Most English verbs may be used with more than one type of complement. The choice of complement type is determined by the particular meaning of a verb. If the meaning of the verb changes, the complement type(s) may change too, and vice versa: If the complement type changes, the verb's meaning often changes.

To illustrate the interconnection between verb meaning and complement type, consider the complements for the verb *hide*.

hide *keep oneself out of sight, conceal oneself*	The kids were hiding behind the tree.
	The thief hid in an abandoned warehouse.
hide _____ *put out of sight, conceal*	
OBJECT	The old lady hid **her money** under her mattress.
	Janet hid **her face** behind the newspaper.
hide _____ *keep secret*	
OBJECT	I tried to hide **my confusion** by changing the subject.
WH-CLAUSE	They wanted to hide **what they had done.**
hide _____ *keep from being seen*	
OBJECT	A sign hid **the entrance to his office.**
PASSIVE	My iPod had been hidden by a stack of books.

There are as many entries for a verb as there are distinct meanings, four in the case of *hide*. Each entry has its own group of complements that can be used with that particular meaning, including the possibility of no complement, as in the first entry for *hide*.

If a verb is followed by a blank line (_____), the verb with that particular meaning requires a complement to make the sentence grammatical. The types of complements that the meaning requires are given in small capital letters as subentries. For example, the third meaning of *hide* ("keep secret") can take either of two different complements: an OBJECT or a WH-CLAUSE (a noun clause beginning with a *wh*-word). To the right of the complement type are one or more sentences illustrating use of the complement. The words of the sentence that correspond to the complement are in bold. Using the third entry for *hide*, **my confusion** is an example of an OBJECT complement and **what they had done** is an example of a WH-CLAUSE complement. (See "Guide to Complements and Phrasal Verbs" on page 19.)

If a verb is NOT followed by a blank line, it is **intransitive**, that is, it does not require a complement to make the sentence grammatical. In this book, the intransitive meanings of a verb are listed before the meanings that require complements. In the example of *hide*, the fact that the first meaning ("keep oneself out of sight, conceal oneself") is not followed by a blank line means that the verb with this particular meaning is intransitive. In the example sentence *The kids were hiding behind the tree*, the adverbial expression *behind the tree* is not obligatory; the sentence would still be grammatical if we deleted it.

> The kids were hiding.

Most of the complement types in this book will be familiar to you, but some may require further explanation. Following is a list of special terms that you will encounter in the description of complements.

> THAT-CLAUSE This is a noun clause beginning with *that*.

>> I thought **that dinner was good, but a little too heavy.**

> PRESENT PARTICIPLE This term includes both present participles and gerunds (present participles modified by a possessive noun or pronoun).

>> Nothing beats **having lots of money in your wallet.** (PRESENT PARTICIPLE)
>> That beats **my trying to do it myself.** (GERUND)

> WH-CLAUSE This is a noun clause beginning with a *wh*-word (*who, whom, whose, what, which, when, where, why,* and *how* (which does not actually begin with *wh*)), as well as compounds of these words (*whoever, whomever, whatever,* etc.).

>> Did you hear **who won the game?**
>> We will grow **what sells the best.**
>> They will drink **whatever is available.**

> WH-INFINITIVE This is a noun clause beginning with a *wh*-word followed by an infinitive.

>> I told them **where to go.**
>> Dad taught us **how to tie knots.**

Complement Types

This book uses 16 basic, or single-element, complement types, which appear in bold in the example sentences. Many of these basic complement types can be combined and used together.

Single Grammatical Element Complements

ADVERB OF TIME	The fiscal year runs **from July 1 to June 30.**
ADVERB OF PLACE	He felt **in his pockets** for the key.
ADVERB OF PLACE TO/FROM	The refugees fled **into the woods.**
ADVERB OF MANNER	He reads **too softly for everyone to hear.**
OBJECT	I hurt **my shoulder.**
*for/in/of/to/with/*etc. OBJECT	The condemned man was pleading **for his life.** The problem lies **with senior management.**
REFLEXIVE PRONOUN	I flung **myself** into jazz.
PREDICATE NOUN	Her father was **a famous artist.**
PREDICATE ADJECTIVE	The moon was **bright.**
INFINITIVE	We sought **to find a better solution for the problem.**
THAT-CLAUSE	The police proved **that the driver was lying.**
WH-CLAUSE	We will soon know **who will get the job.** We will soon know **where the new office will be.**
WH-INFINITIVE	The author forgot **where to put the quotation marks.** I forget **how to change my password.**
PRESENT PARTICIPLE	I can't stand **not knowing what happened.**
PAST PARTICIPLE	We felt **overwhelmed by the experience.**
DIRECT QUOTATION	**"Good morning,"** she said. **"We're glad you're here."**

Multiple Grammatical Element Complements

The following multiple element complements are commonly used. One complement (usually the first) is in bold and the other in bold italic.

OBJECT + ADVERB OF PLACE	We left **the children** *at home.*
OBJECT + ADVERB OF PLACE TO/FROM	He drove **us** *to the station.*
	A policeman directed **the traffic** *onto a side street.*
INDIRECT OBJECT + DIRECT OBJECT	The driver gave *us* **directions.**
	He did *us* **a big favor.**
to PARAPHRASE	The driver gave **directions** *to us.*
for PARAPHRASE	He did **a big favor** *for us.*
OBJECT + PREDICATE NOUN	The accident left **him** *a broken man.*
OBJECT + PREDICATE ADJECTIVE	The movie left **me** *confused.*
OBJECT + INFINITIVE	I found **the new job** *to have its limitations.*
OBJECT + BASE-FORM INFINITIVE	I had **the kids** *put away their toys.*
OBJECT + THAT-CLAUSE	We bet **five dollars** *that you can't eat the entire cake.*
OBJECT + WH-CLAUSE	I told **my friends** *what they should expect.*
OBJECT + WH-INFINITIVE	I told **my friends** *what to expect.*
OBJECT + PRESENT PARTICIPLE	I caught **them** *sleeping on the job.*
OBJECT + PAST PARTICIPLE	Someone must have seen **the car** *stolen.*

Other combinations may be used by certain verbs. Note that OBJECT is divided into INDIRECT OBJECT and DIRECT OBJECT complements for certain verbs, like *give* and *do* above.

PHRASAL VERBS

A **phrasal verb** is a verb + particle (an adverb or preposition) combination that has a meaning different from the combined meanings of the verb and particle. For example, the verb *put* can mean "place, set," "insert," "cause to be in a certain condition/state," and "express, say." When combined with *on*, it can have several different meanings. Four of the meanings for *put on* are given here with example sentences.

deceive [someone]	Don't believe him; he's just **putting** you **on.**
dress in [clothing]	Will I need to **put** my coat **on?**
add	Uncle Nelson has **put on** quite a bit of weight.
start [something] playing	We **put on** some rock music for Dad.

None of the ordinary meanings of *put* and *on* indicate that these words used together would have the meanings above. That is why we call phrasal verbs **idiomatic.**

English abounds with phrasal verbs. In fact, there are many more phrasal verbs in English than nonphrasal verbs. Because they are idiomatic, phrasal verbs can be difficult for English learners.

Not all verb + particle combinations are phrasal verbs. In some cases, the particle is used as a preposition that doesn't change the basic meaning of the verb. *Dive for* is an example.

dive _____ *plunge quickly, lunge*	
for OBJECT	The shortstop dove **for the ball.**

In the sentence above, *for* doesn't change the meaning of *dive.* For this reason, *dive for* is not considered a phrasal verb, and it is included in the Complements section instead.

Some verbs, when followed by a complement, must always be used with a particular preposition; for example, *cling* is always used with *to*.

cling _____ *adhere, hold on tightly*

to OBJECT

He clung **to the ledge** until he was rescued.
The ivy was clinging **to the wall**.

Since *cling* must always be used with *to* when it is followed by a complement, *cling to* is included in the Complements section.

Separable and Inseparable Phrasal Verbs

Many phrasal verbs take no object.

catch on *become popular*

Jazz caught on in the early 1900s.

give out *wear out, stop operating*

The refrigerator gave out after 21 years.

For these phrasal verbs, the particle must be placed immediately after the verb.

Most phrasal verbs, however, take an object. For some of these, the particle can be placed after the object—away from the verb—and for others, the particle must be placed directly after the verb. There are no simple rules for determining whether the particle is placed after the verb or after the object.

Generally, if the particle is considered a preposition, it must be placed after the verb; this type of phrasal verb is called **inseparable**. However, if the particle is considered an adverb, it can, and sometimes MUST, be placed after the object; this type of phrasal verb is called **separable**. Most phrasal verbs are separable.

INSEPARABLE PHRASAL VERB

Our success **is riding on** the merger. ("depend on")

SEPARABLE PHRASAL VERB

My brother **is putting on** his coat. ("dress in")

In the first sentence, *on* is considered a preposition, and therefore it cannot be placed after the object *the merger*.

✗ Our success **is riding** the merger **on**.

In the second example, *on* is considered an adverb, and therefore it can be placed after the object *his coat*.

My brother **is putting** his coat **on**.

For separable phrasal verbs, the particle can be placed after the verb or after the object. There is an important exception, however: If the object is a pronoun, the particle MUST be placed after the object.

My brother **is putting** it **on**.
✗ My brother **is putting on** it.

You can test whether a phrasal verb is separable or inseparable by using a pronoun as its object: If the particle MUST be placed after the pronoun object, the phrasal verb is separable; otherwise, it is inseparable.

Note that if the object of a separable phrasal verb is a long noun phrase, it is better to place the particle after the verb.

Don't **throw away** the lamp that I spent four hours fixing.
? Don't **throw** the lamp that I spent four hours fixing **away**.

You can often determine whether a phrasal verb is separable by knowing whether the particle is considered an adverb or a preposition. In examples on the preceding page, *on* is used both as a preposition (*ride on*) and as an adverb (*put on*). However, some particles are almost always used as prepositions; these generally form inseparable phrasal verbs.

across	into
after	of
against	to
at	upon
between	with
for	

The club **leaped at** Kyle's offer.
X The club **leaped** Kyle's offer **at**.

Acid was **eating into** the countertop.
X Acid was **eating** the countertop **into**.

Some particles are almost always used as adverbs; these particles generally form separable phrasal verbs.

ahead	forth
aside	in
away	off
back	out
down	up

We **put off** the meeting until Friday.
We **put** the meeting **off** until Friday.
We **put** it **off**.

A young attorney **drew up** my will.
A young attorney **drew** my will **up**.
A young attorney **drew** it **up**.

Other particles are separable with some verbs and inseparable with others.

about	on
along	over
around	through
behind	under
by	

See the examples with *ride on* and *put on* on the previous page.

To indicate a separable phrasal verb, a blank line with SEP is used for the complement (object).

break _SEP_ up *put an end to*   Two students broke the fight up.
Two students broke up the fight.
Two students broke it up.

An inseparable phrasal verb is indicated by a blank line (without SEP) after the particle.

break for _____ *interrupt one's activities for*   Let's break for lunch at 12 o'clock.

A phrasal verb may have more than one particle. If there are two or more particles, the last particle is almost always a preposition with its own object. For phrasal verbs like this, the object follows the last particle.

break up with _____ *end a romance with*   Allison broke up with Todd.

The Most Common Phrasal Particles

Following is a list, with examples, of the particles most commonly used in phrasal verbs.

across
> come across _____ *find by accident*   She **came across** her high school yearbook.

after
> keep after _____ *nag, harass*   Mom **keeps after** us about our homework.

along
> bring _SEP_ along *have [someone]*   Be sure to **bring** a friend **along** on the tour.
> come along

around
> get around _____ *avoid*   He **got around** the problem by installing new software.

aside
> cast _SEP_ aside *discard, throw away*   The soldier **cast aside** his rifle and ran.

at
> leap at _____ *accept eagerly*   The class **leaped at** Hilary's offer to bake a cake.

away
> dream _SEP_ away *spend [time] idly*   Let's sit on the riverbank and **dream away** the day.

back
> cut _SEP_ back *shorten*   We must **cut** the shrubs **back** after they flower.

behind
> fall behind (on _____) *lag behind*   They **were falling behind on** the rent.

between
> come between _____ *cause trouble between*   We can't let a silly quarrel **come between** us.

down
> shut _SEP_ down *close permanently*   Management **shut** the garment factory **down**.

for
> go for _____ *be attracted by*   She **goes for** men with beards.

forth
> put _SEP_ forth *propose, suggest*   Johanna **put forth** her plan to save the black-footed ferret.

in
> hold _SEP_ in *suppress*   The candidate is good at **holding** his emotions **in**.

in on
> break in on _____ *interrupt*   I hate to **break in on** your conversation, but I'm starving.

into
> get into _____ *be admitted to*   Our daughter **got into** medical school.

of
> come of _____ *result from*   What **came of** your threat to retire?

off
> run _SEP_ off *print, make copies of*   I **ran** several extra sets **off** for you.

on
    bring __SEP__ on *cause to appear*   It's time to **bring on** the final act.

out
    leave __SEP__ out *omit, exclude*   Please **leave out** the reference to Uncle Harold.

out of
    get out of _____ *avoid, escape*   She **got out of** piano lessons three weeks in a row.

over
    make __SEP__ over *change the appearance of*   The programmer **made over** his cubicle with movie posters.

through
    come through _____ *survive*   The hostages **came through** the ordeal unhurt.

to
    see to _____ *take care of*   The janitor **saw to** the overturned trash cans.

under
    fall under _____ *be influenced/ controlled by*   The princess **fell under** the power of the wicked queen.

up
    wind __SEP__ up *bring to an end*   We **wound up** the meeting by 8 o'clock.

up on
    catch _____ up on *bring up-to-date about*   The assistant will **catch** the actor **up on** the news.

upon
    hit upon _____ *discover*   She **hit upon** the idea of extending Medicare to people 55 and over.

with
    bear with _____ *be patient with*   Please **bear with** me while I think this over.

Note the double particles *in on, out of,* and *up on* in the list above.

Verbs of Motion

Verbs of motion typically form many phrasal verbs with particles considered to be adverbs. This is listed as the first entry in the Phrasal Verbs section.

keep away/back/down/in/off/out/etc. *remain in a specified location*   Keep away from the edge of the bluff. My parents are coming—keep down!

keep __SEP__ **away/back/down/in/off/ out**/etc. *cause to remain in a specified location*   Can you keep the squirrels away from the corn? It's raining; keep the children in.

EXPRESSIONS

An Expressions section is often included on verb pages where space permits. The entries are common idiomatic set phrases that are especially useful to the English learner.

GUIDE TO CONJUGATIONS

(1) (2) (3) (4)
118 (**send**) send | sends · sent · have sent ☑ IRREGULAR

---

(5) **PRESENT**

I send	we send
you send	you send
he/she/it sends	they send

(7) • *The firm sends letters by registered mail.*

PAST

I sent	we sent
you sent	you sent
he/she/it sent	they sent

• *They sent us a nice note.*

(6) **PRESENT PROGRESSIVE**

I am sending	we are sending
you are sending	you are sending
he/she/it is sending	they are sending

• *I am sending you an e-mail.*

PAST PROGRESSIVE

I was sending	we were sending
you were sending	you were sending
he/she/it was sending	they were sending

• *She was sending her children to a private school.*

(8)
PRESENT PERFECT	... have | has sent
PAST PERFECT	... had sent

FUTURE	... will send
FUTURE PROGRESSIVE	... will be sending
FUTURE PERFECT	... will have sent

(9) **PAST PASSIVE**

I was sent	we were sent
you were sent	you were sent
he/she/it was sent	they were sent

• *The letter was sent to the wrong address.*

---

1 This is the verb number.

2 This is the base form of the verb. If this were a Top 30 Verb, there would be an additional page for Complements, Phrasal Verbs, and Expressions, and both pages would have a Top 30 Verb icon at the bottom.

3 These are the principal parts of the verb: present | third-person singular present · past · past perfect (containing the past participle).

4 This indicates whether a verb may form its past and past participle regularly. Some verbs, like *shine* (No. 125), have both regular and irregular forms.

5 Five tense paradigms are shown in the table format familiar to most English learners, where row and column represent verb person and number, respectively. These five tenses were chosen because they are the most frequently used.

6 Some verbs are never used in the progressive tenses, like *know* (No. 86). For these verbs, the progressive forms are not given. We only show forms that an English learner might be expected to use in ordinary conversation or writing.

7 An example sentence is supplied for each tense shown.

8 The forms for these five tenses are displayed in single lines with no pronouns. Thus, all nine simple, progressive, and perfect tenses in the active voice are shown (see pages 6–9), plus the most frequently used passive tense.

9 Some verbs are never used in the passive voice, like *lie* (No. 92); no forms are given for these. Other verbs cannot have a personal subject in the passive voice, like *knit* (No. 85); only *it* and *they* forms are given for these. Some writers, of course, may use these personal passive forms in highly figurative or poetic senses. However, because an English learner might be led to use these forms incorrectly, we do not show them.

Some verbs are only used in the passive voice when they are part of a phrasal verb, like *dream* (No. 46). Because this is a valid use of the passive, all forms are shown for these verbs.

GUIDE TO COMPLEMENTS AND PHRASAL VERBS

1 This meaning of *give* requires no complement.

2 The blank line indicates that this meaning of *give* requires a complement. Either the single complement OBJECT or the double complement INDIRECT OBJECT + DIRECT OBJECT may be used.

3 The object in the example sentence is bold.

4 One element in a double complement is italicized to distinguish the two complements. The INDIRECT OBJECT + DIRECT OBJECT construction may have a *for* PARAPHRASE, as shown below.

5 The direct object is bold, and the indirect object is bold italic (corresponding to the italic in the complement name).

6 A passive-voice variation is often given for an example sentence.

7 This use of *give out* as a phrasal verb requires no complement.

8 This use of *give out* as a phrasal verb requires a complement. The SEP on the blank line indicates that the phrasal verb is separable (see pages 14–15).

9 This use of *give out* as a phrasal verb requires a complement. The blank line without SEP indicates that the phrasal verb is inseparable (see pages 14–15).

Complement types are not identified in the Phrasal Verbs section, since virtually every complement of a phrasal verb functions as an object of the verb, whether it is an OBJECT, REFLEXIVE PRONOUN, or PRESENT PARTICIPLE. Bold and bold italic are not used in example sentences in the Phrasal Verbs section.

The Expressions section (not shown here) includes a blank line for a required complement.

COMPLEMENTS

(1) give *yield, collapse*
The floor might give if we put that much weight on it.

give __(2)__ *host*
OBJECT
(3)
We will give **the reception** in his honor.

(4) INDIRECT OBJECT + DIRECT OBJECT
I gave *my parents* **a surprise party.**
We gave *the seniors* **a graduation party. (5)**

for PARAPHRASE
I gave **a surprise party** *for my parents.*
We gave **a graduation party** *for the seniors.*

(6) PASSIVE
A graduation party was given for the seniors.
The seniors were given a graduation party.

give ___ *devote*
OBJECT + *to* OBJECT
Marvin gave **his whole life** *to the cause of justice.*

PHRASAL VERBS

give __SEP__ away *betray*
A club member gave away our secret meeting place.

give in (to ___) *surrender*
(to [someone/something])
After arguing for two hours, our opponents gave in.
Senator Blather gave in to pressure from his colleagues.

(7) give out *come to an end*
The settlers' food gave out after three weeks.

give out *wear out, stop operating*
After 203,000 miles, our 1979 Oldsmobile finally gave out.

(8) give __SEP__ out *distribute*
C.J. gave out the president's itinerary.

(9) give out ___ *produce*
This old furnace gives out a lot of heat.

give __SEP__ up *stop, cease*
Mom and Dad gave up smoking at the same time.

give __SEP__ up *surrender, yield*
Within an hour, the gunman gave up two hostages.
An hour later, he gave himself up.

188

ENGLISH IRREGULAR VERBS

Conjugations
Complements
Phrasal Verbs
Expressions

TOP 30 VERBS

The following thirty verbs have been selected because of their semantic and syntactic richness, both in their basic meanings and complements and in their phrasal verbs. A full page of example sentences provides guidance on correct usage and immediately precedes or follows the conjugation/complements page.

PRESENT

I arise	we arise
you arise	you arise
he/she/it arises	they arise

• *He arises every morning at the same time.*

PRESENT PROGRESSIVE

I am arising	we are arising
you are arising	you are arising
he/she/it is arising	they are arising

• *George is slowly arising from the sofa.*

PAST

I arose	we arose
you arose	you arose
he/she/it arose	they arose

• *I always arose before seven on school days.*

PAST PROGRESSIVE

I was arising	we were arising
you were arising	you were arising
he/she/it was arising	they were arising

• *He was just arising when the phone rang.*

| **PRESENT PERFECT** | ... have \| has arisen |
| **PAST PERFECT** | ... had arisen |

FUTURE	... will arise
FUTURE PROGRESSIVE	... will be arising
FUTURE PERFECT	... will have arisen

PAST PASSIVE

Arise is never used in the passive voice.

──────────────────────────────(COMPLEMENTS)──

NOTE: The verb *arise* is interchangeable with *rise* in most meanings and uses. See verb No. 111.

arise *get out of bed*

I usually arise around six.
Nobody arises early on weekends.

arise *stand/spring up, move upward*

The audience always arises when the president enters the room.
Rebecca arose from the sofa gracefully.
The dolphins arose from the water.
A cloud of dust arose from the ruins.
He arose out of inner-city poverty to become mayor.

arise *come into being*

The rumor arose when Rob had to appear in court.
A new controversy about ethanol has arisen since the meeting.

arise _____ *originate*

ADVERB OF PLACE TO/FROM

The spring arises **behind our house.**
These glaciers arise **in the Alps.**
Birds arose **from small specialized dinosaurs.**
Prejudice arises **from ignorance and unfamiliarity.**

awake(n)

awake | awakes · awaked · have awaked ☑ REGULAR
awake | awakes · awoke · have awoken ☑ IRREGULAR
awaken | awakens · awakened · have awakened ☑ REGULAR

PRESENT		PRESENT PROGRESSIVE	
I awake	we awake	I am awaking	we are awaking
you awake	you awake	you are awaking	you are awaking
he/she/it awakes	they awake	he/she/it is awaking	they are awaking

• *He awakes every morning at seven.*   • *He is awaking to the danger.*

PAST		PAST PROGRESSIVE	
I awoke	we awoke	I was awaking	we were awaking
you awoke	you awoke	you were awaking	you were awaking
he/she/it awoke	they awoke	he/she/it was awaking	they were awaking

• *It awoke bad memories for me.*   • *They were awaking to a hot morning.*

PRESENT PERFECT	... have | has awoken
PAST PERFECT	... had awoken

FUTURE	... will awake
FUTURE PROGRESSIVE	... will be awaking
FUTURE PERFECT	... will have awoken

PAST PASSIVE

I was awoken	we were awoken
you were awoken	you were awoken
he/she/it was awoken	they were awoken

• *We were awoken by the storm.*

(COMPLEMENTS)

NOTE: *Awake* and *awaken* have the same meanings and uses. They are similar to *wake/waken* (verb No. 179), with this difference: *Wake* is used with *up* (*Jane woke up at 7 o'clock*), but *awake, awaken,* and *waken* are not.

awake *quit sleeping*   The children awoke early.

awake *become aroused*   The crowd's anger suddenly awoke.
                                         Excitement awoke in everyone.

awake _____ *arouse from sleeping*

   OBJECT   The storm awoke **the children** early.
                                         He will awake **everybody in the house** with his snoring.

   WH-CLAUSE   The commotion awoke **whoever was still asleep**.

awake _____ *stir up*

   OBJECT   The crisis has awoken **memories of the 1960s**.
                                         Sam awoke **Stella's interest in China**.

   WH-CLAUSE   It awoke **what had been long forgotten**.
                                         I awoke **whatever concern he had felt**.

(PHRASAL VERBS)

awake from _____ *wake up out of*   Ned awoke from a sound sleep.

awake to _____ *wake up to*   Patsy awoke to the aroma of freshly brewed coffee.
                                            The corporal awoke to the sound and fury of battle.

awake to _____ *become aware of*   She awoke to the possibilities that technology offered.
                                            Dad awoke to the reality of the moment.

PRESENT

I am	we are
you are	you are
he/she/it is	they are

• *William is here.*

PAST

I was	we were
you were	you were
he/she/it was	they were

• *He was the manager for eight years.*

PRESENT PERFECT ... have | has been
PAST PERFECT ... had been

PRESENT PROGRESSIVE

I am being	we are being
you are being	you are being
he/she/it is being	they are being

• *You are being very difficult.*

PAST PROGRESSIVE

I was being	we were being
you were being	you were being
he/she/it was being	they were being

• *They were only being helpful.*

FUTURE ... will be
FUTURE PROGRESSIVE ... will be being
FUTURE PERFECT ... will have been

PAST PASSIVE

Be is never used in the passive voice.

—(**COMPLEMENTS**)—

NOTE: *Be* is also used as a helping verb
• to form the progressive tenses

   be + PRESENT PARTICIPLE   They were driving down the wrong street.
• to form the passive voice

   be + PAST PARTICIPLE   You will be arrested if you drive drunk.

be *exist*   "I think, therefore I am." [RENÉ DESCARTES]
     Oh, let it be.

be _____ *exist*

   there + *be* + PREDICATE NOUN   There was **a policeman** on the corner.

be _____ *have the identity, a property, or a characteristic of*

ADVERB OF TIME	The meeting is **at ten**. My birthday is **in September**. The time is **now**.
ADVERB OF PLACE	The principal is **out of the office**. My parents have never been **to Singapore**.
PREDICATE NOUN	Greg is **a bachelor**. It is **a streetcar**. It is **I**, Mother. [FORMAL] / It's **me**, Mom. [INFORMAL]
PREDICATE ADJECTIVE	Everett is **handsome and rich**. The school is **excellent**.

be _____ *must*

INFINITIVE	You are **to report to the office**. Gary is **to be ready at seven**.

—(**PHRASAL VERBS**)—

NOTE: Many of the following phrasal verbs are used informally.

be against _____ *oppose*   The group is against gun control.

be along *arrive* [USED ONLY IN THE FUTURE TENSE]   Fred will be along any minute now.

be around *exist*   Dinosaurs were around for 150 million years.

be around _____ *be located*   The keys are around here somewhere.

be away *be absent*   The sales clerk is away for a moment.

be behind *lag*   He's behind in his studies.

be down *not be operating*   The server is down, and I can't get my files.

NOTE: Many of the following phrasal verbs are used informally.

be down *be depressed*

I asked her why she was down.

be down on _____ *be angry with*

Why are you always down on your brother?

be down with _____ *be sick due to*

Ellery is down with the flu.

be for _____ *support*

I was for Robert in the last election.
I am for fixing the building up, not tearing it down.

be in *be in one's home/office*

The doctor is in.

be in *be in fashion*

Ruffles are in, pleats are out.

be in on _____ *share in*

Four seniors were in on the prank.

be into _____ *be interested/involved in*

Katrina was into gymnastics in a big way.

be off *not be at work*

The workers will be off for the next three days.

be off *not be operating*

The lights were off in the auditorium.

be off *be less*

Sales are off for the third month in a row.

be off *be wrong*

These estimates are off by 50%.

be off *not be taking place*

Tomorrow's meeting is off.

be on *be operating*

The television is on.

be on *be in effect*

I hope Saturday's party is still on.

be onto _____ *be aware of*

Oscar is onto your tricks.

be onto _____ *be about to discover*

The detective was onto something.

be out *not be inside*

You can lock the doors after everyone is out.

be out *be made public*

The news is out that Alison broke her engagement.

be out *be out of fashion*

Sitcoms are out, documentaries are in.

be out *be asleep/unconscious*

He went to bed and was out within two minutes.

be out *not be permitted*

You can eat apples, but chocolate is out.

be out and about *travel around*

Philip is out and about with his friends.

be out of _____ *no longer possess*

We're out of coffee—would you like tea?

be out (with _____ **)** *be absent (due to [an illness])*

Half of the third graders are out with the flu.

be out (with _____ **)** *be unable to play/work (due to [an injury, illness])*

He was out for two weeks with a bruised elbow.

be over *be finished*

The baseball game is finally over.

be through (with _____ **)** *be finished (with [something])*

We were through with our homework by 7 o'clock.

be up *be finished*

Turn in the exam—your time is up.

be up *be more/greater*

Food prices are up seven percent.

be up *be risen, be put up*

We'll leave for Kentucky once the sun is up.
The for sale sign has been up for six months.

be up and about/around *be out of bed and moving around*

I had a cold, but I was up and about on the third day.

be up for _____ *be a candidate for*

Samantha is up for class president.
George is up for re-election.

be up for _____ *be available for*

The neighbor's house is up for sale again.

be up for _____ *be ready and willing for*

Are you up for a game of cards?

be up for _____ *be on trial for [a crime]*

Tori is up for armed robbery.

be up on _____ *be knowledgeable about*

Veronica is up on all the latest CD releases.

be up to _____ *be able to*

Are you up to cleaning your room today?

top 30 verb

PRESENT		PRESENT PROGRESSIVE	
I bear	we bear	I am bearing	we are bearing
you bear	you bear	you are bearing	you are bearing
he/she/it bears	they bear	he/she/it is bearing	they are bearing

• *Alice bears a lot of responsibility for this.* • *They are bearing up well.*

PAST		PAST PROGRESSIVE	
I bore	we bore	I was bearing	we were bearing
you bore	you bore	you were bearing	you were bearing
he/she/it bore	they bore	he/she/it was bearing	they were bearing

• *The monk bore his suffering in silence.* • *We were bearing a heavy load.*

PRESENT PERFECT	... have	has borne
PAST PERFECT	... had borne

FUTURE	... will bear
FUTURE PROGRESSIVE	... will be bearing
FUTURE PERFECT	... will have borne

PAST PASSIVE

I was borne/born	we were borne/born
you were borne/born	you were borne/born
he/she/it was borne/born	they were borne/born

• *The charges were borne out in today's testimony.*
• *I was born in Richland.*

NOTE: *Born* is the past participle in the sense "give birth to" in the passive voice. *Borne* is used in all other senses.

───────────────────────────────(COMPLEMENTS)───

bear *produce fruit*

In Ecuador, apple trees bear twice a year.

bear _____ *produce*
   OBJECT

These apple trees won't bear **fruit** for three years.

bear _____ *go*
   ADVERB OF PLACE TO/FROM

This road bears **to the left**.
Bear **right** at the next stoplight.

bear _____ *carry*
   OBJECT

"Beware of Greeks who bear **gifts**." [VERGIL]

bear _____ *carry/move along*
   OBJECT

A strong current bore **the ship** out to sea.

bear _____ *support*
   OBJECT

The pillars bear **the weight of the roof**.

bear _____ *be accountable for*
   OBJECT

The engineers bear **a heavy responsibility for the disaster**.

bear _____ *endure*
   OBJECT

He can't bear **the pain**.
He will bear **a substantial financial loss**.

   for OBJECT + INFINITIVE
   INFINITIVE
   (it) THAT-CLAUSE
   PRESENT PARTICIPLE

I can't bear **for you** *to leave so soon*.
I can't bear **to hear such a sad story**.
I can't bear *(it)* **that you have to leave so soon**.
I can't bear **hearing such a sad story**.

bear _____ *carry in one's mind*
   OBJECT

He bears **a real grudge** against them.
I bear **no hard feelings** toward them.

   INDIRECT OBJECT + DIRECT OBJECT
   against PARAPHRASE

I bear *him* **no malice**.
I bear **no malice** *against him*.

bear _____ *give birth to*
   OBJECT   She bore **a son** in 1982.
                                               Lois has borne **three children.**

   PASSIVE   Three children have been born to Lois.

bear _____ *have as a characteristic*
   OBJECT   Rory bears **a scar** on his left arm.
                                               Sasha bears **a strong resemblance** to her mother.

bear _____ *have as an identification*
   OBJECT   All three wills bore **Uncle Leland's signature.**

bear _____ *behave*
   REFLEXIVE PRONOUN + ADVERB OF MANNER   He's bearing **himself** *with dignity.*

bear _____ *take care of, pay for*
   OBJECT   My parents bore **all the expenses of my college
                                               education.**

bear _____ *call for, require*
   OBJECT   The committee bears **watching.**

PHRASAL VERBS

bear down *try hard*   If you bear down, you'll get
                                       an "A" in the course.

bear down on _____ *press down on*   Bear down on the pen—you're making four copies.

bear off _____ *turn off*   Bear off the gravel road when you see a large barn.

bear on _____ *have to do with*   These observations don't bear on the matter at all.

bear SEP **out** *prove right*   The testimony will bear this out.

bear up *survive, endure*   Lila bore up well in spite of the criticism.
                                       The bridge couldn't bear up under such heavy traffic.

bear with _____ *be patient with*   Please bear with us while we discuss the matter.

EXPRESSIONS

bear arms *possess a weapon*   A citizen may bear arms to
                                       protect himself.

bear fruit *yield satisfactory results*   The discussions will hopefully bear fruit soon.

bear _____ **in mind** *consider, remember*   Our representatives should bear in mind that their
                                       decisions affect millions of people.

bear [one's] cross *endure one's troubles*   The cancer took its toll, but Nick bore his cross bravely.

bear the brunt of _____ *endure the worst*   The walnut trees bore the brunt of the storm.
part of

grin and bear it *endure an unpleasant*   We got laid off, and all we can do is grin and bear it.
surprise with good humor

PRESENT		PRESENT PROGRESSIVE	
I beat	we beat	I am beating	we are beating
you beat	you beat	you are beating	you are beating
he/she/it beats	they beat	he/she/it is beating	they are beating

· *In the long run, you never beat the odds.* · *I am beating some eggs.*

PAST		PAST PROGRESSIVE	
I beat	we beat	I was beating	we were beating
you beat	you beat	you were beating	you were beating
he/she/it beat	they beat	he/she/it was beating	they were beating

· *He beat the rugs outside.* · *He was beating back a nasty infection.*

PRESENT PERFECT	... have | has beaten
PAST PERFECT	... had beaten

FUTURE	... will beat
FUTURE PROGRESSIVE	... will be beating
FUTURE PERFECT	... will have beaten

PAST PASSIVE

I was beaten	we were beaten
you were beaten	you were beaten
he/she/it was beaten	they were beaten

· *The record was beaten by three of the swimmers.*

(COMPLEMENTS)

beat *pulsate, throb*
My pulse was beating rapidly.
The drums were beating again.

beat _____ *strike repeatedly*
OBJECT
I beat **the drum** in time to the music.
The jockeys beat **their horses** in the final lap.
The blacksmith beat **the iron** into swords.
The sergeant beat **the recruits** into submission.

beat _____ *mix by stirring*
OBJECT
Beat **the batter** with a wooden spoon.

beat _____ *defeat, win*
OBJECT
The Phillies have beaten **the Red Sox.**
You beat **the record** easily.

beat _____ *be better than*
OBJECT
Good home cooking always beats **restaurant food.**
WH-CLAUSE
Your idea beats **what I was trying to do.**
PRESENT PARTICIPLE
Nothing beats **having lots of money in your wallet.**
That beats **my trying to do it myself.**

beat _____ *confuse, puzzle*
OBJECT + WH-CLAUSE
It beats **me** *how anyone can understand these instructions.*

beat _____ *flap*
OBJECT
A hummingbird beats **its wings** up to 70 times per second.

(PHRASAL VERBS)

beat _____ **back/down/in/out/up**/etc.
arrive at a specified location sooner than
My sister beat me back to the station.
They raced to the top of the hill, and Ben beat the others up.

beat ^{SEP} **back** *drive back*
Our platoon beat back the enemy's attack.

beat ^{SEP} **down** *cause to collapse*
The warriors beat the doors down with clubs.

beat down (on _____**)** *fall (on)*
A driving rain beat down on the stadium crowd.
A blazing sun beat down on the spectators.

beat ^{SEP} **off** *drive away*
She beat the would-be robbers off with pepper spray.

beat ^{SEP} **up** *attack savagely*
Gang members beat the man up and took his car.

PRESENT

I become	we become
you become	you become
he/she/it becomes	they become

• *Jackson becomes cross when he's hungry.*

PRESENT PROGRESSIVE

I am becoming	we are becoming
you are becoming	you are becoming
he/she/it is becoming	they are becoming

• *The kids are becoming tired.*

PAST

I became	we became
you became	you became
he/she/it became	they became

• *The situation became a real mess.*

PAST PROGRESSIVE

I was becoming	we were becoming
you were becoming	you were becoming
he/she/it was becoming	they were becoming

• *His old jokes were becoming quite tiresome.*

PRESENT PERFECT ... have | has become
PAST PERFECT ... had become

FUTURE ... will become
FUTURE PROGRESSIVE ... will be becoming
FUTURE PERFECT ... will have become

PAST PASSIVE

Become is never used in the passive voice.

COMPLEMENTS

become _____ *grow/come to be*

PREDICATE NOUN	The recording became **a huge success.**
	Alice became **chair of the department.**
PREDICATE ADJECTIVE	Robert became **quite friendly.**
	The weather became **stormy.**
WH-CLAUSE	It became **what we feared the most.**
	He will become **whoever he needs to be.**

become _____ *enhance the appearance of, look good on*

OBJECT	Moonlight becomes **her.**
	His sneering attitude really doesn't become **him.**

PHRASAL VERBS

become of _____ *happen to*

Whatever became of your plan to
    start your own business?
I don't know what has become of Mary.

EXPRESSIONS

be becoming on _____ *look good on*

This shade of blue is very becoming on you.

becoming *attractive*

Your dress is very becoming.
That is a most becoming dress you are wearing.

becoming *suitable to*

She gave a eulogy becoming the occasion of her father's
    funeral.

PRESENT			PRESENT PROGRESSIVE		
—	—		—	—	
—	—		—	—	
it befalls	they befall		it is befalling	they are befalling	

· Sorrow and pain befall the broken-hearted.   *· A financial crisis is befalling the country.*

PAST			PAST PROGRESSIVE		
—	—		—	—	
—	—		—	—	
it befell	they befell		it was befalling	they were befalling	

· Hardship befell the Jamestown colony.   *· An ecological disaster was befalling the world.*

PRESENT PERFECT	... have | has befallen
PAST PERFECT	... had befallen

FUTURE	... will befall
FUTURE PROGRESSIVE	... will be befalling
FUTURE PERFECT	... will have befallen

PAST PASSIVE

Befall is never used in the passive voice.

─(**COMPLEMENTS**)─

befall *happen (usually something bad)*

Who knows what evil things might befall?

They blamed him for everything that befell.

befall _____ *happen (usually something bad)*

OBJECT

A tragedy had befallen **the unfortunate family**.

Who knows what terrible curse befell **them**?

A catastrophic earthquake befell **the city** a few years later.

PRESENT

I beget	we beget
you beget	you beget
he/she/it begets	they beget

• *Success begets success.*

PRESENT PROGRESSIVE

I am begetting	we are begetting
you are begetting	you are begetting
he/she/it is begetting	they are begetting

• *His mistakes are begetting a new crop of problems.*

PAST

I begot/begat	we begot/begat
you begot/begat	you begot/begat
he/she/it begot/begat	they begot/begat

• *The king eventually begat an heir.*

PAST PROGRESSIVE

I was begetting	we were begetting
you were begetting	you were begetting
he/she/it was begetting	they were begetting

• *The rain was begetting millions of mosquitoes.*

PRESENT PERFECT ... have | has begotten/begot
PAST PERFECT ... had begotten/begot

FUTURE ... will beget
FUTURE PROGRESSIVE ... will be begetting
FUTURE PERFECT ... will have begotten/begot

PAST PASSIVE

I was begotten/begot	we were begotten/begot
you were begotten/begot	you were begotten/begot
he/she/it was begotten/begot	they were begotten/begot

• *A son was finally begotten by the old king.*

COMPLEMENTS

beget _____ *father, sire*

OBJECT — Henry VIII begat **one son** by his third wife, Queen Jane.

PASSIVE — Mythological monsters were begotten by witches and demons.

beget _____ *cause to exist/happen*

OBJECT — Bad behavior only begets **trouble**.

His amazingly good luck begat **envy and resentment** among his co-workers.

PASSIVE — Their successes were begotten by a lot of hard work.

PRESENT

I begin	we begin
you begin	you begin
he/she/it begins	they begin

• *He always begins breakfast with coffee.*

PRESENT PROGRESSIVE

I am beginning	we are beginning
you are beginning	you are beginning
he/she/it is beginning	they are beginning

• *It is beginning to rain.*

PAST

I began	we began
you began	you began
he/she/it began	they began

• *I began to feel uneasy.*

PAST PROGRESSIVE

I was beginning	we were beginning
you were beginning	you were beginning
he/she/it was beginning	they were beginning

• *We were beginning to get worried.*

PRESENT PERFECT ... have | has begun
PAST PERFECT   ... had begun

FUTURE   ... will begin
FUTURE PROGRESSIVE ... will be beginning
FUTURE PERFECT   ... will have begun

PAST PASSIVE

—	—
—	—
it was begun	they were begun

• *Therapy was begun immediately.*

COMPLEMENTS

begin *start*	His meetings never begin on time.
	Meetings always begin with the reading of the minutes.
	The trouble began when Mack called Thack a fool.
	When does the parade begin?
begin _____ *start [an activity, event, process]*	
OBJECT	The chairperson began **the meeting** promptly at 2 o'clock.
	He began **the discussion** with a joke.
INFINITIVE	I began **to fall asleep** during the long lecture.
	The orchestra began **to play**.
WH-CLAUSE	We only began **what absolutely had to be finished**.
	They began **whatever they needed to do**.
PRESENT PARTICIPLE	I began **falling asleep** during the long lecture.
	The orchestra began **playing**.

PHRASAL VERBS

begin by/with _____ *start a sequence/ process with*	The new owners began by firing all the managers.
	Career planning begins with assessing your strengths.
begin _____ **by/with** *start [a process, event] by [doing something first]*	Let's begin the meeting with a big thank-you to the organizers.
	The song begins with a reference to fields of strawberries.

EXPRESSIONS

beginner *one who is starting to learn something*	He's a beginner when it comes to woodworking.
beginner's luck *luck of an inexperienced person*	Winning my very first case was just beginner's luck.
to begin with *first of all*	To begin with, there were no eyewitnesses.

PRESENT

I behold	we behold
you behold	you behold
he/she/it beholds	they behold

• *In the book, he beholds a heavenly vision.*

PAST

I beheld	we beheld
you beheld	you beheld
he/she/it beheld	they beheld

• *They beheld the ancient tomb in silence.*

PRESENT PERFECT ... have | has beheld
PAST PERFECT ... had beheld

PRESENT PROGRESSIVE

I am beholding	we are beholding
you are beholding	you are beholding
he/she/it is beholding	they are beholding

• *The king is beholding the newborn princess.*

PAST PROGRESSIVE

I was beholding	we were beholding
you were beholding	you were beholding
he/she/it was beholding	they were beholding

• *The troops were beholding the massacre site.*

FUTURE ... will behold
FUTURE PROGRESSIVE ... will be beholding
FUTURE PERFECT ... will have beheld

PAST PASSIVE

I was beheld	we were beheld
you were beheld	you were beheld
he/she/it was beheld	they were beheld

• *A similar scene was beheld by the lunchtime crowd.*

(**COMPLEMENTS**)

behold _____ *observe, look at* [OFTEN USED IN THE IMPERATIVE]

OBJECT
Behold **your king**!
No one had ever beheld **such an amazing sight**.
The children in the village had never beheld
a battery-operated toy before.

PRESENT

I bend	we bend
you bend	you bend
he/she/it bends	they bend

* He always *bends* the rules.

PRESENT PROGRESSIVE

I am bending	we are bending
you are bending	you are bending
he/she/it is bending	they are bending

* He is *bending* over backward to help you.

PAST

I bent	we bent
you bent	you bent
he/she/it bent	they bent

* I *bent* my fishhook.

PAST PROGRESSIVE

I was bending	we were bending
you were bending	you were bending
he/she/it was bending	they were bending

* The kids were *bending* clay into shapes.

PRESENT PERFECT ... have | has bent
PAST PERFECT ... had bent

FUTURE ... will bend
FUTURE PROGRESSIVE ... will be bending
FUTURE PERFECT ... will have bent

PAST PASSIVE

I was bent	we were bent
you were bent	you were bent
he/she/it was bent	they were bent

* The minister's head was *bent* in sorrow.

COMPLEMENTS

bend *become curved/crooked*	The road bends to the right. The trees bent in the wind.
bend *stoop, dip*	I bent to pick up the cat's water bowl. The rod bent under the heavy load.
bend *distort*	His smile bent into an ugly leer.
bend _____ *cause to curve, change the shape of* OBJECT	The archers bent **their bows.** The wind was bending **the trees.** I bent **the wire** into a hook. The magnets bend **the beam of electrons.** The rocks bend **the stream** to the far bank.
bend _____ *distort, cheat* OBJECT	The storm bent **the windmill** out of shape. Politicians bend **the rules** to suit themselves. They bent **the truth** in the run-up to war.

PHRASAL VERBS

bend backward/down/forward/etc. *lean in a specified direction*	Brad bent backward to dodge the ball. She bent down to pet the dog. The girl bent forward to get a better look.
bend ^{SEP} **back/down/over/up/**etc. *change the shape of in a specified direction*	Norvel bent the pins back into place. Adrian bent the corner of the page over.
bend over *lean down at the waist*	The class bent over to touch their toes.
bend over backward *do more than required*	The store bends over backward to please its customers.
bend to _____ *concentrate on*	After a break, Jasper bent to his studies.
bend to _____ *give in to*	He bent to the will of the voters and endorsed the plan.
bend _____ **to** *cause to give in*	Cleopatra bent Antony to her will.
be bent on _____ *be determined [to do]*	Helen was bent on going to law school.

EXPRESSIONS

bend [someone's] ear *talk excessively to*	The stranger bent my ear for 45 minutes.

bereave bereave | bereaves · bereaved · have bereaved
bereave | bereaves · bereft · have bereft

☑ REGULAR
☑ IRREGULAR

PRESENT

— —

it bereaves   they bereave

* War bereaves us of everything we hold dear.

PRESENT PROGRESSIVE

Bereave is never used in the progressive tenses.

PAST

— —

it bereft   they bereft

* Death bereft the family of financial security.

PAST PROGRESSIVE

Bereave is never used in the progressive tenses.

PRESENT PERFECT ... have | has bereft
PAST PERFECT   ... had bereft

FUTURE   ... will bereave
FUTURE PROGRESSIVE —
FUTURE PERFECT   ... will have bereft

PAST PASSIVE

I was bereft   we were bereft
you were bereft   you were bereft
he/she/it was bereft   they were bereft

* She was bereft when her husband died in an accident.

(**COMPLEMENTS**)

bereave _____ *leave alone/desolate, especially by someone's death*

OBJECT   Death bereaves **us all.**

PASSIVE   The widow was bereft when she was only 30 years old.
                   My grandmother was bereft in 1965, the year of my grandfather's
                   death.

OBJECT + of OBJECT   The 1918 flu pandemic bereft **countless families** *of their children*.
                   Colon cancer has bereft **us** *of our father*.

PASSIVE   The children were bereft *of their parents* when they were infants.

bereave _____ *deprive [someone] of [something]*

OBJECT + of OBJECT   Alzheimer's has bereft **him** *of all rationality*.
                   The economic crash bereft **us** *of all our savings*.

PASSIVE   The survivors of the crash were bereft *of all hope*.

PRESENT

I beseech   we beseech
you beseech   you beseech
he/she/it beseeches they beseech

• He beseeches you to be careful.

PRESENT PROGRESSIVE

I am beseeching   we are beseeching
you are beseeching   you are beseeching
he/she/it is beseeching they are beseeching

• I am beseeching you to change your mind.

PAST

I besought   we besought
you besought   you besought
he/she/it besought   they besought

• He earnestly besought her forgiveness.

PAST PROGRESSIVE

I was beseeching   we were beseeching
you were beseeching   you were beseeching
he/she/it was beseeching they were beseeching

• The Times was beseeching us to vote the mayor out.

PRESENT PERFECT ... have | has besought
PAST PERFECT   ... had besought

FUTURE   ... will beseech
FUTURE PROGRESSIVE ... will be beseeching
FUTURE PERFECT   ... will have besought

PAST PASSIVE

I was besought   we were besought
you were besought   you were besought
he/she/it was besought   they were besought

• The company was besought to not relocate their plant.

COMPLEMENTS

beseech _____ request urgently, beg, implore

OBJECT	I beseech **your help in this matter.**
PASSIVE	Emergency relief was besought by all the affected cities.
OBJECT + INFINITIVE	I beseech **you** *to say nothing of this matter.*
	The minister besought **his congregation** *to help the needy.*
	"She besought **him** ... *to speak the truth.*" [RUDYARD KIPLING]
PASSIVE	The senator was besought by her party *to vote against health care reform.*

PRESENT

I beset	we beset
you beset	you beset
he/she/it besets	they beset

• *Crime besets the core of many older cities.*

PRESENT PROGRESSIVE

I am besetting	we are besetting
you are besetting	you are besetting
he/she/it is besetting	they are besetting

• *The enemy fleet is besetting all of our ports.*

PAST

I beset	we beset
you beset	you beset
he/she/it beset	they beset

• *Clouds of flies beset the campers.*

PAST PROGRESSIVE

I was besetting	we were besetting
you were besetting	you were besetting
he/she/it was besetting	they were besetting

• *Creditors were besetting the firm from all sides.*

PRESENT PERFECT ... have | has beset
PAST PERFECT ... had beset

FUTURE ... will beset
FUTURE PROGRESSIVE ... will be besetting
FUTURE PERFECT ... will have beset

PAST PASSIVE

I was beset	we were beset
you were beset	you were beset
he/she/it was beset	they were beset

• *They were beset by a sea of troubles.*

COMPLEMENTS

beset _____ *attack from all sides* [OFTEN USED FIGURATIVELY]

OBJECT	His financial problems beset **him** constantly.
	Peer pressure beset **her** in her struggle to remain drug-free.
	She beset **her parents** with regular requests for money.
PASSIVE	All too often, the elderly are beset by multiple health problems.
	He was beset by self-doubt.
	The owl was beset by a flock of crows.

PRESENT

I bestride	we bestride
you bestride	you bestride
he/she/it bestrides	they bestride

• *He bestrides his horse like a true equestrian.*

PAST

I bestrode	we bestrode
you bestrode	you bestrode
he/she/it bestrode	they bestrode

• *He bestrode the music scene in the 1960s.*

PRESENT PERFECT ... have | has bestridden
PAST PERFECT ... had bestridden

PRESENT PROGRESSIVE

I am bestriding	we are bestriding
you are bestriding	you are bestriding
he/she/it is bestriding	they are bestriding

• *The editor is bestriding two different viewpoints.*

PAST PROGRESSIVE

I was bestriding	we were bestriding
you were bestriding	you were bestriding
he/she/it was bestriding	they were bestriding

• *The hitchhiker was bestriding his backpack.*

FUTURE ... will bestride
FUTURE PROGRESSIVE ... will be bestriding
FUTURE PERFECT ... will have bestridden

PAST PASSIVE

I was bestridden	we were bestridden
you were bestridden	you were bestridden
he/she/it was bestridden	they were bestridden

• *The mountain pass was bestridden by two massive towers.*

COMPLEMENTS

bestride _____ *straddle, sit/stand astride*

OBJECT

The wreck completely bestrode **the narrow country road.**
Our route bestrode **the border between the two countries.**

bestride _____ *tower over, dominate*

OBJECT

"Why, man, he doth bestride **the narrow world** like a Colossus."
[WILLIAM SHAKESPEARE, OF JULIUS CAESAR]
Lately, China has been bestriding **the manufacturing sector.**

PRESENT

I bet	we bet
you bet	you bet
he/she/it bets	they bet

• *Floyd always bets on the Yankees.*

PAST

I bet	we bet
you bet	you bet
he/she/it bet	they bet

• *She bet $20 on Breezy Summit to win.*

PRESENT PERFECT ... have | has bet
PAST PERFECT ... had bet

PRESENT PROGRESSIVE

I am betting	we are betting
you are betting	you are betting
he/she/it is betting	they are betting

• *I'm betting that you are right.*

PAST PROGRESSIVE

I was betting	we were betting
you were betting	you were betting
he/she/it was betting	they were betting

• *They were all betting that he would win.*

FUTURE ... will bet
FUTURE PROGRESSIVE ... will be betting
FUTURE PERFECT ... will have bet

PAST PASSIVE

—	—
—	—
it was bet	they were bet

• *A fortune was bet by professional gamblers.*

COMPLEMENTS

bet *make a wager*

I never bet.
They are always betting.

bet _____ *place as a wager*

OBJECT

Jason bet **a fortune.**
They are betting **a lot of money.**

OBJECT + THAT-CLAUSE
WH-CLAUSE

We bet **five dollars** *that you can't eat the entire cake.*
They will bet **whatever they can afford to lose.**

bet _____ *wager [something] with [someone]*

OBJECT + OBJECT

I bet **Floyd** *10 dollars.*
He bet **me** *dinner at a nice restaurant.*

OBJECT + THAT-CLAUSE

We bet **Robert** *that his team would finish last.*
I bet **you** *that you can't do it.*

bet _____ *assert [that something will/won't happen]*

THAT-CLAUSE

The company bet **that consumers would like the new design.**
Marisa bet **that the Dodgers wouldn't win.**

PHRASAL VERBS

bet on _____ *place a wager on [a contestant]*

I'm betting on the gray stallion.
I'm betting on St. Louis for the convention site.
I'm betting on St. Louis to be the convention site.

EXPRESSIONS

You bet! *Certainly!* [INFORMAL]

"Can you help me move this sofa?"
"You bet!"

PRESENT

I bid	we bid
you bid	you bid
he/she/it bids	they bid

• *He always bids the limit.*

PRESENT PROGRESSIVE

I am bidding	we are bidding
you are bidding	you are bidding
he/she/it is bidding	they are bidding

• *We are bidding on a vacation condo.*

PAST

I bade/bid	we bade/bid
you bade/bid	you bade/bid
he/she/it bade/bid	they bade/bid

• *I bid $200 for the painting.*

PAST PROGRESSIVE

I was bidding	we were bidding
you were bidding	you were bidding
he/she/it was bidding	they were bidding

• *They were bidding more than they could afford.*

PRESENT PERFECT ... have | has bidden/bid
PAST PERFECT ... had bidden/bid

FUTURE ... will bid
FUTURE PROGRESSIVE ... will be bidding
FUTURE PERFECT ... will have bidden/bid

PAST PASSIVE

I was bidden/bid	we were bidden/bid
you were bidden/bid	you were bidden/bid
he/she/it was bidden/bid	they were bidden/bid

• *Twenty-five dollars was just bid.*

―(**COMPLEMENTS**)―

bid *offer to pay a particular price*

I never bid at auctions.
John will bid when it comes on the market.

bid _____ *offer [a price] for*
OBJECT (+ *for* OBJECT)

When bidding began on the dollhouse, Dave bid **$200**.
He bid **$25** *for the rocking chair.*

ON OBJECT

We are bidding **on a first edition of Jane Austen's** *Emma*.

WH-CLAUSE

They will bid **whatever is necessary.**

NOTE: Only *bid* (not *bade* or *bidden*) is used as the past form in the sense "offer as a price."

bid _____ *declare one's intention to take [tricks in a card game]*
OBJECT

I bid **two spades.**

NOTE: Only *bid* (not *bade* or *bidden*) is used as the past form in the sense "declare one's intention to take."

bid _____ *tell [a greeting]*
INDIRECT OBJECT + DIRECT OBJECT
to PARAPHRASE

We bade *them* **farewell.**
We bade **farewell** *to them.*

bid _____ *urge/ask*
OBJECT + INFINITIVE

The butler bid **the guests** *to enter.*
He bid **them** *to be careful.*

PASSIVE

The guests were bidden *to enter.*

―(**PHRASAL VERBS**)―

bid _SEP_ **out** *offer [work] for bids from outside contractors*

The army bid out the construction
of four new barracks.
The ad agency bids out the production of TV commercials.

bid _SEP_ **up** *raise [an auction price] by offering more and more money*

Luana bid the price up on the antique lamp.

―(**EXPRESSIONS**)―

outbid _____ *offer more than*

Laura outbid four other people for the rug.

underbid _____ *offer to do something for less than*

The new firm underbid the others by $5,000.

PRESENT

I bind	we bind
you bind	you bind
he/she/it binds	they bind

• *Duct tape binds the parts together.*

PRESENT PROGRESSIVE

I am binding	we are binding
you are binding	you are binding
he/she/it is binding	they are binding

• *We are binding the reports with staples and tape.*

PAST

I bound	we bound
you bound	you bound
he/she/it bound	they bound

• *I bound the essays before shelving them.*

PAST PROGRESSIVE

I was binding	we were binding
you were binding	you were binding
he/she/it was binding	they were binding

• *The gears were binding against each other.*

PRESENT PERFECT ... have | has bound
PAST PERFECT   ... had bound

FUTURE   ... will bind
FUTURE PROGRESSIVE ... will be binding
FUTURE PERFECT ... will have bound

PAST PASSIVE

I was bound	we were bound
you were bound	you were bound
he/she/it was bound	they were bound

• *They were bound by their promises.*

COMPLEMENTS

bind *stick, become stuck* The pulley was binding.

bind *be uncomfortably tight* This dress is binding.

NOTE: The verb *bind*, when it takes an object, is often used with *together*.

bind _____ *wrap, cover, bandage*
  OBJECT
  We bound **the package** with tape.
  The printer bound **the books** in red leather.
  The doctor bound **my ankle**.

bind _____ *fasten together*
  OBJECT
  The secretary bound **the pages** with a clip.

bind _____ *cause to stick together*
  OBJECT
  The glue binds **the fibers** together.
  The enzyme binds **the calcium ions**.

bind _____ *put an edge/border on*
  OBJECT
  He bound **the rug** with cotton tape to keep the edges
    from raveling.

bind _____ *morally/legally obligate/restrict*
  OBJECT
  My promise binds **me**.
  His father's will binds **the use of the property**.

bind _____ *cause to have an emotional attachment*
  OBJECT
  Duty and honor bound **the company of soldiers** together.

PHRASAL VERBS

bind _SEP_ **off** *cast off* [KNITTING] Be sure to bind off the scarf loosely.

bind _SEP_ **over** *hold on bail* The judge will bind the suspect over for trial.

bind _SEP_ **up** *tie up* The medics bound up the soldiers' wounds.
  The old issues were bound up with twine.

EXPRESSIONS

be bound to _____ *be certain to* It's bound to snow this afternoon.
[do something] Erin is bound to be a great lawyer someday.
  East Junior High is bound to win the math contest.

PRESENT

I bite	we bite
you bite	you bite
he/she/it bites	they bite

• Be careful—the dog bites.

PRESENT PROGRESSIVE

I am biting	we are biting
you are biting	you are biting
he/she/it is biting	they are biting

• The fish are biting this afternoon.

PAST

I bit	we bit
you bit	you bit
he/she/it bit	they bit

• He looks like he bit into a sour lemon.

PAST PROGRESSIVE

I was biting	we were biting
you were biting	you were biting
he/she/it was biting	they were biting

• They were biting off more than they could chew.

PRESENT PERFECT ... have | has bitten
PAST PERFECT ... had bitten

FUTURE ... will bite
FUTURE PROGRESSIVE ... will be biting
FUTURE PERFECT ... will have bitten

PAST PASSIVE

I was bitten	we were bitten
you were bitten	you were bitten
he/she/it was bitten	they were bitten

• I was bitten by dozens of mosquitoes last night.

COMPLEMENTS

bite cut with the teeth	Does your dog bite?
bite sting	The mosquitoes are biting tonight.
	Ouch, that ointment bites.
bite be annoying/objectionable	His criticisms really bite!
bite take the bait, be tricked/cheated	The fish are biting in Big Moose Lake.
	Do you think the customers will bite?
bite _____ seize/wound with the teeth	
OBJECT	I just bit **my tongue**.
	The neighbor's dog bit **Thomas**.
WH-CLAUSE	The puppy was biting **whatever it could reach**.

PHRASAL VERBS

bite into _____ sink one's teeth into	Sammy bit into the orange and got juice all over his face.
bite (into) _____ hurt in a stinging way	The icy wind was biting into my face.
bite SEP **off** remove with the teeth	Susan bit off only a morsel.
bite on _____ chew on	Wade bit on his lip as he decided what to do.
bite on _____ be tricked by	Did Dennis bite on your latest ruse?

EXPRESSIONS

be bitten by the _____ **bug** be obsessed with	Jayne was bitten by the tennis bug.
bite off more than [one] can chew undertake more than one can handle	By opening five stores last year, the owners bit off more than they could chew.
bite [one's] tongue hold back from saying something offensive	Sheila had to bite her tongue to keep from calling her boyfriend a stupid idiot.
bite [someone's] head off speak very angrily to someone	I broke the copier, and my boss bit my head off.
bite the bullet be brave in a painful situation	I bit the bullet and attended my ex-girlfriend's wedding.
bite the dust die, be defeated	How old was the cowboy when he bit the dust?
	My first laptop finally bit the dust.

PRESENT

I bleed	we bleed
you bleed	you bleed
he/she/it bleeds	they bleed

• *His nose bleeds at high altitudes.*

PRESENT PROGRESSIVE

I am bleeding	we are bleeding
you are bleeding	you are bleeding
he/she/it is bleeding	they are bleeding

• *I'm bleeding onto my shirt.*

PAST

I bled	we bled
you bled	you bled
he/she/it bled	they bled

• *His wound bled for quite some time.*

PAST PROGRESSIVE

I was bleeding	we were bleeding
you were bleeding	you were bleeding
he/she/it was bleeding	they were bleeding

• *The company was bleeding money.*

PRESENT PERFECT ... have | has bled
PAST PERFECT ... had bled

FUTURE ... will bleed
FUTURE PROGRESSIVE ... will be bleeding
FUTURE PERFECT ... will have bled

PAST PASSIVE

I was bled	we were bled
you were bled	you were bled
he/she/it was bled	they were bled

• *He was bled dry by the blackmailers.*

COMPLEMENTS

bleed *lose blood*	Her hands and knees were bleeding.
bleed *seep, ooze*	The cut plants bled onto the rug.
	The newsprint is bleeding onto my hands.
bleed *lose money*	The automobile industry is bleeding at an unsustainable rate.
bleed *feel sympathy*	My heart bleeds for the widow.
	Her heart bleeds at her neighbor's misfortune.
bleed _____ *draw blood/fluid from* OBJECT	Doctors used to bleed **their patients** regularly. The mechanic bled **the brake line**.
bleed _____ *extort money from over time* OBJECT	Blackmailers bleed **their victims** of all their money.
bleed _____ *lose rapidly* OBJECT	Newspapers are bleeding **money** at an amazing rate.

PHRASAL VERBS

bleed off _____ *be printed so the image goes off the edge of [a page, sheet]*	The photo of the wolf bleeds off the page.
bleed off _____ *remove the contents of*	Irene bled off the air compressor.
bleed through _____ *show through [a layer]*	The dark blue is bleeding through the coat of white paint.

EXPRESSIONS

bleed _____ **dry/white** *drain of resources*	Legal fees will bleed you dry. The rock star's entourage bled him white.
bleed money *lose money rapidly*	The entire industry is bleeding money.
bleed to death *die from loss of blood*	If the doctors can't stop the bleeding, the boy will bleed to death.
bleeding heart *one who is exceptionally sympathetic toward the underprivileged*	George is a bleeding heart for the homeless.

PRESENT

I blow	we blow
you blow	you blow
he/she/it blows	they blow

  • *The wind always blows in the wintertime.*

PRESENT PROGRESSIVE

I am blowing	we are blowing
you are blowing	you are blowing
he/she/it is blowing	they are blowing

  • *The wind is blowing my hair.*

PAST

I blew	we blew
you blew	you blew
he/she/it blew	they blew

  • *He blew up all the balloons himself.*

PAST PROGRESSIVE

I was blowing	we were blowing
you were blowing	you were blowing
he/she/it was blowing	they were blowing

  • *The fans were blowing the gas out of the chamber.*

PRESENT PERFECT ... have | has blown
PAST PERFECT ... had blown

FUTURE ... will blow
FUTURE PROGRESSIVE ... will be blowing
FUTURE PERFECT ... will have blown

PAST PASSIVE

I was blown	we were blown
you were blown	you were blown
he/she/it was blown	they were blown

  • *The boat was blown off course.*

COMPLEMENTS

blow *move with force*	The wind was blowing softly.
blow *force air out*	The fans were blowing at low speed.
blow *produce a sound by having air forced through it*	The horns were all blowing.
blow *explode, erupt*	The volcano blew with a huge roar.
blow *abruptly fail*	The tire blew when we were going 55 miles an hour.
	The fuse blew when I turned on the iron.

blow _____ *move/carry away with a current of air*

    OBJECT + ADVERB OF PLACE TO/FROM   The fans were blowing **the stale air** *outside*.
    The wind was blowing **dirt** *in my eyes*.
    The breeze blew **the boat** *onto the rocks*.

blow _____ *force air at/into/through, fill with air*

    OBJECT   John blew **his nose**.
    The kids were blowing **bubbles** all afternoon.

    OBJECT + PREDICATE ADJECTIVE   Compressed air blew **the pipes** *clear*.
    She blew **her hair** *dry*.

blow _____ *produce a sound by forcing air through*

    OBJECT   The jazzman blew **the trumpet** with all his might.
    The referee blew **his whistle** before the ball was thrown.

blow _____ *cause to explode*

    OBJECT + PREDICATE ADJECTIVE   He blew **the safe** *open*.

blow _____ *botch, fail to keep*

    OBJECT   I blew **the exam**.
    The actors blew **their lines** repeatedly.
    The Giants blew **a 14-point lead**.

blow _____ *waste [money]*

    OBJECT   Zack blew **his money** on gambling.

blow _____ *leave hurriedly*

    OBJECT   I'm bored—let's blow **this joint**.

PHRASAL VERBS

blow away/off/out/etc. *be carried by a current of air in a specified direction*	Janet's hat blew off.
blow _SEP_ **away** *defeat soundly*	The visitors blew the home team away.
blow _SEP_ **away** *affect intensely*	This new poem of yours blows me away.
blow _SEP_ **away** *kill with a gun*	The gangsters blew the guard away.
blow down *collapse due to a strong current of air*	The shed blew down in the storm.
blow _SEP_ **down** *cause to collapse due to a strong current of air*	The storm blew the shed down.
blow in / (into ____) *arrive unexpectedly (at)*	Well, look who just blew in! Three strangers blew into town on Saturday night.
blow _SEP_ **off** *ignore, choose not to deal with*	Lanny blew off the assignment. Ramona blew off her friends and left town.
blow out *be extinguished*	The candle blew out because of the open windows.
blow out *burst suddenly*	The tire blew out, sounding like a gunshot.
blow _SEP_ **out** *extinguish with a gust of air*	Blow the candle out and go to sleep.
blow _SEP_ **out** *damage severely*	Chuck blew out his knee in the first game.
blow _SEP_ **out** *defeat soundly*	The Lions blew the Tigers out in an exhibition game.
blow [oneself] out *subside*	The guests left after the storm blew itself out.
blow over *subside*	The storm blew over almost as quickly as it arrived. This crisis will blow over soon.
blow up *arrive with wind*	A storm blew up out of the southwest.
blow up *explode*	The truck blew up on contact with a mine.
blow up *lose one's temper*	The teacher will blow up if you don't be quiet.
blow _SEP_ **up** *fill with air*	The clown blew up 20 balloons.
blow _SEP_ **up** *cause to explode*	The soldiers blew the headquarters up with mortars.
blow _SEP_ **up** *enlarge*	Let's blow the map up to 400%.

EXPRESSIONS

blow a fuse/gasket *become extremely angry*	Natalie blew a fuse when her secretary lost the files.
blow off (some) steam *release a pent-up emotion*	The players went to a bar to blow off some steam.
blow [one's] cool *lose one's composure*	I know you're frustrated, but don't blow your cool.
blow [someone's] mind *affect intensely*	The revelation really blows my mind.
blow [one's] (own) horn *praise oneself*	Rebecca is talented, but she never blows her own horn.
blow [one's] top/stack *speak/act very angrily*	The candidate blew his top at the nosy reporter.
blow ____ out of the water *destroy completely*	The new motorcycle will blow its competition out of the water.
blow the whistle (on ____) *report wrongdoing to authorities (about)*	A secretary blew the whistle on the accountant.
blow ____ to bits/ pieces/smithereens *blow completely apart*	A single mortar round blew the police station to pieces.

PRESENT

I break	we break
you break	you break
he/she/it breaks	they break

• *He never breaks his word.*

PRESENT PROGRESSIVE

I am breaking	we are breaking
you are breaking	you are breaking
he/she/it is breaking	they are breaking

• *We are breaking for lunch now.*

PAST

I broke	we broke
you broke	you broke
he/she/it broke	they broke

• *They broke every single agreement.*

PAST PROGRESSIVE

I was breaking	we were breaking
you were breaking	you were breaking
he/she/it was breaking	they were breaking

• *The company was just breaking even.*

PRESENT PERFECT ... have | has broken
PAST PERFECT ... had broken

FUTURE ... will break
FUTURE PROGRESSIVE ... will be breaking
FUTURE PERFECT ... will have broken

PAST PASSIVE

I was broken	we were broken
you were broken	you were broken
he/she/it was broken	they were broken

• *The window was already broken.*

COMPLEMENTS

break *fragment, shatter*	The delicate cup broke into pieces. The waves were breaking close to the shore.
break *fail in strength/resolve/control/ usability*	His health broke. His voice broke with emotion. The criminals broke under questioning. The replacement parts broke too.
break *begin/appear suddenly*	When the storm broke, I was on my bicycle. Dawn is breaking.
break *become publicly known*	The news broke this morning.
break *end suddenly*	Jasmine's fever broke last night.
break *become clear*	I hope the weather breaks soon.
break _____ *fracture, render inoperable* OBJECT	He broke **his left wrist**. They broke **my cell phone**.
break _____ *violate [a rule, agreement]* OBJECT	They broke **the rules**. We broke **our promise to them**.
break _____ *exceed, surpass* OBJECT	He was arrested because he broke **the speed limit**. They broke **the old record** by four seconds.
break _____ *make publicly known* OBJECT	The reporters broke **the news** this morning.
break _____ *disrupt, make ineffective* OBJECT	The soldiers broke **formation**. The noise broke **my concentration**. She broke **the spell**.
break _____ *stop, interrupt* OBJECT	The net broke **the trapeze artist's fall**. Esther broke **the silence** with a scream.
PASSIVE	The deadlock was broken at 3 A.M.

top 30 verb

break _____ *solve, figure out*	
OBJECT	The police broke **the case**.
	The scientists broke **the code**.
break _____ *give the equivalent of in smaller monetary units*	
OBJECT	Can you break **a twenty-dollar bill**?
break _____ *ruin financially*	
OBJECT	One more financial setback will break **the company**.
break _____ *tame, train to obey*	
OBJECT	The cowboys broke **the wild horses**.

(**PHRASAL VERBS**)

break away *leave suddenly*	Helene broke away from the rest of the sprinters.
break down *become inoperative/ineffective*	My car broke down at Sixth and Pine.
	Negotiations broke down after three days.
break down *become upset*	Seth broke down and cried at the news.
break down *give in*	Lonnie broke down and bought an MP3 player.
break _SEP_ **down** *divide into [pieces]*	Let's break the sentence down into subject and predicate.
break for _____ *interrupt one's activities for*	Let's break for lunch at 12 o'clock.
break _SEP_ **in** *train [an employee]*	Has Marilyn broken Mary in yet?
break _SEP_ **in** *use [something] until it functions well*	I have to break in a new pair of shoes.
break into _____ *enter, usually by force*	Thieves broke into the pharmacy.
break into _____ *begin suddenly*	When she's really happy, Gretchen breaks into song.
break into _____ *become engaged in*	Bert broke into show business at the age of four.
break into / in on _____ *interrupt*	I'm sorry to break in on your conversation, but I must go.
break _____ **into** *divide [something] into [pieces]*	We should break the project into individual tasks.
break off *stop suddenly*	Aaron's voice broke off in mid-sentence.
break _SEP_ **off** *discontinue*	The two nations have broken off diplomatic relations.
break out *develop*	Fire broke out in the kitchen area.
break out *be covered with*	Dave broke out in a sweat.
break out (of _____ **)** *escape (from)*	The prisoners broke out of jail in the early morning.
break up *fall apart, scatter*	The partnership broke up on amicable terms.
	The crowd broke up after the speech.
break up *laugh hard*	Every time I hear this monologue, I break up.
break up (with _____ **)** *end a romance (with)*	Have you heard? Alison broke up with Todd.
break _SEP_ **up** *cause to laugh hard*	This monologue just breaks me up.
break _SEP_ **up** *put an end to*	The FBI tried to break up the drug cartel.
	Two students broke the fight up.

(**EXPRESSIONS**)

top 30 verb

break even *achieve a balance between income and expenses*	The firm broke even in 2008.
break the ice *overcome awkwardness/formality*	The president broke the ice with a couple of jokes.

PRESENT

I breed	we breed
you breed	you breed
he/she/it breeds	they breed

• *Uncertainty breeds indecision and delay.*

PRESENT PROGRESSIVE

I am breeding	we are breeding
you are breeding	you are breeding
he/she/it is breeding	they are breeding

• *They are breeding disease-resistant wheat.*

PAST

I bred	we bred
you bred	you bred
he/she/it bred	they bred

• *She bred her dogs to herd sheep.*

PAST PROGRESSIVE

I was breeding	we were breeding
you were breeding	you were breeding
he/she/it was breeding	they were breeding

• *Their ruthless tactics were breeding resentment.*

PRESENT PERFECT ... have | has bred
PAST PERFECT ... had bred

FUTURE ... will breed
FUTURE PROGRESSIVE ... will be breeding
FUTURE PERFECT ... will have bred

PAST PASSIVE

I was bred	we were bred
you were bred	you were bred
he/she/it was bred	they were bred

• *These mice were bred in a laboratory.*

COMPLEMENTS

breed *mate, produce offspring*
Many animals fail to breed in captivity.
Mosquitoes breed in stagnant water.
My guppies are breeding like rabbits.

breed *originate and develop*
Unhappiness breeds on itself.
Fear bred in the streets of the threatened city.

breed _____ *cause to reproduce, especially for specific characteristics*
OBJECT   They breed **show horses** on their ranch.
PASSIVE   The plants were bred to withstand an early frost.

breed _____ *raise [a child], rear, train*
OBJECT   She bred **her daughters** to have perfect manners.
PASSIVE   William Faulkner was born and bred in Mississippi.

breed _____ *cause to happen*
OBJECT   Familiarity breeds **contempt**. [PROVERB]
     Success breeds **success**.
PASSIVE   Speculation is bred by unregulated risk taking.

breed _____ *be the source/origin of*
OBJECT   Silicon Valley breeds **innovation and technological breakthroughs**.
     The Midwest breeds **its share of talented musicians**.

─────────────────────────────────── PHRASAL VERBS ───

bring _SEP_ **about** *cause to happen*	How can we bring about change?
bring _SEP_ **along** *have [someone] come along*	Be sure to bring a friend along on the tour.
bring _SEP_ **around** *cause to regain consciousness*	The medic brought the injured man around.
bring _SEP_ **around** *persuade*	They brought Andy around on going to Cancun.
bring _SEP_ **away** *come away with [information]*	We bring valuable insights away from the speech.
bring _SEP_ **back** *recall*	These photographs bring back lots of memories.
bring ____ **before** *cause to appear before [an authority]*	The guards brought the defendant before Judge Flynn.
bring ____ **before** *introduce for consideration by*	I brought the zoning issue before the city council.
bring _SEP_ **down** *cause to fall*	His own mistakes brought him down.
bring _SEP_ **forth** *give birth to, produce*	Amy expects to bring forth a healthy son. Reinforcements brought forth the historic victory.
bring _SEP_ **forth** *make known*	The lawyer brought forth two good arguments.
bring _SEP_ **in** *produce, earn*	The subsidiary brought in $30 million last year.
bring ____ **in on** *include [someone] in [an activity]*	The president brought them in on the decision.
bring _SEP_ **off** *make happen, accomplish*	He brought off the biggest upset of the day.
bring _SEP_ **on** *cause to appear*	It's time to bring on the clowns.
bring _SEP_ **out** *cause to emerge*	A police siren brings people out into the street.
bring _SEP_ **out** *publish, issue*	She brings out a new novel every two years.
bring _SEP_ **over** *persuade*	Alexandra brought Gil over to our side.
bring ____ **through** *help to endure*	My sister brought her husband through.
bring ____ **to** *cause to regain consciousness*	We brought Anne to before the medics arrived.
bring _SEP_ **together** *cause to gather*	We brought the class together for one last party.
bring _SEP_ **up** *mention*	Jackie brought up the idea of having more parties.
bring _SEP_ **up** *raise [a child]*	It's not easy to bring up twins. Camelia's parents brought her up to be nice.
bring ____ **up on** *provide in [someone's] childhood*	Mom brought us up on the Beatles.
bring ____ **up on / up-to-date on / up to speed on** *inform [someone] about*	Would you like to bring us up on the latest developments?

─────────────────────────────────────── EXPRESSIONS ───

bring ____ **into play** *cause to be a factor*	The campaign is bringing Internet strategies into play.
bring ____ **into question** *cause to be doubted*	Reports have brought his character into question.
bring ____ **into service** *begin to use*	We will bring 30 wind farms into service by May.
bring ____ **into view** *cause to be seen*	The viewfinder brought the mountain into view.
bring ____ **to a head** *cause to reach a crisis*	The theft brings the question of security to a head.
bring ____ **to an end / a close / a climax** *end*	My new book will bring the case to a close.
bring ____ **to life** *give vitality to*	The children want to bring the puppet to life.
bring ____ **to light** *reveal*	The journalist brought the corruption to light.
bring ____ **to mind** *recall*	The reunion brought to mind all the good times we had.
bring ____ **to [someone's] attention** *make aware of*	Citizens have brought the issue to our attention.

I bring   we bring
you bring   you bring
he/she/it brings   they bring
  • *April showers bring May flowers.*

PRESENT PROGRESSIVE

I am bringing   we are bringing
you are bringing   you are bringing
he/she/it is bringing   they are bringing
  • *We are bringing the books with us.*

PAST

I brought   we brought
you brought   you brought
he/she/it brought   they brought
  • *They brought us some good news.*

PAST PROGRESSIVE

I was bringing   we were bringing
you were bringing   you were bringing
he/she/it was bringing   they were bringing
  • *They were bringing the dessert.*

PRESENT PERFECT … have | has brought
PAST PERFECT   … had brought

FUTURE   … will bring
FUTURE PROGRESSIVE   … will be bringing
FUTURE PERFECT   … will have brought

PAST PASSIVE

I was brought   we were brought
you were brought   you were brought
he/she/it was brought   they were brought
  • *This message was brought to you by our sponsor.*

(COMPLEMENTS)

NOTE: The verb *bring* generally indicates movement toward the speaker
or toward the focus of attention; compare with *take* (verb No. 166).

bring _____ *carry, lead*

OBJECT (+ ADVERB OF PLACE TO/FROM)
Who will bring **dessert**?
Bring **the book** *here*, please.
I brought **the visitors** *to their hotel*.
The coupons really brought **a crowd** *to the store*.
You should bring **them** *back*.

INDIRECT OBJECT + DIRECT OBJECT
He brought *me* **my dinner**.
She brought *us* **the new account**.
The sale brought *them* **a small fortune**.

to PARAPHRASE
He brought **my dinner** *to me*.
She brought **the new account** *to us*.
The sale brought **a small fortune** *to them*.

OBJECT + WH-CLAUSE
She brought **us** *whatever she could*.

WH-CLAUSE (+ ADVERB OF PLACE TO/FROM)
Bring **whomever you want**.
Bring **whatever you can** *to the picnic*.

bring _____ *cause to be in a particular state/condition*

OBJECT + *to* OBJECT
I brought **the water** *to a boil*.
They brought **the meeting** *to a conclusion*.

bring _____ *bear as an attribute*

OBJECT
He brought **lots of experience** to the table.

bring _____ *result in*

OBJECT
The storm brought **ten inches of rain**.
The drug will bring **nearly immediate relief**.

bring _____ *cause*

OBJECT + INFINITIVE
What brought **you** *to apply to 8 colleges*?

bring _____ *sell for*

OBJECT
Our old car brought **$350**.
The sale will bring **a lot of money**.

bring _____ *file in court*

OBJECT
He brought **charges** against the owners.

broadcast

broadcast | broadcasts · broadcast/broadcasted · ☑ IRREGULAR
have broadcast/broadcasted ☑ REGULAR

PRESENT

I broadcast	we broadcast
you broadcast	you broadcast
he/she/it broadcasts	they broadcast

• *He broadcasts all of their games.*

PAST

I broadcast	we broadcast
you broadcast	you broadcast
he/she/it broadcast	they broadcast

• *The station broadcast the show for 50 years.*

PRESENT PERFECT ... have | has broadcast
PAST PERFECT ... had broadcast

PRESENT PROGRESSIVE

I am broadcasting	we are broadcasting
you are broadcasting	you are broadcasting
he/she/it is broadcasting	they are broadcasting

• *They are broadcasting the debate live.*

PAST PROGRESSIVE

I was broadcasting	we were broadcasting
you were broadcasting	you were broadcasting
he/she/it was broadcasting	they were broadcasting

• *We were broadcasting from Los Angeles then.*

FUTURE ... will broadcast
FUTURE PROGRESSIVE ... will be broadcasting
FUTURE PERFECT ... will have broadcast

PAST PASSIVE

— —
— —
it was broadcast   they were broadcast

• *The news was broadcast in high definition.*

(COMPLEMENTS)

broadcast *transmit programming via radio/TV*	They broadcast in Latin America. They broadcast in Spanish. We broadcast on the FM dial in stereo. Shhh! They're broadcasting.
broadcast *participate in a broadcast program*	She broadcasts live from Rockefeller Center.
broadcast _____ *transmit via radio/TV*	
OBJECT	They broadcast **news about Asia**. We broadcast **college football games**.
broadcast _____ *communicate via radio/TV*	
OBJECT	The police broadcast **a description of the suspect**. The weather bureau broadcast **a storm warning for the region**.
THAT-CLAUSE	The networks broadcast **that Senator Blather was the likely winner**. The radio broadcast **that all the major downtown freeways were closed**.
WH-CLAUSE	The stations only broadcast **what they think the public wants to hear**.
broadcast _____ *make widely known*	
OBJECT	I'll broadcast **my marriage proposal** on the stadium scoreboard. Please don't broadcast **the rumor** to everyone you see.
THAT-CLAUSE	I model part-time. But I don't go broadcasting **that I do**.
WH-CLAUSE	Don't go broadcasting **why we split up**.

PRESENT

I build	we build
you build	you build
he/she/it builds	they build

• *He builds custom-made furniture.*

PRESENT PROGRESSIVE

I am building	we are building
you are building	you are building
he/she/it is building	they are building

• *They are building a new house.*

PAST

I built	we built
you built	you built
he/she/it built	they built

• *They just built a house near us.*

PAST PROGRESSIVE

I was building	we were building
you were building	you were building
he/she/it was building	they were building

• *We were building passenger cars on truck frames.*

PRESENT PERFECT ... have | has built
PAST PERFECT ... had built

FUTURE ... will build
FUTURE PROGRESSIVE ... will be building
FUTURE PERFECT ... will have built

PAST PASSIVE

—	—
—	—
it was built	they were built

• *Our house was built in 1996.*

COMPLEMENTS

build *increase in size/intensity*	The waves were building ever higher. Our debt was building to scary levels. Excitement is building over who will be elected.
build ____ *construct*	
OBJECT	Tommy built **the wagon** out of parts he found in the garage. We built **a deck** this summer. They are building **a communications network**. We have built **a good plan**. The prosecutor built **a strong case** against the suspect.
INDIRECT OBJECT + DIRECT OBJECT	They built *us* **a two-car garage**. We built *them* **a new investment package**.
for PARAPHRASE	They **built a two-car garage** *for us*. We built **a new investment package** *for them*.
WH-CLAUSE	We can only build **what we can afford**. They will build **whatever the marketplace wants**.
build ____ *increase*	
OBJECT	The campaign built **support** by offering free T-shirts. The company is building **their business** one store at a time.

PHRASAL VERBS

build ____ **in/into** *make [something] an integral part of*	We will build cabinets into the laundry room. The programmers built security into the server software.
build ____ **on/onto** *construct [something] as an addition to*	We built a deck onto the house this summer.
build _SEP_ **up** *increase*	The politicians built up hope among poor people. Steven is building up leg strength by running five miles a day.
build _SEP_ **up** *promote*	The agency built Eileen up as a pop singer.

EXPRESSIONS

build ____ **to order** *construct to individual specifications*	The woodworker builds bookcases to order. Every computer is built to order.

burn

burn | burns · burned · have burned
burn | burns · burnt · have burnt

☑ REGULAR
☑ IRREGULAR

PRESENT

I burn	we burn
you burn	you burn
he/she/it burns	they burn

• *He really burns me up.*

PRESENT PROGRESSIVE

I am burning	we are burning
you are burning	you are burning
he/she/it is burning	they are burning

• *She is burning loveletters from her ex-husband.*

PAST

I burnt	we burnt
you burnt	you burnt
he/she/it burnt	they burnt

• *We burnt oak firewood last winter.*

PAST PROGRESSIVE

I was burning	we were burning
you were burning	you were burning
he/she/it was burning	they were burning

• *A light was burning in the window.*

PRESENT PERFECT ... have | has burnt
PAST PERFECT ... had burnt

FUTURE ... will burn
FUTURE PROGRESSIVE ... will be burning
FUTURE PERFECT ... will have burnt

PAST PASSIVE

I was burnt	we were burnt
you were burnt	you were burnt
he/she/it was burnt	they were burnt

• *My hand was burnt by the hot plate.*

COMPLEMENTS

burn *be on fire*	Get out—the building is burning!
	A small fire was burning in the fireplace.
burn *be destroyed by fire*	Our apartment building burnt last night.
	The paper and kindling burnt quickly.
burn *give off light*	Every lamp in the house was burning.
burn *be/feel hot/painful*	Her forehead was burning.
	My ears were burning from the cold.
burn *become sunburned*	With her fair complexion, she burns easily.
burn _____ *set fire to, destroy by fire*	
OBJECT	We burnt **the trash** in the fireplace.
burn _____ *damage/injure by heat/fire*	
OBJECT	A spark burnt **a hole** in my pants.
	I burnt **my fingers.**
	I burnt **myself** on the stove.
burn _____ *use as fuel/energy*	
OBJECT	Most cars can burn **regular gas.**
	Soccer players burn **more calories** than golfers.
WH-CLAUSE	We burnt **whatever we could get our hands on.**
burn _____ *cause to feel hot*	
OBJECT	The salsa burnt **my mouth.**
burn _____ *record data on*	
OBJECT	We burnt **some new CDs.**
burn _____ *defeat, trick, cheat*	
OBJECT	The quarterback burnt **the defense** on that play.
PASSIVE	I got burnt by the dot-com crash in 2000.
	We were burnt in the commodities market.

PHRASAL VERBS

burn down *burn smaller and smaller*	The candle burnt down and went out.
burn _SEP_ **up** *make very angry*	That nasty remark really burns me up.

PRESENT

I burst	we burst
you burst	you burst
he/she/it bursts	they burst

• *He always bursts into tears.*

PRESENT PROGRESSIVE

I am bursting	we are bursting
you are bursting	you are bursting
he/she/it is bursting	they are bursting

• *I'm bursting to tell you what happened.*

PAST

I burst	we burst
you burst	you burst
he/she/it burst	they burst

• *He burst all of our hopes.*

PAST PROGRESSIVE

I was bursting	we were bursting
you were bursting	you were bursting
he/she/it was bursting	they were bursting

• *We were just bursting after Thanksgiving dinner.*

PRESENT PERFECT ... have | has burst	
PAST PERFECT ... had burst	

FUTURE ... will burst	
FUTURE PROGRESSIVE ... will be bursting	
FUTURE PERFECT ... will have burst	

PAST PASSIVE

—	—
—	—
it was burst	they were burst

• *The dam was burst by the heavy rains.*

COMPLEMENTS

burst *break, rupture*	The balloons all burst. I was afraid that my eardrums would burst from the sudden pressure change.
burst *be filled to the breaking point*	The auditorium was bursting with students.
burst *explode* [OFTEN FIGURATIVE]	The rocket burst above the spectators' heads. The bushes are just bursting with blossoms.
burst *give way to sudden emotion*	I felt like my heart would burst. I was bursting with pride.
burst _____ *cause to break/explode* OBJECT	The explosion burst **the windows**. The older kids burst **all the balloons**. The hurricane burst **the retaining walls**.

burst _____ *be very eager*
     for OBJECT + INFINITIVE
 	
     INFINITIVE
	We are bursting **for him *to tell us***.
	I am bursting **for Mary *to see what we have done***.
	I'm bursting **to know what happened**.
	The kids are bursting **to open their presents**.

PHRASAL VERBS

burst in on _____ *interrupt suddenly*	The secretary burst in on the private meeting.
burst in/into _____ *enter suddenly*	The children burst into the room.
burst onto _____ *emerge suddenly in a location*	The singer burst onto the stage.
burst out *explode outward*	When the glass burst out, I was cut by flying shards.
burst out _____ *begin suddenly [to do]*	We all burst out laughing at the joke.
burst (out) into _____ *begin [an activity] suddenly*	After the accident, Kathleen burst into tears. When I hear bongo drums, I burst out into song.
burst out of _____ *be too big for*	She was embarrassed to be bursting out of her dress.
burst out of _____ *leave quickly*	At midnight, the partygoers burst out of the hall.
burst through _____ *break through with force*	The troops burst through the enemy line.

PRESENT

I buy	we buy
you buy	you buy
he/she/it buys	they buy

• *He always buys locally.*

PRESENT PROGRESSIVE

I am buying	we are buying
you are buying	you are buying
he/she/it is buying	they are buying

• *We are buying a new TV.*

PAST

I bought	we bought
you bought	you bought
he/she/it bought	they bought

• *We bought a new car last week.*

PAST PROGRESSIVE

I was buying	we were buying
you were buying	you were buying
he/she/it was buying	they were buying

• *They were buying it on credit.*

PRESENT PERFECT ... have | has bought
PAST PERFECT ... had bought

FUTURE ... will buy
FUTURE PROGRESSIVE ... will be buying
FUTURE PERFECT ... will have bought

PAST PASSIVE

I was bought	we were bought
you were bought	you were bought
he/she/it was bought	they were bought

• *The house was bought in 1982.*

COMPLEMENTS

buy _____ *purchase*

OBJECT

I bought **take-out** for dinner.
We will buy **500 shares of Apex Corporation.**
A dollar buys **less** than a euro does.

INDIRECT OBJECT + DIRECT OBJECT

I bought *the kids* **some new toys.**
They bought *us* **dinner.**

for PARAPHRASE

I bought **some new toys** *for the kids*.
They bought **dinner** *for us*.

WH-CLAUSE

Mom buys **whichever brand is cheapest.**

buy _____ *accept, believe, agree to/with*

OBJECT

They bought **our proposal.**
Will the students buy **the idea**?
I don't buy **that** at all.

PHRASAL VERBS

buy into _____ *purchase shares of*

Our investment club bought into
the Triangle Corporation.

buy into _____ *agree with, believe in*

I don't buy into his money-making scheme.

buy ⎯SEP⎯ **off** *bribe*

The candidate changed positions; lobbyists bought him off.

buy ⎯SEP⎯ **out** *purchase all assets/
interests of [a business]*

We bought out our competitors.

buy ⎯SEP⎯ **up** *purchase all of*

We bought up every copy of the *Times* that had Tim's
crossword puzzle in it.

EXPRESSIONS

buy _____ **for a song** *purchase cheaply*

She bought this new rocking chair for a song.

buy _____ **on credit/time** *purchase now
and pay later for*

Can we buy this refrigerator on credit?

buy _____ **sight unseen** *purchase
without looking at first*

My parents bought a condo in Florida sight unseen.

buy (some) time *delay an action/decision
in hopes that a situation will improve*

The owner wants to buy some time while he considers
all his options.

PRESENT		PRESENT PROGRESSIVE	
I cast	we cast	I am casting	we are casting
you cast	you cast	you are casting	you are casting
he/she/it casts	they cast	he/she/it is casting	they are casting

• The statue casts a long shadow.   *• I am casting the play this week.*

PAST		PAST PROGRESSIVE	
I cast	we cast	I was casting	we were casting
you cast	you cast	you were casting	you were casting
he/she/it cast	they cast	he/she/it was casting	they were casting

• He cast me in the role of the duke.   *• We were casting off by 6 A.M.*

PRESENT PERFECT	... have | has cast
PAST PERFECT	... had cast

FUTURE	... will cast
FUTURE PROGRESSIVE	... will be casting
FUTURE PERFECT	... will have cast

PAST PASSIVE	
I was cast	we were cast
you were cast	you were cast
he/she/it was cast	they were cast

• The dice were cast.

COMPLEMENTS

cast *throw a fishing line/net into the water*   He cast wherever he could see fish.

cast _____ *throw*
   OBJECT

The fishermen cast **their nets** off their boats.
I cast **a line** to the children in the boat.
The boys cast **stones** into the pond.

cast _____ *direct, focus*
   OBJECT + ADVERB OF PLACE

The fireplace cast **a cheerful light** *into the room.*
He cast **a quick glance** *at his audience.*
The moon cast **its light** *on the shimmering lake.*

cast _____ *convey*
   OBJECT + ADVERB OF PLACE

Recent events cast **doubt** *on our decision.*
His actions cast **suspicion** *on his motives.*

cast _____ *choose actors for*
   OBJECT

Roberta has already cast **the play.**

cast _____ *assign a role to*
   OBJECT + *as* OBJECT

We cast **him** *as the hero's father.*
Senator Blather cast **his opponent** *as a reckless spender.*

   OBJECT + *in* OBJECT

He cast **her** *in the leading role.*
Sally cast **Harry** *in the role of best friend.*

cast _____ *form by pouring liquid into a mold*
   OBJECT

The foundry casts **brass bells.**
We cast **wax candles** with the children.

cast _____ *deposit [a ballot, vote]*
   OBJECT

Samuel cast **his ballot** for the liberal candidate.

PHRASAL VERBS

cast _SEP_ **aside/away/off** *discard, throw away*

Lisa cast aside her winter clothes.
The boss cast off all his doubts about the new salesperson.

cast _SEP_ **back** *direct to the past*   The retired teacher cast his thoughts back to happier days.

cast off *push away from the dock*   The cruise ship cast off at 0900 hours.

cast _SEP_ **out** *expel*   The club cast Ollie out for failure to pay dues.

catch _____ *draw even with, overtake*
   OBJECT

Their Gross Domestic Product is catching **Spain's**.
I tried to catch **him** on the last lap.

catch _____ *take/get quickly*
   OBJECT

Norvel caught **a glimpse of himself** in the mirror.
I caught **sight of Cary** on the subway platform.
Try to catch **some sleep** before you leave.

catch _____ *attract and hold*
   OBJECT

Lori's poster will catch **everybody's attention**.
The new employee caught **her eye**.

PHRASAL VERBS

catch _____ **from** *get [a disease] from [someone/something]*

The whole class caught
   the flu from Jimmy.

catch on *become popular*

The Beatles caught on after *The Ed Sullivan Show*.

catch on (to _____) *figure out, learn*

Dexter finally caught on to what Delia had meant.
Cal is new at the job, but he's catching on quickly.

catch [someone]'s eye *get [someone's] attention*

I caught her eye from across the room.

catch _SEP_ up in *interest/involve [someone] in*

Her husband caught her up in his latest scheme.
The crowd was caught up in all the excitement.

catch _____ up (on) *bring up-to-date about*

The assistant will catch the actor up on the news.

catch up on _____ / get caught up on _____
make oneself current about

I hope to catch up on my reading when I retire.
Tonight we can get caught up on our sleep.

catch up (to/with _____) *get even (with [someone/something])*

Will supply ever catch up to demand?
The taxi caught up with the bus at Skinker Blvd.

EXPRESSIONS

be caught short *be without money when one needs it*

Bill was caught short today
   and couldn't pay for his lunch.

catch a whiff of _____ *smell*

I caught a whiff of sweet perfume.

catch _____ at it *discover [someone doing something wrong]*

They were sneaking cookies, and Mother caught
   them at it.

catch _____ dead *see at any time*
[USUALLY NEGATIVE]

You wouldn't catch me dead in that place.
I wouldn't be caught dead in that place.

catch _____ napping *surprise [someone who is unprepared]*

The enemy caught our platoon napping.

catch _____ off balance/guard *surprise*

The question caught Senator Blather off balance.

catch (on) fire *become ignited*

The kindling finally caught fire.

catch [one's] breath *rest after intense activity*

I just ran four miles—let me catch my breath!

catch [one's] death of cold *become sick with a severe cold*

Put on a jacket or you'll catch your death of cold.

catch _____ red-handed *discover [someone] doing something wrong*

The police caught the thief red-handed.

catch _____ with [someone's] pants down *discover [someone] in an embarrassing situation*

They were taking bribes, and investigators caught
   them with their pants down.

catch wind of _____ *hear about*

We just caught wind of the new energy proposal.

top 30 verb

PRESENT

I catch	we catch
you catch	you catch
he/she/it catches	they catch

• *The basin catches rainwater.*

PRESENT PROGRESSIVE

I am catching	we are catching
you are catching	you are catching
he/she/it is catching	they are catching

• *I am catching the last train.*

PAST

I caught	we caught
you caught	you caught
he/she/it caught	they caught

• *I caught a cold over the weekend.*

PAST PROGRESSIVE

I was catching	we were catching
you were catching	you were catching
he/she/it was catching	they were catching

• *The kids were catching minnows in the pond.*

PRESENT PERFECT … have | has caught
PAST PERFECT … had caught

FUTURE … will catch
FUTURE PROGRESSIVE … will be catching
FUTURE PERFECT … will have caught

PAST PASSIVE

I was caught	we were caught
you were caught	you were caught
he/she/it was caught	they were caught

• *The burglar was finally caught by the police.*

COMPLEMENTS

catch *begin to burn/operate*	The leaves and twigs finally caught.
	The engine coughed twice and caught.
catch *become entangled*	My sleeve caught on a hook.
catch *act as a catcher* [BASEBALL]	Molina caught in all four games of the series.
catch _____ *capture, seize, trap, snag, entangle*	
OBJECT	They caught **the thief**.
	We caught **some trout** for dinner.
	The bushes caught **my jacket**.
PASSIVE	I was caught in traffic for 45 minutes.
	Basil was caught in a hailstorm.
catch _____ *grasp and hold onto (physically)*	
OBJECT	I caught **the ball**.
catch _____ *understand, comprehend*	
OBJECT	I caught **the joke**.
	Sorry, I didn't catch **your name**.
catch _____ *discover [someone doing something wrong]*	
OBJECT + PRESENT PARTICIPLE	I caught **them** *sleeping on the job*.
	We caught **the kids** *smoking in the garage*.
PASSIVE	Zack was caught *breaking into a car*.
catch _____ *board [a vehicle]*	
OBJECT	I have to catch **a plane**.
	I'll catch **a taxi** at the hotel.
catch _____ *become sick with*	
OBJECT	Everyone caught **a cold**.
catch _____ *go to see*	
OBJECT	We caught **the last performance of the day**.
catch _____ *watch, listen to*	
OBJECT	Did you catch **the game** on TV?
catch _____ *meet with*	
OBJECT	I'll catch **you** later.
	We will catch **him** at the meeting tomorrow.

chide

chide | chides · chided · have chided
chide | chides · chid · have chid/chidden

☑ REGULAR
☑ IRREGULAR

PRESENT

I chide	we chide
you chide	you chide
he/she/it chides	they chide

• *She chides me for being gullible.*

PRESENT PROGRESSIVE

I am chiding	we are chiding
you are chiding	you are chiding
he/she/it is chiding	they are chiding

• *We are chiding them about their terrible coffee.*

PAST

I chid	we chid
you chid	you chid
he/she/it chid	they chid

• *The librarian gently chid the children.*

PAST PROGRESSIVE

I was chiding	we were chiding
you were chiding	you were chiding
he/she/it was chiding	they were chiding

• *I was chiding him for spending all his money.*

PRESENT PERFECT ... have | has chid/chidden
PAST PERFECT ... had chid/chidden

FUTURE ... will chide
FUTURE PROGRESSIVE ... will be chiding
FUTURE PERFECT ... will have chid/chidden

PAST PASSIVE

I was chid/chidden	we were chid/chidden
you were chid/chidden	you were chid/chidden
he/she/it was chid/chidden	they were chid/chidden

• *We were chidden for missing the beginning of the meeting.*

COMPLEMENTS

chide *express disapproval/displeasure*

He is an old grouch who chides constantly.
He chides about the morals of "kids these days."

chide _____ *reprimand, scold*

OBJECT

Too many teachers chide **their students** over nothing.
I chid **the people who kept talking during the movie.**

PASSIVE

We were chidden for expressing unpopular opinions.

DIRECT QUOTATION

"Don't act like that," she chid.
"Well," the senator chid, **"we'll see about that!"**

chide _____ *goad, nag*

OBJECT + *into* PRESENT PARTICIPLE

The manager chid **the tenants** *into cleaning up the yard.*
He chid **me** *into doing something I didn't really want to do.*

PASSIVE

We were chid *into filling out a questionnaire.*

PRESENT

I choose	we choose
you choose	you choose
he/she/it chooses	they choose

* *He always chooses to take Amtrak.*

PRESENT PROGRESSIVE

I am choosing	we are choosing
you are choosing	you are choosing
he/she/it is choosing	they are choosing

* *They are choosing someone right now.*

PAST

I chose	we chose
you chose	you chose
he/she/it chose	they chose

* *They chose a new president.*

PAST PROGRESSIVE

I was choosing	we were choosing
you were choosing	you were choosing
he/she/it was choosing	they were choosing

* *They were choosing a new secretary.*

PRESENT PERFECT ... have | has chosen
PAST PERFECT ... had chosen

FUTURE ... will choose
FUTURE PROGRESSIVE ... will be choosing
FUTURE PERFECT ... will have chosen

PAST PASSIVE

I was chosen	we were chosen
you were chosen	you were chosen
he/she/it was chosen	they were chosen

* *My candidate was chosen.*

COMPLEMENTS

choose *make a selection*

You need to choose.
They are still choosing.
You may choose between lemon and cherry Danish.

choose _____ *select, opt for, prefer*

OBJECT	Giuseppe chose **the toasted ravioli**. The delegates chose **Senator Blather**. The residents chose **pumpkin pie** over cheesecake. The bride chose **satin** for her wedding dress.
INDIRECT OBJECT + DIRECT OBJECT	I chose *myself* **a new computer**. My son chose *his mother* **a present**.
for PARAPHRASE	I chose **a new computer** *for myself*. My son chose **a present** *for his mother*.
OBJECT + *as* PREDICATE NOUN	He chose **Ralph** *as his partner*. They chose **Sue** *as captain*.
OBJECT + *for* PREDICATE NOUN	We will choose **Meg** *for treasurer*. She chose **Sarah** *for her maid of honor*.
OBJECT + *to be* PREDICATE NOUN	They chose **him** *to be secretary*.
OBJECT + INFINITIVE	They chose **her** *to give the keynote address*. He chose **Larry** *to be his best man*. You should choose **Kay** *to design your book*.
INFINITIVE	We chose **to fly to Denver**.
WH-CLAUSE	He is choosing **what to take**. We chose **where we would go on vacation**.
PRESENT PARTICIPLE	We chose **flying to Denver** over driving there.

EXPRESSIONS

choose (up) sides *form opposing teams by having captains alternately select players*

Once they chose up sides, they had
  to decide which team would bat first.

pick and choose *select carefully*

Co-op members can pick and choose from a wide
  variety of Dina's produce.

cleave

cleave | cleaves · cleaved · have cleaved   ☑ REGULAR
cleave | cleaves · cleft/clove · have cleft/cloven   ☑ IRREGULAR

PRESENT

I cleave	we cleave
you cleave	you cleave
he/she/it cleaves	they cleave

• *Mica cleaves in absolutely straight lines.*

PRESENT PROGRESSIVE

I am cleaving	we are cleaving
you are cleaving	you are cleaving
he/she/it is cleaving	they are cleaving

• *The boat is cleaving the waves at full speed.*

PAST

I cleft/clove	we cleft/clove
you cleft/clove	you cleft/clove
he/she/it cleft/clove	they cleft/clove

• *He clove the log in half.*

PAST PROGRESSIVE

I was cleaving	we were cleaving
you were cleaving	you were cleaving
he/she/it was cleaving	they were cleaving

• *The war was cleaving the nation.*

PRESENT PERFECT ... have | has cleft/cloven
PAST PERFECT ... had cleft/cloven

FUTURE ... will cleave
FUTURE PROGRESSIVE ... will be cleaving
FUTURE PERFECT ... will have cleft/cloven

PAST PASSIVE

—	—
—	—
it was cleft/cloven	they were cleft/cloven

• *A tunnel was cleft through the hill.*

NOTE: This irregular verb should not be confused with the unrelated regular verb *cleave (to),* meaning "stick/adhere (to)," as in *His tongue cleaved to the roof of his mouth.*

───(COMPLEMENTS)───

cleave *split/separate, usually along natural lines*

The best firewood cleaves with hardly any effort.
We found some slate that clove perfectly.

cleave *move smoothly, as if splitting the air/water*

The birds clove and swooped through the air.
The jet clove through the clouds.

cleave _____ *cut something apart by a splitting blow*

OBJECT

We cleft **the logs** into quarters.
They then clove **the cedar** for roof shakes.

PASSIVE

The rock had been cleft for paving stones.

cleave _____ *penetrate/pierce, as if by splitting*

OBJECT

A bolt of lightning cleft **the night sky**.
The boat clove **the waves,** spraying water to both sides.

PASSIVE

The shield was cloven by the Viking in a single stroke.

PRESENT		PRESENT PROGRESSIVE	
I cling	we cling	I am clinging	we are clinging
you cling	you cling	you are clinging	you are clinging
he/she/it clings	they cling	he/she/it is clinging	they are clinging

• *We cling to our beliefs as long as we can.*   • *He is clinging to life by a thread.*

PAST		PAST PROGRESSIVE	
I clung	we clung	I was clinging	we were clinging
you clung	you clung	you were clinging	you were clinging
he/she/it clung	they clung	he/she/it was clinging	they were clinging

• *He clung to them throughout the ordeal.*   • *The passengers were clinging to the handrails.*

PRESENT PERFECT	... have	has clung
PAST PERFECT	... had clung

FUTURE	... will cling
FUTURE PROGRESSIVE	... will be clinging
FUTURE PERFECT	... will have clung

PAST PASSIVE

—	—
—	—
it was clung	they were clung

• *The story was clung to desperately.*

(**COMPLEMENTS**)

NOTE: The verb *cling*, when not used with an object, is always followed by *together*.

cling *hold on tightly to each other*

The twins clung together under the umbrella.
The socks were clinging together when I removed them from the dryer.

cling _____ *adhere, hold on tightly*
   to OBJECT

He clung **to the ledge** until he was rescued.
The climbers were clinging **to the rope**.
The girl clung **to her father's hand**.
The ivy was clinging **to the wall**.
The price stickers always cling **to the fruit**.
The molecules cling **to each other**.
The office was clinging **to outdated software**.

cling _____ *have a strong emotional attachment*
   to OBJECT

Believers cling **to their faith**.
Elvis's fans always clung **to him** no matter what.

   to WH-CLAUSE

They will cling **to whoever their prophet is**.
They clung **to whatever their leader told them**.

clothe

clothe | clothes · clothed · have clothed
clothe | clothes · clad · have clad

☑ REGULAR
☑ IRREGULAR

PRESENT

I clothe	we clothe
you clothe	you clothe
he/she/it clothes	they clothe

• *He clothes his models in the latest fashions.*

PRESENT PROGRESSIVE

I am clothing	we are clothing
you are clothing	you are clothing
he/she/it is clothing	they are clothing

• *She is clothing her bridesmaids in pastel colors.*

PAST

I clad	we clad
you clad	you clad
he/she/it clad	they clad

• *She clad herself in a dressing gown.*

PAST PROGRESSIVE

I was clothing	we were clothing
you were clothing	you were clothing
he/she/it was clothing	they were clothing

• *He was clothing the actors in medieval costumes.*

PRESENT PERFECT ... have | has clad
PAST PERFECT ... had clad

FUTURE ... will clothe
FUTURE PROGRESSIVE ... will be clothing
FUTURE PERFECT ... will have clad

PAST PASSIVE

I was clad	we were clad
you were clad	you were clad
he/she/it was clad	they were clad

• *The king was clad in beautiful ermine robes.*

(**COMPLEMENTS**)

clothe _____ *put clothes on, dress*

   OBJECT — They always clothe **themselves** in the oddest fashions.

   PASSIVE — He was clad in dirty shorts and a rumpled T-shirt.

clothe _____ *cover, as with clothing*

   OBJECT — The decorators clad **the tables** with linen fabric.

clothe _____ *provide clothing for*

    — He could hardly feed and clothe **his own family**.

   OBJECT — That store clothes **half of the people in the whole town**.

   PASSIVE — The flood victims were clad by relief agencies.

PRESENT

I come	we come
you come	you come
he/she/it comes	they come

- *He comes here on weekends.*

PAST

I came	we came
you came	you came
he/she/it came	they came

- *They came to see you.*

PRESENT PERFECT ... have | has come
PAST PERFECT ... had come

PRESENT PROGRESSIVE

I am coming	we are coming
you are coming	you are coming
he/she/it is coming	they are coming

- *I'm coming as fast as I can.*

PAST PROGRESSIVE

I was coming	we were coming
you were coming	you were coming
he/she/it was coming	they were coming

- *The ships were just coming into view.*

FUTURE ... will come
FUTURE PROGRESSIVE ... will be coming
FUTURE PERFECT ... will have come

PAST PASSIVE

Come is never used in the passive voice.

COMPLEMENTS

come *move toward the speaker*	Please come here. Don't come too close—I have a cold.
come *fare, get along*	How's Harry coming in his new job?
come _____ *arrive/appear in space/time*	
ADVERB OF TIME	The deadline has come **all too soon**.
ADVERB OF PLACE TO/FROM (+ ADVERB OF TIME)	The car came **over the hill** at 60 miles an hour. The class came **to the chapter on ancient Rome**. They come **home** *once a week*.
come _____ *extend, reach*	
ADVERB OF PLACE TO/FROM	Her skirt comes **below her knees**. His property comes **as far as this fence**.
come _____ *originate*	
ADVERB OF PLACE TO/FROM	Doris comes **from a large family**. Most malware comes **from China**.
come _____ *be available*	
ADVERB OF MANNER	The new model comes **in three colors**. The DVD player comes **ready to use**. The computer comes **without a keyboard**.
come _____ *reach a state/conclusion*	
TO OBJECT	The two sides came **to an understanding**. Barney came **to his senses** at last.
INFINITIVE	I came **to like him** after all. We came **to enjoy walking to school**. The time has come **to say good-bye**.
come _____ *arrive in a particular condition*	
PREDICATE ADJECTIVE	He came **ready to work**. They came **eager for the show to begin**.
come _____ *become*	
PREDICATE ADJECTIVE	The steering wheel came **loose** and he lost control of the car. Sandy's dream of becoming an astronaut came **true**.

───(PHRASAL VERBS)───

come away/forward/in/out/up/etc. *approach in a specified direction*	Marcy came up from the basement. Melinda came in through the back door.
come about *happen*	How did the agreement come about?
come across/upon ____ *find/meet by accident*	She came across her high school yearbook. We came upon a deer in the clearing.
come along *appear*	We'll ask the first person who comes along.
come along *make progress*	The project is coming along fairly well.
come (along) with ____ *accompany*	Jayne may come along with us to the grocery. These instructions came with the new monitor.
come around *recover*	I was knocked unconscious, but I soon came around.
come around (to ____**)** *agree finally (to)*	He eventually came around to my point of view.
come at ____ *attack*	Rudy came at the burglar with his fists flying.
come back *be popular again*	Smaller cars are coming back.
come between ____ *cause trouble between*	We can't let a silly quarrel come between us.
come down *decrease* [OF PRICES]	Gasoline prices are coming down.
come down *be demolished*	The historic inn will come down for urban renewal.
come down *be handed down by tradition*	Western philosophy came down to us from the Greeks.
come down to ____ *be a matter of*	The debate comes down to money.
come down with ____ *become sick with*	A third of my classmates came down with a cold.
come from ____ *be caused by*	John's problems come from his lack of control.
come in *become available, arrive*	The election results are coming in now. The new encyclopedias will come in tomorrow.
come in ____ *finish a contest*	Carrie came in second in the 100-meter dash.
come of ____ *result from*	Nothing came of my complaint to the board.
come off ____ *become separated from*	A fender came off my bike today.
come off *happen*	The dinner party came off just as we expected.
come on *be illuminated*	The streetlights come on at dusk.
come on *begin to be broadcast*	When does *Countdown* come on tonight?
come out *be made public*	The facts came out at the afternoon meeting.
come out *declare oneself*	Senator Blather came out in favor of wind farms.
come out *turn out, end up, do*	Everything came out fine in the end.
come (out) to ____ *amount to*	Your repair bill comes out to $227.46. All of Ellery's efforts came to nothing.
come out with ____ *introduce [a product]*	The company came out with three new workstations.
come through ____ *survive*	Randall came through the ordeal of boot camp.
come to *regain consciousness*	Gertie came to before the medics arrived.
come to ____ *be a matter of*	When it comes to idioms, we are the experts.
come up *increase* [OF PRICES]	Stock prices have come up over the past week.
come up *appear for consideration*	The issue comes up every few months. Did the issue of slavery come up in history class?
come up against ____ *encounter, confront*	The activists came up against a lot of opposition.
come up for ____ *be in line for*	These antique lamps don't come up for sale very often. The position comes up for election every four years.
come up with ____ *find, produce*	She came up with two quarters for the parking meter. Has the detective come up with a motive yet?

top 30 verb

PRESENT

I cost	we cost
you cost	you cost
he/she/it costs	they cost

* *The scarves cost more than 50 dollars.*

PRESENT PROGRESSIVE

I am costing	we are costing
you are costing	you are costing
he/she/it is costing	they are costing

* *The delay is costing us a fortune.*

PAST

I cost	we cost
you cost	you cost
he/she/it cost	they cost

* *That mistake cost us dearly.*

PAST PROGRESSIVE

I was costing	we were costing
you were costing	you were costing
he/she/it was costing	they were costing

* *You were costing the company a lot of money.*

PRESENT PERFECT ... have | has cost
PAST PERFECT ... had cost

FUTURE ... will cost
FUTURE PROGRESSIVE ... will be costing
FUTURE PERFECT ... will have cost

PAST PASSIVE

Cost is rarely used in the passive voice.

COMPLEMENTS

cost *be expensive*

Going to college really costs.
Hybrid cars cost, but so does gasoline.
Lack of training costs dearly.
Cheap mattresses cost in the long run.

cost _____ *have a price of*
   OBJECT

The new house cost **half a million dollars**.
My books cost **$200 a semester**.

cost _____ *cause the loss of*
   OBJECT

Starvation costs **25,000 lives** a day.
It cost **my job**.
It cost **his self-respect**.

   INDIRECT OBJECT + DIRECT OBJECT

The battle cost *the army* **a lot of good soldiers**.
The accident cost *me* **a fortune**.
The mistake cost *us* **the contract**.

cost _____ *cause suffering/loss to*
   OBJECT

My hesitation certainly cost **me**.

PHRASAL VERBS

cost _SEP_ **out** *estimate, set a value on/for*

I will cost the entire project out.
We were costing out the Johnston contract.

EXPRESSIONS

cost a fortune *be very expensive*

It would cost a fortune to move
   that printing press.

cost a pretty penny *be very expensive*

I'll bet that car cost a pretty penny.

cost an arm and a leg *be very expensive*

This watch cost me an arm and a leg.

PRESENT

I creep	we creep
you creep	you creep
he/she/it creeps	they creep

• *Time creeps by when you're bored.*

PRESENT PROGRESSIVE

I am creeping	we are creeping
you are creeping	you are creeping
he/she/it is creeping	they are creeping

• *The fog is creeping into the hollow.*

PAST

I crept	we crept
you crept	you crept
he/she/it crept	they crept

• *Old age crept up on us.*

PAST PROGRESSIVE

I was creeping	we were creeping
you were creeping	you were creeping
he/she/it was creeping	they were creeping

• *The soldiers were creeping past the guards.*

PRESENT PERFECT ... have | has crept
PAST PERFECT ... had crept

FUTURE ... will creep
FUTURE PROGRESSIVE ... will be creeping
FUTURE PERFECT ... will have crept

PAST PASSIVE

Creep is never used in the passive voice.

COMPLEMENTS

creep *move along close to the ground*

Bob crept away from his pursuers.
The lion crept toward the antelope.

creep *move cautiously/stealthily*

We crept down the stairs.
I crept into the kids' room, trying not to wake them.

creep *grow along a surface*

Weeds were creeping into the flower beds.

creep *shiver from fear/dread*

The scream made my flesh creep.

creep _____ *advance slowly*
  ADVERB OF PLACE TO/FROM

Daylight crept **in through the windows**.
Water from the clogged drain crept **across the floor**.

creep _____ *appear gradually*
  ADVERB OF PLACE TO/FROM

A sense of urgency crept **through the crowd**.

PHRASAL VERBS

creep by *pass slowly*

The years crept by when Lawrence
  was in prison.

creep in/into _____ *enter inconspicuously*

A note of resentment crept into his voice.
Negativity crept into his later writing.

creep up on _____ *advance slowly and imperceptibly toward*

The cat crept up on the mouse.

EXPRESSIONS

creep out of the woodwork *appear after being gone for a long time*

Well, look who's crept out of the woodwork—it's Percy!

PRESENT

I cut	we cut
you cut	you cut
he/she/it cuts	they cut

• *He cuts the lawn every weekend.*

PRESENT PROGRESSIVE

I am cutting	we are cutting
you are cutting	you are cutting
he/she/it is cutting	they are cutting

• *I'm cutting class today.*

PAST

I cut	we cut
you cut	you cut
he/she/it cut	they cut

• *I cut myself shaving.*

PAST PROGRESSIVE

I was cutting	we were cutting
you were cutting	you were cutting
he/she/it was cutting	they were cutting

• *We were cutting the staff by ten percent.*

PRESENT PERFECT … have | has cut
PAST PERFECT … had cut

FUTURE … will cut
FUTURE PROGRESSIVE … will be cutting
FUTURE PERFECT … will have cut

PAST PASSIVE

I was cut	we were cut
you were cut	you were cut
he/she/it was cut	they were cut

• *Our budget was cut substantially.*

COMPLEMENTS

cut *hurt someone's feelings*	His criticisms really cut. He really knows how to cut.
cut _____ *make an incision, separate* ADVERB OF MANNER	A sharp knife cuts **safely**. His ax cuts **like a razor**.
cut _____ *undergo an incision/separation* ADVERB OF MANNER	The dried wood cuts **easily**.
cut _____ *penetrate with a sharp object* OBJECT	Jill cut **her finger** on a knife.
cut _____ *sever, separate into pieces (slice, mow, pare, trim, dig, etc.)* OBJECT	I cut **the cake**. My husband cut **the grass** this morning. I need to cut **my fingernails**. The new barber cut **my hair**. The backhoe cut **a trench** for a new waterline.
cut _____ *make by chopping/hacking* OBJECT	We cut **a path** through the dense woods.
cut _____ *reduce the size/number of* OBJECT	They will cut **my hours** after Christmas. We have to cut **the budget**. The authors had to cut **the manuscript** by a third.
cut _____ *remove [from a group]* OBJECT	The coach cut **three players** from the squad. The director cut **five scenes** from the movie.
cut _____ *change direction suddenly* ADVERB OF PLACE TO/FROM	Cut **to the right** just before the railroad tracks.
cut _____ *go directly, take a shortcut* ADVERB OF PLACE TO/FROM	We can cut **across Mr. Applegate's property**. The highway cuts **through a national park**. The seniors cut **to the front of the line**.
cut _____ *dilute* OBJECT	That bartender cuts **whiskey** with tap water.

top 30 verb

cut ＿＿＿ *break, stop*	
OBJECT	The storm cut **the telephone lines.**
	Please cut **all the noise.**
	He cut **the engine.**
cut ＿＿＿ *skip without permission*	
OBJECT	We cut **class** to watch the inauguration.
cut ＿＿＿ *record*	
OBJECT	She is cutting **a new album.**
cut ＿＿＿ *fill out and issue*	
OBJECT	The secretary cut **a check for $50.23.**
cut ＿＿＿ *handle* [USUALLY NEGATIVE]	
OBJECT	I can't cut **the 45-minute drive to work** anymore.
PRESENT PARTICIPLE	Tom can't cut **being a police officer** anymore.

───────── **PHRASAL VERBS** ─────────

cut across ＿＿＿ *transcend*	The president's economic proposal cuts across party lines.
cut back *reverse direction*	The receiver cut back to the middle of the field.
cut ^SEP^ **back** *shorten*	We must cut back the shrubs after they flower.
cut back (on) ＿＿＿ *reduce*	The department cut back spending in April.
cut ^SEP^ **down** *chop/saw and cause to fall*	Our neighbors cut two elm trees down.
cut down (on) ＿＿＿ *reduce*	The doctor told Ed to cut down on caffeine.
cut in *begin operating*	We pulled the crank six times before the motor cut in.
cut in *interrupt*	The reporter cut in before I finished my first sentence.
cut in *move into a line out of turn*	The motorist cut in just before his lane ended.
cut ^SEP^ **in** *mix in*	Cut in the shortening with a pastry blender.
cut in on ＿＿＿ *interrupt*	The actress cut in on the director.
cut ^SEP^ **off** *interrupt*	The protester cut me off in mid-sentence.
cut ^SEP^ **off** *move suddenly in front of, block*	A driver cut me off at the curve. The policeman cut the robbers off at the bridge.
cut ^SEP^ **off** *shorten*	Gerry cut off the knotty end of the board.
cut ^SEP^ **off** *shut off*	When his car overheated, the driver cut off the engine.
cut off/out *stop suddenly, shut off*	The water heater cuts off at 120 degrees.
cut out *go away quickly*	This party is boring; let's cut out.
cut ^SEP^ **out** *eliminate*	I will cut out afternoon snacks for two weeks.
cut up *joke, clown, behave wildly*	Ken always cuts up when the teacher leaves the room.
cut ^SEP^ **up** *separate into sections with a sharp object*	Cut the mushrooms up, and then we'll add them to the sauce.

───────── **EXPRESSIONS** ─────────

cut ＿＿＿ **down to size** *humiliate*	His opponent cut him down to size.
cut ＿＿＿ **some slack** *make an allowance for*	He wasn't feeling well, so the boss cut him some slack.
cut ＿＿＿ **to the quick** *badly hurt the feelings of*	Your nasty remarks cut me to the quick.
cut [one's] teeth on ＿＿＿ *learn/do as a beginner*	The journalist cut her teeth on writing obituaries.
cut ^SEP^ **short** *stop suddenly*	The president cut the press conference short.

PRESENT

I deal	we deal
you deal	you deal
he/she/it deals	they deal

• *He deals in antique furniture.*

PAST

I dealt	we dealt
you dealt	you dealt
he/she/it dealt	they dealt

• *I dealt myself a bad hand.*

PRESENT PERFECT ... have | has dealt
PAST PERFECT ... had dealt

PRESENT PROGRESSIVE

I am dealing	we are dealing
you are dealing	you are dealing
he/she/it is dealing	they are dealing

• *I'm dealing this hand.*

PAST PROGRESSIVE

I was dealing	we were dealing
you were dealing	you were dealing
he/she/it was dealing	they were dealing

• *They were dealing illegal drugs.*

FUTURE ... will deal
FUTURE PROGRESSIVE ... will be dealing
FUTURE PERFECT ... will have dealt

PAST PASSIVE

I was dealt	we were dealt
you were dealt	you were dealt
he/she/it was dealt	they were dealt

• *Justice was dealt to everyone.*

COMPLEMENTS

deal *distribute cards in a game*	Who's dealing?
	I will deal as soon as everyone sits down.
deal *engage in bargaining/negotiation*	The union will never deal.
	He only deals if the price is right.
deal _____ *distribute [cards]*	
OBJECT	I will deal **five cards** to each player.
	He deals **the cards** until none are left.
INDIRECT OBJECT + DIRECT OBJECT	You dealt *me* an awful hand.
	He dealt *her* three aces.
to PARAPHRASE	You dealt **a bad hand** *to me*.
	He dealt **three aces** *to her*.
deal _____ *sell [illegal drugs]*	
OBJECT	He deals **marijuana** to teenagers.
	The gang deals **stolen prescription drugs**.
deal _____ *deliver, administer*	
INDIRECT OBJECT + DIRECT OBJECT	Spike dealt *the intruder* **a blow to the head**.
	Fate dealt *him* **a terrible blow**.
	Life has dealt *them* **some bad times**.
to PARAPHRASE	Fate dealt **a terrible blow** *to him*.
	Life has dealt **some bad times** *to them*.

PHRASAL VERBS

deal in _____ *buy and sell*	The real estate broker deals only in commercial properties.
deal _SEP_ **in** *allow to take part*	Maurice has free time; let's deal him in.
deal _SEP_ **out** *distribute piece by piece*	Agnes dealt the cards out three at a time.
deal with _____ *behave toward, treat in a particular way*	The coach dealt fairly with his players.
deal with _____ *handle, take care of*	The board agreed to deal with financial matters later.
deal with _____ *have to do with, concern*	The article deals with early French-American customs.
deal with _____ *try to accept/reconcile*	Meg dealt with three deaths in her family last year.

PRESENT

I dig	we dig
you dig	you dig
he/she/it digs	they dig

 • *He really digs in at suppertime.*

PRESENT PROGRESSIVE

I am digging	we are digging
you are digging	you are digging
he/she/it is digging	they are digging

 • *I'm digging as fast as I can.*

PAST

I dug	we dug
you dug	you dug
he/she/it dug	they dug

 • *They dug up a lot of information.*

PAST PROGRESSIVE

I was digging	we were digging
you were digging	you were digging
he/she/it was digging	they were digging

 • *The kids were digging in the backyard.*

| **PRESENT PERFECT** | ... have \| has dug |
| **PAST PERFECT** | ... had dug |

FUTURE	... will dig
FUTURE PROGRESSIVE	... will be digging
FUTURE PERFECT	... will have dug

PAST PASSIVE

—	—
—	—
it was dug	they were dug

 • *The foundation was dug last week.*

(COMPLEMENTS)

dig *turn up / remove soil by hand, tool, or machine*	I have been digging all afternoon. We will dig tomorrow.
dig *search [for something]*	Nicole dug in her suitcase for the shampoo. I am digging everywhere I can think of. The accountants are really digging.
dig _____ *create [a hole] by removing soil* OBJECT	The road crew was digging **a trench**. The dog dug **a hole** in our front lawn. They have dug **the foundation**.
dig _____ *remove from the soil* OBJECT	The farmer dug **potatoes** in the field. Miners can dig **coal** from the slopes.
dig _____ *notice, understand, like* [INFORMAL] OBJECT	Did you dig **that crazy shirt**? I couldn't dig **all that technical talk**. Kids don't dig **classical music**.
WH-CLAUSE	Did you dig **what he was saying**? I can't dig **what the teacher is saying**. Did you dig **who was in that movie**?

(PHRASAL VERBS)

dig at _____ *criticize*	He's always digging at me for my conservatism.
dig down/deep *be generous*	We all must dig down to feed the poor.
dig in *start to work intensively*	There were 23 court cases to study, and the lawyers dug in.
dig in *start eating*	Supper's on the table. Dig in!
dig into _____ *investigate thoroughly*	The detectives dug into the suspect's background.
dig into _____ *start eating*	The workmen dug into the stew and biscuits.
dig _SEP_ **out** *uncover by digging*	Tim dug his car out with a snow shovel.
dig _SEP_ **out** *obtain by searching*	Let's dig out the family photo albums.
dig _SEP_ **up** *uncover by digging*	We dug 23 arrowheads up in one afternoon.
dig _SEP_ **up** *obtain by searching*	Reporters dug up a lot of information about the mayor.

I dive   we dive
you dive   you dive
he/she/it dives   they dive

• *The market dives after bad economic news.*

PRESENT PROGRESSIVE

I am diving   we are diving
you are diving   you are diving
he/she/it is diving   they are diving

• *I'm diving into the bond market.*

PAST

I dove   we dove
you dove   you dove
he/she/it dove   they dove

• *I never dove from the highest board.*

PAST PROGRESSIVE

I was diving   we were diving
you were diving   you were diving
he/she/it was diving   they were diving

• *We were diving for lobsters.*

PRESENT PERFECT   ... have | has dived
PAST PERFECT   ... had dived

FUTURE   ... will dive
FUTURE PROGRESSIVE   ... will be diving
FUTURE PERFECT   ... will have dived

PAST PASSIVE

Dive is never used in the passive voice.

COMPLEMENTS

dive *plunge into water headfirst*

She dove into the pool.
I dove from the 10-meter board.
I dove with my eyes closed.
Michael has been diving since he was four years old.

dive *go/swim underwater*

The submarine dove to 75 meters.
The ducks were diving in the pond.
The whale dove as soon as the boat approached.
We were diving in wet suits.

dive *fall sharply and quickly*

The plane dove under the clouds.
The temperature dives at nightfall.
The market dove on the news.

dive _____ *plunge quickly, lunge*
    for OBJECT

The soldiers dove **for cover**.
The shortstop dove **for the ball**.

PHRASAL VERBS

dive in *start doing something energetically*

We put the craft materials on the
    table and told the kids to dive right in.

dive into _____ *start doing energetically*

Becky dove into the new design project.
New arrivals are diving right into the discussion.

do _____ travel [a distance] / visit [a place] / spend [time]
OBJECT

Hikers can do **20 miles a day.**
His car can do **100 miles an hour.**
We will do **several museums** this afternoon.
I did **three years** in the Navy.

do _____ be right/proper [USUALLY NEGATIVE]
INFINITIVE

It won't do **to be late for the meeting.**
It will never do **to come in over budget.**

do _____ cause, have as an effect
OBJECT
INDIRECT OBJECT + DIRECT OBJECT

The wind did **a lot of damage.**
A nap will do *you* **some good.**

do _____ create, produce, play a role in
OBJECT

The author is doing **a biography of Abraham Lincoln.**
The artist is doing **portraits of famous people.**
The actress did **three movies** last year.

─(**PHRASAL VERBS**)─

do away with _____ eliminate

I did away with my landline phone at home.
The company did away with employee bonuses.

do away with _____ murder

He did away with three wives before he was caught.

do _SEP_ **in** make very tired

Driving for three hours does me in.

do _SEP_ **in** cause the death/failure of, kill

Pneumonia finally did him in.
The mob tried to do in the entire police force.
The politician was done in by greed.

do [someone] out of _____ prevent [someone]
from getting

The con artist did investors out of their life's savings.

do _SEP_ **over** repeat

I misspelled a word and had to do the sign over.

do _SEP_ **over** decorate differently

The couple did over the living room last summer.

do _SEP_ **up** wrap [a package]

Would you do up this gift for me?

do _SEP_ **up** fasten [clothing]

She did up her son's coat.

do _SEP_ **up** decorate, dress up

We will do up the office for the boss's birthday.
Anya really did herself up for the party.

do without _____ get along without

We can't do without your help.

─(**EXPRESSIONS**)─

could do with _____ want, need

I could do with some ice cream
  right now.

do a job/number on _____ damage, harm

The kids really did a job on our furniture.
The committee did a number on his budget proposal.

do _____ **dirty** treat poorly

The team did him dirty by trading him to the Lions.

do _____ **for a living** earn money on which
to live by doing

"What does she do for a living?" "She does web
  design."

do the trick be exactly what is needed

Lowering interest rates does the trick every time.
This pocketknife will do the trick.

do well to _____
be lucky in doing

Nancy does well to give a speech without crying.
Gordon did well to escape the fire uninjured.

have to do with _____
concern, be about

What does my zip code have to do with my car
  insurance?
The problem has something to do with the cable
  service.

top
30
verb

PRESENT		PRESENT PROGRESSIVE	
I do	we do	I am doing	we are doing
you do	you do	you are doing	you are doing
he/she/it does	they do	he/she/it is doing	they are doing

   • *He always does his best.*   • *I'm doing what I can.*

PAST		PAST PROGRESSIVE	
I did	we did	I was doing	we were doing
you did	you did	you were doing	you were doing
he/she/it did	they did	he/she/it was doing	they were doing

   • *I did everything you asked.*   • *We were doing just fine until we had an accident.*

PRESENT PERFECT	... have | has done
PAST PERFECT	... had done

FUTURE	... will do
FUTURE PROGRESSIVE	... will be doing
FUTURE PERFECT	... will have done

PAST PASSIVE	
I was done	we were done
you were done	you were done
he/she/it was done	they were done

   • *The job was done in record time.*

(COMPLEMENTS)

NOTE: *Do* is also used with the base form of a verb

• to ask questions in the simple present and past tenses

   Do you want some candy?

• to form negative statements with *not* in the simple present and past tenses

   I do not think we will win.

• to emphasize what one is saying

   I do wish Mary would attend.

do *manage, get along*		"How is your son doing in school?" "He's doing well, thanks."
do *be adequate/right*		A couple of hours will do. Ten dollars will do. Your blue suit will do for the party.
do _____ *perform, finish working on*		
	OBJECT	I did **some errands** after lunch. I was just doing **my job**. We always do **the crossword puzzle** together. The kids should do **their homework** soon.
	WH-CLAUSE	I did **what needed to be done**. We will do **whatever job we are assigned**.
do _____ *perform [for someone's benefit]*		
	INDIRECT OBJECT + DIRECT OBJECT	Do *me* **a favor**. He did *them* **a good deed**. They did *the company* **a real service**.
	for PARAPHRASE	Do **a favor** *for me*. He did **a good deed** *for them*. They did **a real service** *for the company*.
do _____ *prepare, clean, decorate, arrange*		
	OBJECT	We did **the table** before the guests came. I did **a nice roast** for dinner. I did **the dishes** afterwards. My husband does **the laundry**. We did **the living room** in pale blue. She does **my hair**.

PRESENT

I draw	we draw
you draw	you draw
he/she/it draws	they draw

• *He draws a grim picture of the economy.*

PRESENT PROGRESSIVE

I am drawing	we are drawing
you are drawing	you are drawing
he/she/it is drawing	they are drawing

• *The play is drawing well.*

PAST

I drew	we drew
you drew	you drew
he/she/it drew	they drew

• *Her presentation drew a large audience.*

PAST PROGRESSIVE

I was drawing	we were drawing
you were drawing	you were drawing
he/she/it was drawing	they were drawing

• *We were drawing up a new will.*

PRESENT PERFECT ... have | has drawn
PAST PERFECT ... had drawn

FUTURE ... will draw
FUTURE PROGRESSIVE ... will be drawing
FUTURE PERFECT ... will have drawn

PAST PASSIVE

I was drawn	we were drawn
you were drawn	you were drawn
he/she/it was drawn	they were drawn

• *The sketches were drawn by Leonardo da Vinci.*

COMPLEMENTS

draw *create a picture*	She draws beautifully.
	Art students must draw every day.
draw *attract an audience*	Costume dramas rarely draw well.
draw *show a handgun*	Policemen are trained to draw and aim, but hold their fire.
draw _____ *create [a picture]*	
OBJECT	The children drew **pictures of their families**.
	The architects have drawn **a floor plan**.
INDIRECT OBJECT + DIRECT OBJECT	The children drew *them* pictures.
	The economist drew *us a scary picture of the future*.
for PARAPHRASE	The children drew **pictures** *for them*.
	The economists **drew a scary picture of the future** *for us*.
draw _____ *create a picture of*	
OBJECT	The artist drew **the Taj Mahal**.
	I'd like to draw **Queen Victoria without her crown**.
draw _____ *drag, pull, extract*	
OBJECT	The teacher drew **the children** away from the window.
	I drew **the curtains** across the windows.
	The archers drew **their bows**.
	The nurse needs to draw **a blood sample**.
	He drew **the winning number**.
draw _____ *move steadily*	
ADVERB OF PLACE TO/FROM	The robber drew **closer to his victim**.
	My business day was drawing **to a close**.
draw _____ *attract*	
OBJECT	Water always draws **mosquitoes**.
	He usually draws **a big crowd**.
draw _____ *form*	
OBJECT	Voters must draw **their own conclusions** from the debate.

PHRASAL VERBS

draw _SEP_ **up** *write, formulate*	A young attorney drew up my will.
	Our family drew up an evacuation plan.

PRESENT

I dream	we dream
you dream	you dream
he/she/it dreams	they dream

- *He dreams of getting rich.*

PRESENT PROGRESSIVE

I am dreaming	we are dreaming
you are dreaming	you are dreaming
he/she/it is dreaming	they are dreaming

- *If I'm dreaming, don't wake me up.*

PAST

I dreamt	we dreamt
you dreamt	you dreamt
he/she/it dreamt	they dreamt

- *I dreamt that I ate a giant marshmallow.*

PAST PROGRESSIVE

I was dreaming	we were dreaming
you were dreaming	you were dreaming
he/she/it was dreaming	they were dreaming

- *I was dreaming that I was late to work.*

PRESENT PERFECT ... have | has dreamt
PAST PERFECT   ... had dreamt

FUTURE   ... will dream
FUTURE PROGRESSIVE ... will be dreaming
FUTURE PERFECT   ... will have dreamt

PAST PASSIVE

I was dreamt	we were dreamt
you were dreamt	you were dreamt
he/she/it was dreamt	they were dreamt

- *It was never even dreamt of 50 years ago.*

COMPLEMENTS
---

dream *have thoughts and images while one sleeps*	I think I was dreaming. We can all dream, can't we? I must have been dreaming.
dream *pass time idly*	Sorry, I was just dreaming.

dream _____ *have [thoughts and images] while one sleeps*

about OBJECT	Last night I dreamt **about my grandmother.** Do rabbits dream **about carrots?** She dreamt **about Cassie and Pookie.** I never dream **about my childhood.**
THAT-CLAUSE	I dreamt **that I had gotten lost in the woods.** Cinderella dreamt **that she had met her prince.**
about PRESENT PARTICIPLE	I dreamt **about losing my job.** He dreamt **about their moving back home.**

dream _____ *imagine, wish*

of OBJECT	We all dream **of a better future for our children.** Everyone dreams **of world peace.**
THAT-CLAUSE	Everyone dreams **that they will be rich and famous.** People always dream **that tomorrow will be better than today.**
of PRESENT PARTICIPLE	Cubs fans could only dream **of winning the World Series.** Actors always dream **of getting the big break.**

dream _____ *consider possible/proper* [ALWAYS NEGATIVE]

of PRESENT PARTICIPLE	We wouldn't dream **of going to the party without you.** He would never dream **of eating meat.**

PHRASAL VERBS
---

dream _SEP_ **away** *spend [time] idly*	Let's sit on the riverbank and dream away the day.
dream _SEP_ **up** *invent, concoct*	Our board dreamt up a plan to avoid bankruptcy. My brother and I dream up all kinds of wacky ideas.

PRESENT

I drink	we drink
you drink	you drink
he/she/it drinks	they drink

• *John drinks white wine.*

PRESENT PROGRESSIVE

I am drinking	we are drinking
you are drinking	you are drinking
he/she/it is drinking	they are drinking

• *I'm only drinking green tea these days.*

PAST

I drank	we drank
you drank	you drank
he/she/it drank	they drank

• *I drank two cups of coffee.*

PAST PROGRESSIVE

I was drinking	we were drinking
you were drinking	you were drinking
he/she/it was drinking	they were drinking

• *They were drinking in the hotel bar.*

PRESENT PERFECT ... have | has drunk
PAST PERFECT ... had drunk

FUTURE ... will drink
FUTURE PROGRESSIVE ... will be drinking
FUTURE PERFECT ... will have drunk

PAST PASSIVE

—	—
—	—
it was drunk	they were drunk

• *Orange juice was always drunk at breakfast.*

COMPLEMENTS

drink *take a liquid in one's mouth and swallow it*	Is the patient able to drink? He is drinking without any trouble now. Don't try to drink too soon.
drink *consume alcoholic beverages*	Jack is drinking again. They never drink. We drink only on special occasions.
drink _____ *consume [a liquid]*	
OBJECT	I like to drink **sparkling water.** He only drinks **imported beer.** Their kids never drink **soda pop.**
WH-CLAUSE	We will drink **what is already open.** I'll drink **whatever is on tap.**
drink _____ *cause [oneself] to be in a particular state as a result of excessive alcohol consumption*	
REFLEXIVE PRONOUN + *into* OBJECT	He drank **himself** *into oblivion.* The college students drank **themselves** *into a stupor.*
REFLEXIVE PRONOUN + *to* OBJECT	One of my neighbors drank **himself** *to death.*
REFLEXIVE PRONOUN + PREDICATE ADJECTIVE	He drank **himself** *stupid.* They drank **themselves** *blind.* I drank **myself** *senseless.*

PHRASAL VERBS

drink _SEP_ **away** *consume alcohol to relieve oneself of*	The lonely widower drank his troubles away.
drink _SEP_ **down** *swallow [a liquid] completely*	Mother told me to drink the syrup down in one gulp.
drink _SEP_ **in** *absorb with the mind/senses*	He drinks in knowledge like a sponge. The tourists drank in the mountain scenery. We drank in the sights and sounds of New Year's Eve.
drink to _____ *make a toast to*	Let's drink to the couple's health and happiness. I'll drink to that!
Drink up! *Start/keep drinking!*	There's more wine in the cellar. Drink up!
drink _SEP_ **up** *consume all of [a liquid]*	My teenage sons drank up all the milk.

PRESENT

I drive	we drive
you drive	you drive
he/she/it drives	they drive

• *He drives a blue Toyota.*

PRESENT PROGRESSIVE

I am driving	we are driving
you are driving	you are driving
he/she/it is driving	they are driving

• *I'm driving home this afternoon.*

PAST

I drove	we drove
you drove	you drove
he/she/it drove	they drove

• *I drove the kids to school.*

PAST PROGRESSIVE

I was driving	we were driving
you were driving	you were driving
he/she/it was driving	they were driving

• *We were driving to Seattle.*

PRESENT PERFECT ... have | has driven
PAST PERFECT ... had driven

FUTURE ... will drive
FUTURE PROGRESSIVE ... will be driving
FUTURE PERFECT ... will have driven

PAST PASSIVE

I was driven	we were driven
you were driven	you were driven
he/she/it was driven	they were driven

• *The decision was driven by the need to be more cost-effective.*

COMPLEMENTS

drive *operate a vehicle*
Who can drive?
My grandmother never drives at night.

drive *move with great force/speed*
The rain was driving across the road.
The army drove forward relentlessly.

drive _____ *operate [a vehicle (equipped with)]*
OBJECT
He is driving **an old pickup truck**.
We drove **a rented convertible** in Hawaii.
Who can drive **a stick shift**?

drive _____ *cause to go [to a specific place]*
OBJECT + ADVERB OF PLACE TO/FROM
I drove **the car** *into the garage*.
Can you drive **me** *home*?
The waves drove **the boat** *onto the rocks*.
The farmers were driving **their sheep** *to pasture*.

drive _____ *press forcefully*
OBJECT
The company drives **its sales force** hard.
The jockeys drove **their horses** as hard as they could.

drive _____ *force into a specific condition/behavior*
OBJECT + to OBJECT
Reading Dr. King's speeches drove **him** *to a life of service*.
OBJECT + PREDICATE ADJECTIVE
You are driving **me** *crazy*.
His behavior drove **his parents** *mad*.
OBJECT + INFINITIVE
The bad reviews drove **the author** *to entirely revise the play*.
Famine drove **the peasants** *to revolt*.

drive _____ *shape, propel*
OBJECT
National interest always drives **foreign policy**.
Opposition to slavery drove **public opinion in the North**.
Oil prices now drive **the value of the dollar**.

PHRASAL VERBS

drive _SEP_ **down** *cause to decrease*
Foreclosures are driving down home prices.

drive _SEP_ **up** *cause to increase*
Limiting oil production will drive prices up.

drive _____ **on** *cause to move forward to success*
It is the memory of my mother that drives me on.

I eat · we eat
you eat · you eat
he/she/it eats · they eat

• He only eats cereal for breakfast.

PAST

I ate · we ate
you ate · you ate
he/she/it ate · they ate

• I ate breakfast early this morning.

PRESENT PERFECT ... have | has eaten
PAST PERFECT ... had eaten

PRESENT PROGRESSIVE

I am eating · we are eating
you are eating · you are eating
he/she/it is eating · they are eating

• We are eating out tonight.

PAST PROGRESSIVE

I was eating · we were eating
you were eating · you were eating
he/she/it was eating · they were eating

• I was eating lunch when I got the news.

FUTURE ... will eat
FUTURE PROGRESSIVE ... will be eating
FUTURE PERFECT ... will have eaten

PAST PASSIVE

— · —
— · —
it was eaten · they were eaten

• Only a third of the cat food was eaten.

COMPLEMENTS

eat *take food in one's mouth and swallow it*

The children usually eat around noon.
I eat too much when I get stressed.
I'll call you back, we're eating now.
Let's eat!

eat ___ *consume [food]*

OBJECT

The kids love to eat **pizza**.
My wife will never eat **liver**.

WH-CLAUSE

Can we eat **what was left over from last night**?
The dog eats **whatever the children drop on the floor**.

eat ___ *bear the expense of*

OBJECT

We will have to eat **the cost overrun**.
They are just going to eat **the overhead costs**.
You will have to eat **the rest of the contract**.

eat ___ *make as if by eating*

OBJECT

The paint remover ate **a hole** in my glove.

PHRASAL VERBS

eat (at) ___ *bother, annoy*

His criticisms have been eating at me all day.

eat at / away at / into ___ *wear away, corrode*

Rust was eating away at the exterior of my car.
Acid was eating into the countertop.

eat in *have a meal at home*

The weather is awful. Let's eat in.

eat out *have a meal in a restaurant*

I don't feel like cooking. Let's eat out.

Eat up! *Start/keep eating!*

Dinner is getting cold. Eat up!

eat _SEP_ up *bite all over*

Mosquitoes are eating the campers up.

eat _SEP_ up *use up, consume, waste*

The boss's lavish lifestyle ate up the company's profit.

eat _SEP_ up *enjoy greatly*

The singer told awful jokes, but the audience ate it up.

eat _SEP_ up *believe [something]*

My aunt ate up everything she read in the tabloids.

EXPRESSIONS

eat ___ **out of house and home**
consume all the food in [someone's] home

Our three sons are eating us out of house and home.

PRESENT

I fall	we fall
you fall	you fall
he/she/it falls	they fall

• *Night falls early this time of year.*

PAST

I fell	we fell
you fell	you fell
he/she/it fell	they fell

• *The market fell like a rock yesterday.*

PRESENT PERFECT	... have | has fallen
PAST PERFECT	... had fallen

PRESENT PROGRESSIVE

I am falling	we are falling
you are falling	you are falling
he/she/it is falling	they are falling

• *Look out! It's falling.*

PAST PROGRESSIVE

I was falling	we were falling
you were falling	you were falling
he/she/it was falling	they were falling

• *The snow was falling heavily.*

FUTURE	... will fall
FUTURE PROGRESSIVE	... will be falling
FUTURE PERFECT	... will have fallen

PAST PASSIVE

Fall is never used in the passive voice.

COMPLEMENTS

fall *drop downward*	I fell on the ice.
	He fell to his knees.
	The valley fell in front of him.
fall *become lower/weaker/less*	The temperature has fallen into the 20s.
	His voice always falls at the end of his sentences.
	Their expectations are falling.
	The wind usually falls at sunset.
	The market fell today.
	Our productivity fell last quarter.
fall *be wounded/killed in battle*	Fifty thousand soldiers fell at the Battle of Gettysburg.
fall _____ *pass [into a specific state/condition], become*	
PREDICATE ADJECTIVE	Dad falls **asleep** in front of the news.
	Ursula fell **sick** after eating potato salad at the picnic.
	The crowd fell **silent** as she approached the podium.

PHRASAL VERBS

fall away/back/down/in/off/out/etc. *fall in a specified direction*	The castle walls are falling down.
	My hat fell off when I stood up.
fall apart/through *fail, come to nothing*	Our party plans fell through at the last minute.
fall back *retreat*	The regiment fell back to the new fort.
fall back on _____ *turn back to for help*	The Dickersons fell back on their savings.
fall behind (on _____**)** *lag behind*	On the third lap, the American swimmers fell behind.
	The doctor fell further behind as the day went on.
	My roommates and I are falling behind on the rent.
fall for _____ *become strongly attracted to*	Patrick fell for Tammy on their first date.
fall for _____ *be deceived by*	We won't fall for the politician's lies anymore.
fall in with _____ *associate with*	Our son fell in with computer nerds at school.
fall off *decline, diminish*	Attendance at our church has fallen off dramatically.
fall on _____ *happen on*	Christmas falls on a Saturday this year.
	The meeting falls on my day off.
fall out (with _____**)** *quarrel (with [someone])*	Nick fell out with the project director.
fall under _____ *be influenced/controlled by*	The princess fell under the power of the wicked queen.
fall (up)on/to _____ *become the duty of*	Organization of the meeting fell to the secretary.

PRESENT	
I feed	we feed
you feed	you feed
he/she/it feeds	they feed

• He feeds the birds every day.

PRESENT PROGRESSIVE	
I am feeding	we are feeding
you are feeding	you are feeding
he/she/it is feeding	they are feeding

• I'm feeding the documents into the shredder.

PAST	
I fed	we fed
you fed	you fed
he/she/it fed	they fed

• I fed the cat two hours ago.

PAST PROGRESSIVE	
I was feeding	we were feeding
you were feeding	you were feeding
he/she/it was feeding	they were feeding

• They were feeding us misinformation.

PRESENT PERFECT	... have | has fed
PAST PERFECT	... had fed

FUTURE	... will feed
FUTURE PROGRESSIVE	... will be feeding
FUTURE PERFECT	... will have fed

PAST PASSIVE	
I was fed	we were fed
you were fed	you were fed
he/she/it was fed	they were fed

• The children were fed earlier.

COMPLEMENTS

feed *eat*
How often do they feed?
The birds were feeding on our plum tree.
Lions only feed when they are hungry.

feed *supply [food/materials]*
The zookeepers feed every morning and evening.
Don't feed too fast, or the shredder will jam.

feed _____ *give food to, supply materials to*

OBJECT
We feed **the homeless** at a downtown shelter.
You should only feed **the goldfish** once a week.
Keep feeding **the boiler** until we have enough steam.

INDIRECT OBJECT + DIRECT OBJECT
Feed *me* **some more rope**.

to PARAPHRASE
Feed **some more rope** *to me*.

feed _____ *send [an electric current, a signal]*

OBJECT
The sensor feeds **a signal** to the computer.
The station feeds **the broadcast** to a satellite.

PASSIVE
The current is fed to the circuit breaker.

feed _____ *foster, support*

OBJECT
Resentment feeds **hostility**.
Rumors are feeding **the confusion**.
Music feeds **the soul**.

PASSIVE
The mind can only be fed by education.

feed _____ *supply*

INDIRECT OBJECT + DIRECT OBJECT
We fed *the chickens* **corn**.
The company fed *the press* **misleading information**.
The director fed *the actress* **her lines**.
This cable feeds *the factory* **its power**.

to PARAPHRASE
We fed **corn** *to the chickens*.
The company fed **misleading information** *to the press*.
The director fed **the actress's lines** *to her*.
This cable feeds **power** *to the factory*.

feed _____ *move/push [into/through an opening]*

OBJECT + ADVERB OF PLACE TO/FROM
The nurse fed **the breathing tube** *into the patient's windpipe*.
The tourist fed **quarters** *into the vending machine*.

PRESENT		PRESENT PROGRESSIVE	
I feel	we feel	I am feeling	we are feeling
you feel	you feel	you are feeling	you are feeling
he/she/it feels	they feel	he/she/it is feeling	they are feeling

· *My arm feels just fine, thanks.*   · *I'm feeling tired.*

PAST		PAST PROGRESSIVE	
I felt	we felt	I was feeling	we were feeling
you felt	you felt	you were feeling	you were feeling
he/she/it felt	they felt	he/she/it was feeling	they were feeling

· *They felt sorry for her.*   · *We were feeling our way through the cave.*

PRESENT PERFECT	... have | has felt
PAST PERFECT	... had felt

FUTURE	... will feel
FUTURE PROGRESSIVE	... will be feeling
FUTURE PERFECT	... will have felt

PAST PASSIVE

—   —
—   —
it was felt   they were felt

· *The loss was felt by everyone.*

───────────────────────────────(**COMPLEMENTS**)───

feel _____ *perceive oneself to be*

   PREDICATE NOUN
     Sally felt **a complete fool**.
     I felt **a victim of circumstances**.

   PREDICATE ADJECTIVE
     John felt **foolish**.
     We all felt **sad at the news**.
     The situation felt **all wrong**.
     Are you feeling **better** today?
     I don't feel **well**.

   PAST PARTICIPLE
     The team felt **defeated** after losing their best pitcher.
     We felt **overwhelmed** by the experience.

feel _____ *have an emotion/opinion*

   ADVERB OF MANNER
     He felt **badly** about what had happened.
     Robert always feels **strongly** about political issues.

feel _____ *seem*

   it + *feel* + PREDICATE ADJECTIVE +
     INFINITIVE
     It felt **good** *to go to class again.*
     It feels **weird** *to be in the presence of so many geeks.*

feel _____ *seem to the sense of touch*

   PREDICATE ADJECTIVE
     The water feels **too cold**.

feel _____ *search by touch*

   ADVERB OF PLACE
     I felt **everywhere**.
     He felt **in his pockets** for the key.
     She felt **under the cushions**.

feel _____ *seek by touching*

   OBJECT
     The burglars felt **their way** along the corridor.

feel _____ *touch in order to examine*

   OBJECT
     I felt **his swollen ankle**.
     The detective felt **the suspect** for a gun.
     She carefully felt **the dog's injured leg**.

feel _____ *be aware of, sense*

   OBJECT
     They felt **the impact of the explosion**.
     I felt **a rock in my shoe**.
     Ron felt **a pang of jealousy**.

feel ⎯⎯⎯ *be aware of, sense* [continued]	
OBJECT + PRESENT PARTICIPLE	They felt the **boat** *getting under way*.
	I felt **myself** *getting sick*.
	The speaker felt **the audience** *losing interest*.
feel ⎯⎯⎯ *believe, think*	
OBJECT + INFINITIVE	The coach felt **the team** *to be ready for the game*.
	John felt **them** *to be completely mistaken*.
	I always felt **myself** *to be a good sport*.
THAT-CLAUSE	I feel **that I am right about it.**
	We feel **that we should go ahead as planned.**
	Sam felt **that he deserved a bigger raise.**
feel ⎯⎯⎯ *experience, have grief/pity because of*	
OBJECT	We felt **Grandma's death** keenly.

PHRASAL VERBS

feel (about/around) for ⎯⎯⎯ *seek by touching*	I felt for the light switch.
	She was feeling around in the dark for her glasses.
feel for ⎯⎯⎯ *sympathize with*	I really feel for the team that lost.
feel ˢᴱᴾ **out** *find out the views of*	Senator Blather felt out the voters about the tax increase.

EXPRESSIONS

feel at home *feel comfortable/accepted*	My friends feel at home here.
feel ⎯⎯⎯ **in [one's] bones** *sense by intuition*	I feel it in my bones that he's going to hit a home run tonight.
feel like ⎯⎯⎯ *desire, want*	I feel like pizza for dinner.
	I feel like drinking lemonade.
feel like ⎯⎯⎯ *seem to be*	This feels like real wood.
	It feels like January, even though it's only September.
feel like / as if / as though ⎯⎯⎯ *believe/sense that*	I feel like it's going to rain.
	We feel as if we're never going to pay off the mortgage.
feel like a million (bucks/dollars) *feel physically and mentally strong*	An early-morning walk through the woods makes me feel like a million bucks.
feel like a new person *feel refreshed/renewed*	After a shower and shave, the hobo felt like a new person.
feel like death warmed over *feel very sick*	The flu made him feel like death warmed over.
feel like [oneself] *perceive oneself to be in a normal state*	After having a cold for a week, I feel like myself again.
feel no pain *be drunk*	After drinking a six pack, Meredith is feeling no pain.
feel [one's] oats *be lively*	The salesman danced a jig around the office; he's feeling his oats since he landed that big contract.
feel out of place *feel awkward*	Gordon feels out of place at wine-and-cheese parties.
feel the pinch *have too little money*	My parents want to vacation in Spain, but they're feeling the pinch.
feel up to ⎯⎯⎯ *perceive oneself to be capable of*	Do you feel up to going shopping?

PRESENT

I fight	we fight
you fight	you fight
he/she/it fights	they fight

• *He always fights for the underdog.*

PRESENT PROGRESSIVE

I am fighting	we are fighting
you are fighting	you are fighting
he/she/it is fighting	they are fighting

• *I'm fighting a nasty cold.*

PAST

I fought	we fought
you fought	you fought
he/she/it fought	they fought

• *The senator fought against corruption.*

PAST PROGRESSIVE

I was fighting	we were fighting
you were fighting	you were fighting
he/she/it was fighting	they were fighting

• *They were fighting a rearguard action in the hills.*

PRESENT PERFECT	... have | has fought
PAST PERFECT	... had fought

FUTURE	... will fight
FUTURE PROGRESSIVE	... will be fighting
FUTURE PERFECT	... will have fought

PAST PASSIVE

I was fought	we were fought
you were fought	you were fought
he/she/it was fought	they were fought

• *The battle of Gettysburg was fought in July 1863.*

─(COMPLEMENTS)─

fight *engage in combat/argument*

It is useless to fight with City Hall.
The damaged ship will never fight again.
It is noble to fight for one's country.
The media was fighting for access to the court transcripts.
What married couple doesn't fight occasionally?
She was fighting against other committee members.

fight _____ *contend/struggle against, oppose*

OBJECT

The Spanish fought **Napoleon's armies** savagely.
I am fighting **a terrible sore throat**.
The company is fighting **the judge's ruling**.
We will fight **the takeover bid**.
The neighborhood fought **the new development**.
The opposition is fighting **Senator Blather's amendment**.

WH-CLAUSE

We have fought **what we considered to be wrong**.
They will fight **whomever we nominate**.
We will fight **whatever forces are arrayed against us**.

fight _____ *wage, be engaged in*

OBJECT

We are fighting **a war on poverty**.
He is fighting **the good fight**.
They fought **a running battle** for a week.

─(PHRASAL VERBS)─

fight back *retaliate*

She may lose the argument,
    but she'll find a way to fight back.

fight SEP **back** *resist, struggle against*

Ruth fought back her tears after hearing about his death.

fight SEP **off** *repel an attack by*

I'm trying to fight off a bout of the flu.
The platoon fought off a much larger force.

fight on *continue to fight*

Although surrounded, Colonel Travis's men fought on.

fight SEP **out** *settle by struggle*

The rival gangs fought it out with guns.
Beth and Seth fought out their differences in court.

fight over _____ *struggle to obtain*

The classmates fought over who would get the award.
Jayne and Eve fought over Humphrey.

find _____ *declare as a legal verdict* OBJECT + PREDICATE ADJECTIVE	The jury found **the defendant** *guilty*.
find _____ *obtain* OBJECT	You must find **time to study**. Charlotte and Kathy found **an apartment** on Walnut Street. Our product found **lots of buyers** among senior citizens. Grandma finds **comfort** in her photo albums.

<hr>

PHRASAL VERBS

find for _____ *decide in favor of*	The jury found for the defendant.
find out *learn the truth*	Your mother will find out. I'll search the Internet and find out for you.
find ᴸᴱᴾ **out** *learn*	I found out what makes Jason tick. What did you find out about the boss's husband?

<hr>

EXPRESSIONS

find a way around _____ *discover a way to avoid [something]*	The computer engineer found a way around the error message. My attorney found a way around the regulation.
find fault (with _____ **)** *discover something wrong with [someone/something]*	My landlord finds fault with everyone. The moderator found fault with both candidates' arguments.
find favor with _____ *win the approval of*	Vergil found favor with the emperor Augustus.
find it in [one's] heart / in [oneself] _____ *have the courage/compassion*	We found it in our hearts to forgive them. The voters found it in themselves to elect a black president.
find neither hide nor hair of _____ *fail to detect any sign of*	The detectives found neither hide nor hair of the suspect.
find [one's] bearings *determine where one is*	After wandering in the woods for four hours, we found our bearings.
find [one's] tongue/voice *determine what to say*	The candidate finally found her voice, but it was too late.
find [one's] way *discover the route*	We eventually found our way to the log cabin.
find [oneself] *become aware of what one wants to be/do in life*	Melanie found herself in her sophomore year of college.
find out the hard way *discover something by (usually unpleasant) experience*	Senator Blather found out the hard way how much voters oppose tax hikes.
find the/[one's] mark *discover a way to win / defeat someone*	She found her mark midway through the second period and scored four goals after that.

PRESENT

I find	we find
you find	you find
he/she/it finds	they find

* *He finds his new job interesting.*

PRESENT PROGRESSIVE

I am finding	we are finding
you are finding	you are finding
he/she/it is finding	they are finding

* *I'm finding it hard to concentrate.*

PAST

I found	we found
you found	you found
he/she/it found	they found

* *We found a really great babysitter.*

PAST PROGRESSIVE

I was finding	we were finding
you were finding	you were finding
he/she/it was finding	they were finding

* *They were finding more support than expected.*

PRESENT PERFECT ... have | has found
PAST PERFECT ... had found

FUTURE ... will find
FUTURE PROGRESSIVE ... will be finding
FUTURE PERFECT ... will have found

PAST PASSIVE

I was found	we were found
you were found	you were found
he/she/it was found	they were found

* *The murderer was never found.*

(COMPLEMENTS)

find _____ discover, come upon by chance

OBJECT	I finally found **my missing wallet.**
	The hikers found **a path back to camp.**
	Astronomers found **a new moon orbiting Jupiter.**
INDIRECT OBJECT + DIRECT OBJECT	I found *Jane* **a great birthday present.**
	We found *the kittens* **a nice home.**
for PARAPHRASE	I found **a great birthday present** *for Jane.*
	We found **a nice home** *for the kittens.*
OBJECT + INFINITIVE	I found **the new job** *to have its limitations.*
	Larry found **the restaurant** *to get a lot of repeat customers.*
OBJECT + PRESENT PARTICIPLE	I found **myself** *holding my breath.*
	They found **the kids** *playing in the backyard.*
	Harriet found **Jim** *working in the garage.*
OBJECT + PAST PARTICIPLE	I found **the dog** *covered with mud.*
	We found **our car** *damaged beyond repair.*
	I found **myself** *drained by the experience.*
THAT-CLAUSE	I found **that there was no simple solution.**
	We all find **that we get tired more easily as we get older.**
	Amy found **that she liked living in Montana.**
	I find **that the new job has its limitations.**
WH-CLAUSE	We found **what we had been looking for.**
	I never found **why the computer failed.**
	The police will find **whoever did this.**

find _____ consider

OBJECT + (to be) PREDICATE NOUN	I found **him** *(to be) a poor listener.*
	The teacher found **the class** *(to be) good students.*
	They found **the car** *(to be) a piece of junk.*
OBJECT + (to be) PREDICATE ADJECTIVE	I found **myself** *(to be) upset with him.*
	We found **him** *(to be) amused at it.*
	They found **the situation** *(to be) very satisfactory.*

fit | fits · fit · have fit
fit | fits · fitted · have fitted

☑ IRREGULAR
☑ REGULAR

PRESENT

I fit	we fit
you fit	you fit
he/she/it fits	they fit

• *The theory fits all the facts.*

PRESENT PROGRESSIVE

I am fitting	we are fitting
you are fitting	you are fitting
he/she/it is fitting	they are fitting

• *I am fitting them in as best I can.*

PAST

I fit	we fit
you fit	you fit
he/she/it fit	they fit

• *We fit eight people at the table before.*

PAST PROGRESSIVE

I was fitting	we were fitting
you were fitting	you were fitting
he/she/it was fitting	they were fitting

• *We were fitting in very nicely, I thought.*

PRESENT PERFECT ... have | has fit
PAST PERFECT ... had fit

FUTURE ... will fit
FUTURE PROGRESSIVE ... will be fitting
FUTURE PERFECT ... will have fit

PAST PASSIVE

I was fit	we were fit
you were fit	you were fit
he/she/it was fit	they were fit

• *Millions of transistors were fit onto a single chip.*

COMPLEMENTS

NOTE: For the following six meanings, *fit* is not used in the progressive tenses.

fit *be the right size and shape*

The sweater fits perfectly.
Will the new rug fit in the living room?

fit *be accommodated*

How many students can fit in a phone booth?
These bags won't fit in the dumpster.

fit ____ *be the right size and shape for*
  OBJECT

The new suit fits **me** perfectly.
The old frame won't fit **the new picture**.

fit ____ *be appropriate/suitable for*
  OBJECT

Your hat fits **the rest of your outfit**.
The class fits **my schedule** pretty well.
The punishment must fit **the crime**.

fit ____ *accommodate*
  OBJECT

Can we fit **24 children** in the classroom?

fit ____ *manage to insert*
  OBJECT

We can fit **four skeins of yarn** in this box.

NOTE: For the following four meanings, *fit* may be used in the progressive tenses.

fit ____ *adjust to the right size and shape*
  OBJECT

You need to fit **the rug** to the room.

fit ____ *measure for the right size*
  OBJECT

The tailor is fitting **Dad** for a new suit.
  PASSIVE

Dad was fitted for a new suit.

fit ____ *make appropriate/suitable*
  OBJECT + to OBJECT

Does a songwriter fit **words *to music*** or **music *to words***?

fit ____ *supply, equip*
  OBJECT + with OBJECT

The shipyard will fit **the boat *with everything it needs***.

PHRASAL VERBS

fit in *be in accord/harmony*

Our new neighbors fit in just fine.

fit _SEP_ **in** *provide a place for*

The hostess will fit the two unexpected guests in.

I flee	we flee
you flee	you flee
he/she/it flees	they flee

• *Everyone flees from imminent danger.*

PRESENT PROGRESSIVE

I am fleeing	we are fleeing
you are fleeing	you are fleeing
he/she/it is fleeing	they are fleeing

• *They are fleeing as fast as they can.*

PAST

I fled	we fled
you fled	you fled
he/she/it fled	they fled

• *I never fled from a fight.*

PAST PROGRESSIVE

I was fleeing	we were fleeing
you were fleeing	you were fleeing
he/she/it was fleeing	they were fleeing

• *The animals were fleeing from the forest fire.*

PRESENT PERFECT   ... have | has fled
PAST PERFECT   ... had fled

FUTURE   ... will flee
FUTURE PROGRESSIVE   ... will be fleeing
FUTURE PERFECT   ... will have fled

PAST PASSIVE

Flee is rarely used in the passive voice.

(COMPLEMENTS)

flee *move/run away from danger/ unpleasantness, escape*

The fish fled when my shadow fell
     across the pond.
The deer fled when they heard the shot.
The birds fled before the coming storm.
The refugees fled into the woods.
The soldiers were fleeing back into the trenches.
The reporters had fled to the press bar.
Civilians were fleeing from the rampaging soldiers.

flee *move away swiftly, vanish*

The moon fled behind the clouds.
The ghostly shape fled from view.
Our shadows fled before us.

flee _____ *run away from*
    (*from*) OBJECT

The survivors quickly fled **(from) the scene of the explosion.**
The reporters fled **(from) the room** when the senator began
     his lengthy speech.
The entire city fled **(from) the rapidly rising floodwaters.**
The animals fled **(from) the burning barn.**
I fled **(from) the noisy, overcrowded arena.**

PRESENT

I fling	we fling
you fling	you fling
he/she/it flings	they fling

• *She flings her hair back if she's angry.*

PRESENT PROGRESSIVE

I am flinging	we are flinging
you are flinging	you are flinging
he/she/it is flinging	they are flinging

• *The dog is flinging dirt everywhere.*

PAST

I flung	we flung
you flung	you flung
he/she/it flung	they flung

• *He flung his clothes all over room.*

PAST PROGRESSIVE

I was flinging	we were flinging
you were flinging	you were flinging
he/she/it was flinging	they were flinging

• *The kids were flinging toys out the car window.*

PRESENT PERFECT	... have | has flung
PAST PERFECT	... had flung

FUTURE	... will fling
FUTURE PROGRESSIVE	... will be flinging
FUTURE PERFECT	... will have flung

PAST PASSIVE

I was flung	we were flung
you were flung	you were flung
he/she/it was flung	they were flung

• *The protesters were flung into police vans.*

COMPLEMENTS

fling _____ move suddenly, scatter
    ADVERB OF PLACE TO/FROM

Roberta flung **out of the room.**
The leaves were flinging **all over the lawn.**

fling _____ throw recklessly
    OBJECT + ADVERB OF PLACE TO/FROM

The kids had flung **their books** *everywhere.*
I flung **myself** *onto the sofa.*
The rioters had flung **the furniture** *in every direction.*
The wind was flinging **my raked leaves** *all over the lawn.*

fling _____ cast, throw
    OBJECT + ADVERB OF PLACE TO/FROM

He flung **a rope** *over a tree limb.*
The cadets will fling **their caps** *into the air.*
I flung **a blanket** *over the shivering children.*
The fisherman is flinging **his net** *into the pond.*
The guards flung **him** *into an empty cell.*
The reporter flung **his shoe** *at the president.*

fling _____ devote oneself entirely to
    REFLEXIVE PRONOUN + *into* OBJECT

I flung **myself** *into jazz.*
We flung **ourselves** *into the social scene.*
Freshmen tend to fling **themselves** *into too many
    activities.*
Frank flung **himself** *into his work.*

PHRASAL VERBS

fling _SEP_ **around/aside/away/down/
in/off/out/up/etc.** *throw in a specified
direction*

The burglar flung away his loot as
    soon as he saw the cop.
Bill opened the car door and flung his jacket in.

EXPRESSIONS

fling caution to the wind *take a serious
risk*

Harry flung caution to the wind and
    jumped into the lake with all his clothes on.

fling [one's] head back *tilt one's head
back suddenly*

Don flung his head back and laughed.

PRESENT

I fly	we fly
you fly	you fly
he/she/it flies	they fly

• *Cathy flies to New York once a month.*

PAST

I flew	we flew
you flew	you flew
he/she/it flew	they flew

• *I never flew in such a small plane before.*

PRESENT PERFECT	… have	has flown
PAST PERFECT	… had flown

PRESENT PROGRESSIVE

I am flying	we are flying
you are flying	you are flying
he/she/it is flying	they are flying

• *I am flying back tonight.*

PAST PROGRESSIVE

I was flying	we were flying
you were flying	you were flying
he/she/it was flying	they were flying

• *The kids were flying kites in the park.*

FUTURE	… will fly
FUTURE PROGRESSIVE	… will be flying
FUTURE PERFECT	… will have flown

PAST PASSIVE

I was flown	we were flown
you were flown	you were flown
he/she/it was flown	they were flown

• *The flags were flown at half-mast.*

COMPLEMENTS

fly *move through the air*	My hat flew into the air.
	The birds flew around us, screeching and squawking.
	The plane was flying at 36,000 feet.
fly *travel by aircraft*	Amelia Earhart was the first woman to fly solo across the Atlantic.
	When are you flying to Paris?
	Whoever thought that we could fly to the moon?
fly *wave/float in the air*	Flags were flying in the breeze.
	His shirttail was flying in the wind as he ran down the hill.
fly *move/spread/go/pass quickly*	The wood chips flew as the chain saw bit into the log.
	The door flew open, and in walked Grandmother.
	Rumors were flying everywhere.
	I'm already late for the meeting; I have to fly.
	My, how time flies.
fly *win acceptance*	His proposal will never fly with the voters.
	"Do you think the plan will fly?" "I think it will fly."
fly _____ *pilot / travel in [an aircraft]*	
OBJECT	My grandfather flew **fighter planes** in World War II.
	I flew **United** to Chicago.
fly _____ *transport by aircraft*	
OBJECT	We flew **the children** to England, where they would be safe.
	They flew **the engine** back to the manufacturer.
PASSIVE	The replacement parts were flown from Sweden.
fly _____ *cause to move through the air*	
OBJECT	Didn't you fly **paper airplanes** when you were a kid?
	We always fly **the flag** on Memorial Day.

PHRASAL VERBS

fly away/back/down/in/out/over/up/etc. *fly in a specified direction*	The robin flew down from its nest.
	The planes flew over in formation.
fly by *go quickly past*	Did you see the wild geese fly by, heading home again?
	January really flew by.

PRESENT

I forbear	we forbear
you forbear	you forbear
he/she/it forbears	they forbear

• *He forbears from talking about his wealth.*

PAST

I forbore	we forbore
you forbore	you forbore
he/she/it forbore	they forbore

• *I forbore my usual coffee after dinner.*

PRESENT PERFECT ... have | has forborne
PAST PERFECT ... had forborne

PAST PASSIVE

—	—
—	—
it was forborne	they were forborne

• *A scathing reply was forborne with difficulty.*

PRESENT PROGRESSIVE

I am forbearing	we are forbearing
you are forbearing	you are forbearing
he/she/it is forbearing	they are forbearing

• *We are forbearing from taking any action.*

PAST PROGRESSIVE

I was forbearing	we were forbearing
you were forbearing	you were forbearing
he/she/it was forbearing	they were forbearing

• *The critics were forbearing in their comments.*

FUTURE ... will forbear
FUTURE PROGRESSIVE ... will be forbearing
FUTURE PERFECT ... will have forborne

COMPLEMENTS

forbear *be patient/tolerant*

We know there have been some problems,
  but please forbear.
To forbear in the face of provocation is admirable.
Where someone else might seek revenge, he forbears.

forbear _____ *refrain (from), resist*

OBJECT

I will forbear **my uncle's company** when he is in town.
She forbears **mention of his name** around her ex-boyfriend.

PASSIVE

An exercise of presidential power couldn't be forborne
  any longer.

(*from*) PRESENT PARTICIPLE

We are forbearing **(from) saying anything about the accident.**
I will forbear **(from) replying to your rude comments.**
Only a saint would forbear **(from) getting angry.**

PRESENT

I forbid	we forbid
you forbid	you forbid
he/she/it forbids	they forbid

 • *The law forbids the sale of handguns.*

PRESENT PROGRESSIVE

I am forbidding	we are forbidding
you are forbidding	you are forbidding
he/she/it is forbidding	they are forbidding

 • *Sally's mother is forbidding any more parties.*

PAST

I forbade	we forbade
you forbade	you forbade
he/she/it forbade	they forbade

 • *The police forbade parking on the street.*

PAST PROGRESSIVE

I was forbidding	we were forbidding
you were forbidding	you were forbidding
he/she/it was forbidding	they were forbidding

 • *The company was forbidding smoking in the area.*

PRESENT PERFECT ... have | has forbidden
PAST PERFECT   ... had forbidden

FUTURE   ... will forbid
FUTURE PROGRESSIVE ... will be forbidding
FUTURE PERFECT   ... will have forbidden

PAST PASSIVE

I was forbidden	we were forbidden
you were forbidden	you were forbidden
he/she/it was forbidden	they were forbidden

 • *The lawyers were forbidden to talk to the press.*

COMPLEMENTS

forbid _____ *prohibit, not allow*

OBJECT	The law forbids **the sale of alcohol to minors**.
	Most religions forbid **marriage between close relatives**.
	My parents forbid **books at the dinner table**.
	Lack of time forbids **further explanation**.
PASSIVE	Campfires are forbidden in this area.
OBJECT + INFINITIVE	I forbid **you *to talk to me like that***.
	Some churches forbid **priests *to marry***.
	Jane's mother forbade **her *to go to the party***.
PASSIVE	I was forbidden *to take pictures there*.
PRESENT PARTICIPLE	The new law forbids **smoking in public places**.
	The rules of soccer forbid **tripping an opponent**.
	My mother forbids **watching TV before finishing homework**.
	Space forbids **covering all the issues**.
PASSIVE	Using a cell phone in class is strictly forbidden.

EXPRESSIONS

God/Heaven forbid! *I hope it will not happen.*

God forbid that Mark should fall asleep
    and have an accident.
"Your ex-boyfriend is coming to the party."
    "Heaven forbid!"

forecast

forecast | forecasts · forecast · have forecast ☑ IRREGULAR
forecast | forecasts · forecasted · have forecasted ☑ REGULAR

PRESENT

I forecast	we forecast
you forecast	you forecast
he/she/it forecasts	they forecast

• *His newsletter forecasts economic disaster.*

PRESENT PROGRESSIVE

I am forecasting	we are forecasting
you are forecasting	you are forecasting
he/she/it is forecasting	they are forecasting

• *The weather bureau is forecasting more snow.*

PAST

I forecast	we forecast
you forecast	you forecast
he/she/it forecast	they forecast

• *The weatherman forecast rain for today.*

PAST PROGRESSIVE

I was forecasting	we were forecasting
you were forecasting	you were forecasting
he/she/it was forecasting	they were forecasting

• *Economists were forecasting a strong market.*

PRESENT PERFECT ... have | has forecast
PAST PERFECT ... had forecast

FUTURE ... will forecast
FUTURE PROGRESSIVE ... will be forecasting
FUTURE PERFECT ... will have forecast

PAST PASSIVE

—	—
—	—
it was forecast	they were forecast

• *Earnings were forecast to rise.*

(**COMPLEMENTS**)

forecast *make a prediction*

Who can forecast in such a turbulent economy?
He is reluctant to forecast until more data is available.

forecast _____ *predict*

OBJECT

The weather service is forecasting **heavy rain** for tonight.
Most economists have forecast **a good fourth quarter**.

PASSIVE

The sudden breakup of their marriage had not been forecast
by anybody.

THAT-CLAUSE

Computer models have forecast **that the earth will get warmer**.
I forecast **that it will take months to sell the house**.

PASSIVE

That the dollar would weaken has long been forecast.

WH-CLAUSE

No one can truly forecast **what will happen next**.
They are trying to forecast **how much rain we will get**.

forecast _____ *foreshadow*

OBJECT

High voter turnout forecasts **trouble for the incumbents**.
Scary music in a movie always forecasts **danger**.

PASSIVE

Some people think that earthquakes can be forecast by the
behavior of animals.

PRESENT

I forget	we forget
you forget	you forget
he/she/it forgets	they forget

• *He always forgets to put the milk away.*

PRESENT PROGRESSIVE

I am forgetting	we are forgetting
you are forgetting	you are forgetting
he/she/it is forgetting	they are forgetting

• *I'm always forgetting something.*

PAST

I forgot	we forgot
you forgot	you forgot
he/she/it forgot	they forgot

• *I forgot his first name.*

PAST PROGRESSIVE

I was forgetting	we were forgetting
you were forgetting	you were forgetting
he/she/it was forgetting	they were forgetting

• *I was forgetting what I was about to do.*

PRESENT PERFECT ... have | has forgotten
PAST PERFECT   ... had forgotten

FUTURE   ... will forget
FUTURE PROGRESSIVE   ... will be forgetting
FUTURE PERFECT   ... will have forgotten

PAST PASSIVE

I was forgotten	we were forgotten
you were forgotten	you were forgotten
he/she/it was forgotten	they were forgotten

• *The incident certainly wasn't forgotten.*

COMPLEMENTS

forget *fail to remember*

Don't forget!
He never forgets.
They won't forget, will they?

forget _____ *fail to remember*

OBJECT

I forgot **his e-mail address.**
You must never forget **your password.**
Don't forget **the flowers.**

INFINITIVE

I forgot **to water the plants.**
Don't forget **to run the dishwasher.**
The kids always forget **to hang their coats up.**

THAT-CLAUSE

We forgot **that we were having dinner with the Smiths tonight.**
I forgot **that the meeting had been canceled.**
She forgot **that she had to pick up the cat at the vet.**

WH-CLAUSE

I forgot **what I was about to say.**
He forgot **where he had put his car keys.**
I will never forget **where we stayed in Florida.**

WH-INFINITIVE

The author forgot **where to put the quote marks.**
I forget **how to change my password.**

PRESENT PARTICIPLE

I can't forget **taking her to the hospital.**
He won't soon forget **doing that.**
Did he forget **running into a tree?**

forget _____ *leave behind*

OBJECT

Darn it. I forgot **my briefcase.**
Don't forget **your hat** when you leave.
People always forget **things** when they get off the plane.

forget _____ *neglect, disregard*

(*about*) OBJECT

Don't forget **(about) your friends** when you send holiday cards.
Sam forgot **(about) the ice cream in the trunk.**

EXPRESSIONS

Forget it! *Disregard it.*

"Do I have to clean the bathroom?"
"Forget it! I'll do it myself."

PRESENT

I forgive	we forgive
you forgive	you forgive
he/she/it forgives	they forgive

• *He forgives anything his daughter does.*

PRESENT PROGRESSIVE

I am forgiving	we are forgiving
you are forgiving	you are forgiving
he/she/it is forgiving	they are forgiving

• *I'm forgiving part of their debt.*

PAST

I forgave	we forgave
you forgave	you forgave
he/she/it forgave	they forgave

• *I forgave him for forgetting my birthday.*

PAST PROGRESSIVE

I was forgiving	we were forgiving
you were forgiving	you were forgiving
he/she/it was forgiving	they were forgiving

• *They were always forgiving my mistakes.*

PRESENT PERFECT ... have | has forgiven
PAST PERFECT ... had forgiven

FUTURE ... will forgive
FUTURE PROGRESSIVE ... will be forgiving
FUTURE PERFECT ... will have forgiven

PAST PASSIVE

I was forgiven	we were forgiven
you were forgiven	you were forgiven
he/she/it was forgiven	they were forgiven

• *You were forgiven for making such a mistake.*

(COMPLEMENTS)

forgive *pardon*

He forgives readily.
She can forgive without being superior about it.
I can't forgive so easily.

forgive _____ *excuse, pardon, stop feeling angry/punitive about/toward*

OBJECT

I tried to forgive **his insensitive behavior.**
Some people never forgive **even the smallest slight.**

PASSIVE

My sister was always forgiven, no matter what she had done.

OBJECT + *for* OBJECT

I forgave **Don** *for his thoughtless remark.*
Please forgive **me** *for this interruption.*

OBJECT + *for* PRESENT PARTICIPLE

Will she forgive **him** *for forgetting their anniversary*?
Can you forgive **me** *for being so late*?
I'll never forgive **her** *for eating the last piece of cake.*

forgive _____ *cancel payment of [a debt]*

OBJECT

Many parents forgive **their children's loans.**
The bank may temporarily forgive **interest payments on house loans.**
Some schools will forgive **a percentage of student loans.**

(EXPRESSIONS)

Forgive and forget. [PROVERB]
Pardon an offense, and forget it ever happened.

You could punish him forever—
  or just forgive and forget.

PRESENT

I forgo	we forgo
you forgo	you forgo
he/she/it forgoes	they forgo

• *He forgoes dessert when he is dieting.*

PRESENT PROGRESSIVE

I am forgoing	we are forgoing
you are forgoing	you are forgoing
he/she/it is forgoing	they are forgoing

• *We are forgoing our usual trip to Hawaii.*

PAST

I forwent	we forwent
you forwent	you forwent
he/she/it forwent	they forwent

• *No college student ever forwent free food.*

PAST PROGRESSIVE

I was forgoing	we were forgoing
you were forgoing	you were forgoing
he/she/it was forgoing	they were forgoing

• *The emcee was forgoing lengthy introductions.*

PRESENT PERFECT ... have | has forgone
PAST PERFECT   ... had forgone

FUTURE   ... will forgo
FUTURE PROGRESSIVE ... will be forgoing
FUTURE PERFECT   ... will have forgone

PAST PASSIVE

—	—
—	—
it was forgone	they were forgone

• *The registration fee was forgone to boost attendance.*

NOTES: (1) *Forgo* may also be spelled *forego*: *forego* | *foregoes · forewent · have foregone.*
(2) An archaic verb **forego** (always spelled with *e* and meaning "to go before") survives only as a present participle / adjective (as in *The **foregoing** statement was a paid political announcement*) and as a past participle (in the phrase ***foregone** conclusion*).

──(**COMPLEMENTS**)──

forgo _____ *decline the use/enjoyment of, do without*

OBJECT
We must forgo **the reception** tonight.
The doctor told him that he must forgo **all fatty foods.**
I forwent **the nasty response that popped into my mind.**
The accused has forgone **his right to a jury trial.**

PRESENT PARTICIPLE
We must forgo **meeting you for dinner.**
I couldn't forgo **seeing how the movie turned out.**
We are trying to get the kids to forgo **watching so much TV.**

PRESENT

I forsake	we forsake
you forsake	you forsake
he/she/it forsakes	they forsake

* *The movie forsakes any semblance of plot.*

PRESENT PROGRESSIVE

I am forsaking	we are forsaking
you are forsaking	you are forsaking
he/she/it is forsaking	they are forsaking

* *You are forsaking some of your oldest friends.*

PAST

I forsook	we forsook
you forsook	you forsook
he/she/it forsook	they forsook

* *They forsook allegiance to their country.*

PAST PROGRESSIVE

I was forsaking	we were forsaking
you were forsaking	you were forsaking
he/she/it was forsaking	they were forsaking

* *The professors were forsaking their teaching duties.*

PRESENT PERFECT ... have | has forsaken
PAST PERFECT ... had forsaken

FUTURE ... will forsake
FUTURE PROGRESSIVE ... will be forsaking
FUTURE PERFECT ... will have forsaken

PAST PASSIVE

I was forsaken	we were forsaken
you were forsaken	you were forsaken
he/she/it was forsaken	they were forsaken

* *This principle was forsaken in their greed for power.*

COMPLEMENTS

forsake _____ *abandon, desert*

OBJECT

The bridegroom forsook **all of his old habits.**
He would never forsake **Susan.**
"And forsaking **all others**, I will be faithful...." [WEDDING VOW]

PASSIVE

All of his promises were forsaken.

forsake _____ *renounce, give up*

PRESENT PARTICIPLE

He forsook **smoking and drinking.**
I will forsake **eating meat** for a month.
John will never forsake **riding his motorcycle.**
Because of my knee injury I have forsaken **playing tennis.**

PRESENT

I freeze	we freeze
you freeze	you freeze
he/she/it freezes	they freeze

   • *It usually freezes by mid-October.*

PAST

I froze	we froze
you froze	you froze
he/she/it froze	they froze

   • *The bank froze their assets.*

PRESENT PERFECT	... have | has frozen
PAST PERFECT	... had frozen

PRESENT PROGRESSIVE

I am freezing	we are freezing
you are freezing	you are freezing
he/she/it is freezing	they are freezing

   • *I'm freezing out here.*

PAST PROGRESSIVE

I was freezing	we were freezing
you were freezing	you were freezing
he/she/it was freezing	they were freezing

   • *They were freezing raspberries from their garden.*

FUTURE	... will freeze
FUTURE PROGRESSIVE	... will be freezing
FUTURE PERFECT	... will have frozen

PAST PASSIVE

I was frozen	we were frozen
you were frozen	you were frozen
he/she/it was frozen	they were frozen

   • *The specimens were frozen at −70°C.*

(**COMPLEMENTS**)

freeze *harden into ice, become solid due to cold*	The muddy roads would soon freeze. The rivers all froze that dreadful winter.
freeze *become uncomfortably/ dangerously cold*	Put on a hat or your ears will freeze. Turn up the heat; the room is freezing. The mountain climbers nearly froze to death.
freeze *be at or below 32° Fahrenheit*	The weatherman says it will freeze tonight.
freeze *be preserved in a very cold place*	Girl Scout cookies freeze well.
freeze *become motionless*	The rabbits froze when they heard the hawk. His face froze when he heard us coming.
freeze *be damaged/destroyed by frost*	My petunias all froze last night.
freeze _____ *cause (the contents of) to harden into ice or other solid* OBJECT	We froze **a couple of trays of ice.** The cold snap froze **our garden hoses.**
freeze _____ *chill, make uncomfortably/dangerously cold* OBJECT	The wind was freezing **my fingers.** The driving rain froze **the crowd watching the game.**
freeze _____ *preserve in a very cold place* OBJECT	We can freeze **the leftover vegetable soup.**
freeze _____ *cause to become motionless* OBJECT	The shout froze **everyone** in the store. The peace agreement froze **the armies** in place. The accident froze **traffic** for hours.
freeze _____ *fix at a certain level* OBJECT	The Federal Reserve froze **the interest rate** today.
freeze _____ *prohibit, restrict* OBJECT	The government froze **foreign assets** today.

(**PHRASAL VERBS**)

freeze up *stop functioning*	If there is a power surge, my computer completely freezes up. I just freeze up when I have to talk to a group of people.

PRESENT

I gainsay	we gainsay
you gainsay	you gainsay
he/she/it gainsays	they gainsay

• *He gainsays every proposal to raise taxes.*

PRESENT PROGRESSIVE

I am gainsaying	we are gainsaying
you are gainsaying	you are gainsaying
he/she/it is gainsaying	they are gainsaying

• *They are not gainsaying your idea.*

PAST

I gainsaid	we gainsaid
you gainsaid	you gainsaid
he/she/it gainsaid	they gainsaid

• *They gainsaid whatever we wanted to do.*

PAST PROGRESSIVE

I was gainsaying	we were gainsaying
you were gainsaying	you were gainsaying
he/she/it was gainsaying	they were gainsaying

• *He wasn't gainsaying the importance of the bill.*

PRESENT PERFECT ... have | has gainsaid
PAST PERFECT ... had gainsaid

FUTURE ... will gainsay
FUTURE PROGRESSIVE ... will be gainsaying
FUTURE PERFECT ... will have gainsaid

PAST PASSIVE

I was gainsaid	we were gainsaid
you were gainsaid	you were gainsaid
he/she/it was gainsaid	they were gainsaid

• *The defendant's statement was gainsaid by three witnesses.*

COMPLEMENTS

gainsay _____ contradict, deny, declare false [OFTEN NEGATIVE]

OBJECT	I don't gainsay **the impact of the recession.**
	Nobody is gainsaying **your conclusions.**
	I will not gainsay **a member of the club**, even if he is wrong.
PASSIVE	The high risk is being gainsaid by informed people.
THAT-CLAUSE	I won't gainsay **that his ideas have some merit.**
	Even his opponents don't gainsay **that he is trying to do the right thing.**
	Can you really gainsay **that interest rates have fallen?**
WH-CLAUSE	No one will gainsay **what the president recommends.**
	I am not gainsaying **how risky the venture is.**
	Senator Blather will gainsay **whatever you propose.**

PRESENT		PRESENT PROGRESSIVE	
I get	we get	I am getting	we are getting
you get	you get	you are getting	you are getting
he/she/it gets	they get	he/she/it is getting	they are getting

• *He gets to sleep late on weekends.*   • *I'm getting ready now.*

PAST		PAST PROGRESSIVE	
I got	we got	I was getting	we were getting
you got	you got	you were getting	you were getting
he/she/it got	they got	he/she/it was getting	they were getting

• *We got good feedback on the proposal.*   • *The plan was getting a lot of criticism.*

PRESENT PERFECT	... have	has got/gotten
PAST PERFECT	... had got/gotten

FUTURE	... will get
FUTURE PROGRESSIVE	... will be getting
FUTURE PERFECT	... will have got/gotten

PAST PASSIVE

I was got/gotten	we were got/gotten
you were got/gotten	you were got/gotten
he/she/it was got/gotten	they were got/gotten

• *Permission was gotten from the authorities.*

──────────────────────────────(COMPLEMENTS)──

NOTE: *Get* is also used as a helping verb to form the passive voice.

get + PAST PARTICIPLE	The burglar got caught by police.
	I got injured playing football.
	Bobby got sent to the principal's office.
	We'll get married in October.

get _____ *receive, obtain*

OBJECT	They got **permission** to leave early.
	I got **a "B"** in Social Studies last quarter.
	I got **a traffic ticket** last night.
	The company got **an award for community service.**
	I'm getting **a busy signal.**
	We are getting **a new car.**
PASSIVE	Permission to leave early was gotten.

get _____ *bring*

INDIRECT OBJECT + DIRECT OBJECT	Get *me* **a coffee**, will you?
	I will get *her* **a blanket.**
for PARAPHRASE	Get **a coffee** *for me*, will you?
	I will get **a blanket** *for her.*

get _____ *notice, understand*

OBJECT	Did you get **that smirky look on his face?**
	"Did you get **the joke?**" "Yes, I got **it.**"
WH-CLAUSE	I got **what he was trying to say.**
	Did you get **how he avoided talking to us?**

get _____ *become*

PREDICATE ADJECTIVE	He really got **angry** about it.
	I got **sick** on the way back.
	The dogs got **loose** and headed for the barn.

get _____ *begin, start*

PRESENT PARTICIPLE	Let's get **going.**

get _____ *have the opportunity, receive permission*

INFINITIVE	We will get **to meet them at the reception.**
	The kids get **to stay up late tonight.**

get _____ *cause/persuade [to do/be]*

OBJECT + PREDICATE ADJECTIVE	Get **your hands** *clean* before coming to the table.
	I got **the computer screen** *dirty*.
OBJECT + INFINITIVE	I got **the kids** *to clean up their room*.
	We finally got **the truck** *to start*.
OBJECT + PRESENT PARTICIPLE	I got **the kids** *cleaning up their room*.
	It got **me** *thinking about a new solution*.
OBJECT + PAST PARTICIPLE	I finally got **my computer** *fixed*.
	We got **our house** *painted*.

get _____ *arrive at*

ADVERB OF PLACE TO/FROM	Our parents got **home** early.
	We can get **to the office** in 15 minutes.

get _____ *travel*

ADVERB OF PLACE TO/FROM	Did you get **to Paris** last summer?
	I got **as far as Chicago**.

get _____ *cause to move*

OBJECT + ADVERB OF PLACE TO/FROM	Can you get **me** *to the airport* in 30 minutes?
	I got **the car** *out of the garage*.

get _____ *be affected/infected by*

OBJECT	I got **the hiccups** just before I went on stage.
	Can you get **the flu** from a flu shot?

NOTE: For the following two meanings, *get* is used only in the present perfect tense.

get _____ *have, possess*

OBJECT	I've got **a terrible cold**.
	I've only got **about $20** on me.

get _____ *must*

INFINITIVE	I've got **to go now**.
	He has got **to be more careful**.

(PHRASAL VERBS)

get across/back/down/in/out/up/etc. *move in a specified direction*	The police ordered the crowd to get back.
	She opened the car door and told him to get in.
get _SEP_ **in/out/etc.** *take/bring in a specified direction*	Did you get the firewood in?
	He got the cheese and crackers out.
get around/out *become known*	The news got around that they were divorced.
get around _____ *avoid*	I got around the problem by installing new software.
get away with _____ *do without being punished*	The company got away with selling pirated software.
get back to _____ *respond to*	I must get back to Anthony tomorrow.
get behind (on _____ **)** *be late making payments (on [something])*	Lots of people have gotten behind on their mortgages.
get by (on/with _____ **)** *manage to survive/do (with [something])*	Amos gets by on $750 a month.
	Our neighbors get by with just one car.
get in/into _____ *be admitted to*	Our son got into nursing school.
get out of _____ *avoid, escape*	Harold got out of doing dishes four nights in a row.
get over _____ *recover from*	Pat got over the flu in three days.
get up *rise*	It's 7 o'clock—time to get up.
	Please get up and get me a fork.
get _____ **up** *cause to rise*	Mom got us up before dawn.

top
30
verb

PRESENT

I gird	we gird
you gird	you gird
he/she/it girds	they gird

• She girds the coarse robe with a thick cord.

PRESENT PROGRESSIVE

I am girding	we are girding
you are girding	you are girding
he/she/it is girding	they are girding

• The centurion is girding his cloak before leaving.

PAST

I girt	we girt
you girt	you girt
he/she/it girt	they girt

• He girt himself for a fight.

PAST PROGRESSIVE

I was girding	we were girding
you were girding	you were girding
he/she/it was girding	they were girding

• The army was girding itself for battle.

PRESENT PERFECT ... have | has girt
PAST PERFECT ... had girt

FUTURE ... will gird
FUTURE PROGRESSIVE ... will be girding
FUTURE PERFECT ... will have girt

PAST PASSIVE

I was girt	we were girt
you were girt	you were girt
he/she/it was girt	they were girt

• The Parthenon was girt by 46 pillars.

COMPLEMENTS

gird _____ *fasten with a belt/strap/cord*

OBJECT
He girt **his sword** around his waist.
We girt **all of the drapes** with blue sashes.

PASSIVE
The garment was girt tightly around her.

gird _____ *surround, encircle*

OBJECT
A deep moat girds **the castle**.
Trees have completely girt **the old barn**.

PASSIVE
The city is girt by two beltways.

gird _____ *prepare [oneself/someone] [for action / a challenge]*

OBJECT + *for* OBJECT
The president is girding **the nation** *for war*.
The company girt **the employees** *for another round of layoffs*.

(REFLEXIVE PRONOUN +) *for* OBJECT
The soldiers girt (**themselves**) *for the summer campaign*.
Toy stores are girding (**themselves**) *for the Christmas rush*.
I girt (**myself**) *for a confrontation with my boss*.

OBJECT + *for* WH-CLAUSE
The candidate girt **his supporters** *for what was in store*.

(REFLEXIVE PRONOUN +) *for* WH-CLAUSE
We all girt (**ourselves**) *for whatever was to come*.
Jayne girt (**herself**) *for what might happen to her job*.

(REFLEXIVE PRONOUN +) INFINITIVE
He girt (**himself**) *to cross the shaky footbridge*.
Senator Blather is girding (**himself**) *to run for president*.
The government is girding (**itself**) *to take action against counterfeiters*.

EXPRESSIONS

gird (up) [one's] loins *prepare oneself [for action / a challenge]*

State universities are girding their loins for cutbacks in public funding.

give _____ *perform*
OBJECT

The symphony gave **a concert** last night.
The band gave **a free concert** to benefit AIDS victims.

give _____ *cause to have*
INDIRECT OBJECT + DIRECT OBJECT

Loud music gives *me* **a headache.**

give _____ *pay*
OBJECT

Michelle gave **$125** for her outfit.

give _____ *administer*
INDIRECT OBJECT + DIRECT OBJECT

Freddie gave *the guard* **a punch in the mouth.**
Darla's mom gave *her* **some cough syrup.**

to PARAPHRASE

Darla's mom gave **some cough syrup** *to her.*

give _____ *cause*
OBJECT + INFINITIVE

You gave **me** *to understand that you would support us.*
He gave **Jackson** *to believe that the problem was solved.*

give _____ *sentence to*
INDIRECT OBJECT + DIRECT OBJECT

The judge gave *the criminal* **30 days in jail.**

give _____ *sacrifice*
OBJECT + *for* OBJECT

"It is sweet and right to give **your life** *for your country.*"
[HORACE]

give _____ *devote*
OBJECT + *to* OBJECT

Marvin gave **his whole life** *to the cause of justice.*

─────(PHRASAL VERBS)───

give <u>SEP</u> **away** *betray*

A club member gave away our
secret meeting place.

give <u>SEP</u> **back** *return*

You'll have to give the engagement ring back.

give in (to _____) *surrender*
(to [someone/something])

After arguing for two hours, our opponents gave in.
Senator Blather gave in to pressure from his colleagues.

give it to _____ *scold, punish*

My boss really gave it to me when I walked in late.

give off _____ *release, emit*

The compost is giving off an earthy smell.
The laptop gives off a lot of heat.

give out *come to an end*

The settlers' food gave out after three weeks.

give out *wear out, stop operating*

After 203,000 miles, our 1979 Oldsmobile finally gave out.

give <u>SEP</u> **out** *distribute*

C.J. gave out the president's itinerary.

give <u>SEP</u> **out** *make known*

Don't give out your cell phone number.

give out _____ *produce*

This old furnace gives out a lot of heat.

give <u>SEP</u> **up** *stop, cease*

Mom and Dad gave up smoking at the same time.

give <u>SEP</u> **up** *surrender, yield*

Within an hour, the gunman gave up two hostages.
An hour later, he gave himself up.

give up (on _____) *admit failure*
(with [something])

Sheila finally gave up on the crossword puzzle.
I tried four times to reach Lisa, then gave up.

give up (on _____) *stop trying ([to do])*

Ainsley finally gave up on trying to convince Sam.

PRESENT

I give	we give
you give	you give
he/she/it gives	they give

  • *He gives 10% of his income to charity.*

PRESENT PROGRESSIVE

I am giving	we are giving
you are giving	you are giving
he/she/it is giving	they are giving

  • *I'm giving up on it.*

PAST

I gave	we gave
you gave	you gave
he/she/it gave	they gave

  • *The company gave me a car to use.*

PAST PROGRESSIVE

I was giving	we were giving
you were giving	you were giving
he/she/it was giving	they were giving

  • *We were giving a party that evening.*

PRESENT PERFECT ... have | has given
PAST PERFECT ... had given

FUTURE ... will give
FUTURE PROGRESSIVE ... will be giving
FUTURE PERFECT ... will have given

PAST PASSIVE

I was given	we were given
you were given	you were given
he/she/it was given	they were given

  • *All of the employees were given entry cards.*

COMPLEMENTS

give *make a gift/donation*	How much can you give? They always give generously to the homeless shelter.
give *yield, collapse*	For the deadlock to be broken, something has to give. The floor might give if we put that much weight on it.
give _____ *make a gift of, donate*	
INDIRECT OBJECT + DIRECT OBJECT	Terry gave *Dan* **a new computer.** Spanky gave *Alfalfa* **the high sign.**
to PARAPHRASE	Terry gave **a new computer** *to Dan.* Spanky gave **the high sign** *to Alfalfa.*
give _____ *convey physically*	
OBJECT	She gave **a little smile** at the news.
INDIRECT OBJECT + DIRECT OBJECT	Leo gave *the president* **a copy of the report.** She gave *the boys* **a dirty look.**
to PARAPHRASE	Leo gave **a copy of the report** *to the president.* She gave **a dirty look** *to the boys.*
give _____ *provide*	
OBJECT	Soy-based inks give **good results.**
INDIRECT OBJECT + DIRECT OBJECT	Give *me* **a chance to prove myself.** This gives *gays and lesbians* **the right to marry.** The boss gave *his cousin* **a job.**
to PARAPHRASE	The boss gave **a job** *to his cousin.*
give _____ *host*	
OBJECT	We will give **the reception** in his honor.
INDIRECT OBJECT + DIRECT OBJECT	I gave *my parents* **a surprise party.** We gave *the seniors* **a graduation party.**
for PARAPHRASE	I gave **a surprise party** *for my parents.* We gave **a graduation party** *for the seniors.*
PASSIVE	A graduation party was given for the seniors. The seniors were given a graduation party.
give _____ *present*	
OBJECT	The senator is giving **a speech** on TV.

go _____ *engage in [a sport/leisure activity]*
   PRESENT PARTICIPLE

   We plan to go **skiing** in Idaho.
   They went **dancing** last night.

go _____ *do [something inadvisable]* [USED ONLY IN THE NEGATIVE; INFORMAL]
   PRESENT PARTICIPLE

   Don't go **telling everyone about it.**
   We won't go **running to him with all our problems.**

go _____ *belong*
   ADVERB OF PLACE

   Coats go **in the closet**, not **on the floor.**

go _____ *be sent*
   to OBJECT

   The proposal went by e-mail **to all department heads.**

go _____ *be given/sold*
   to OBJECT

   The prize goes **to the lady in the blue sweater.**
   The antique lamp goes **to bidder No. 17.**

(PHRASAL VERBS)

go back/down/in/out/up/etc.
move in a specified direction
   He went back to check the furnace.
   Ed went out to watch the sunset.

go against _____ *oppose, be contrary to*
   She'll go against the incumbent in the fall election.
   Dispensing birth control pills goes against his conscience.

go along with _____ *agree with*
   The president went along with his staff on the issue.

go away *end*
   My headache went away before lunch.

go back to _____ *date back to*
   The New Year's Eve custom goes back to Druid times.

go back to _____ *resume*
   It's four in the morning—go back to sleep.

go by _____ *be known as*
   His real name is Meredith, but he goes by Snuffy.

go down *decrease*
   The swelling has slowly gone down.
   The temperature went down 18 degrees in one hour.

go down *stop functioning*
   Cable service went down at 9:36 this morning.

go for _____ *be attracted by*
   She goes for men with beards.

go for _____ *do [an activity]*
   Let's go for a swim.

go for _____ *sell for [an amount]*
   How much did the dining room set go for?

go into _____ *begin a career in*
   Steve went into electronics, and Stuart went into medicine.

go off *explode, fire*
   The gun went off accidentally.

go off *take place, happen*
   The surprise party went off as planned.

go on *be switched on*
   All of a sudden, the lights went on.

go on *happen*
   What went on at yesterday's meeting?
   What's going on?

go on (_____) *continue ([doing])*
   Forrest Gump just went on running.
   How long will the concert go on?

go out *be extinguished*
   The lights went out one by one.

go through _____ *examine*
   She went through her mail during supper.

go through _____ *spend, consume*
   We go through $5,000 a month.
   Our son goes through two gallons of milk a week.

go under *fail*
   A third of all small businesses go under.

go up *be built*
   A new mall is going up on the edge of town.

go up *increase*
   The stock market has gone up 225 points.

go with _____
harmonize with
   This tie would go well with your blue suit.
   That paisley shirt doesn't go with anything.

go without _____
manage without
   The prisoners went without food for nine days.

top 30 verb

$\quad$ **COMPLEMENTS**

go *depart, leave*

Please go.
I'm going as soon as I can get packed.
The seasons come and go.

go *function*

The engine won't go.

go *become worse, fail*

I think my hearing is going.
For most athletes, the knees are the first thing to go.

go *be eliminated/discarded*

I'm afraid that Smith will have to go.

go *be worded/sung*

The song goes like this ... la la di la la, la la di da.

go ____ *travel*
ADVERB OF PLACE TO/FROM

I'm going **to Dallas** tomorrow.
We are going **to lunch** now.
Where do they go on vacation?

go ____ *proceed, move*
ADVERB OF MANNER

The car in the left lane is going **too slow**.
I'm going **as fast as I can**.

go ____ *extend, lead*
ADVERB OF PLACE TO/FROM

Route 66 originally went **from Chicago to Los Angeles**.
Delta goes **everywhere in the Southeast**.
That door goes **to the kitchen**.

go ____ *pass*
ADVERB OF MANNER

The evening went **too quickly**.

go ____ *progress*
ADVERB OF MANNER

The meeting is going **well**.
How is it going?

go ____ *be, become, turn out*
PREDICATE ADJECTIVE

The soldiers went **hungry** for days.
I think the cheese has gone **bad**.
How many banks have gone **bankrupt**?
My e-mails to her have all gone **unanswered**.

go ____ *attend*
TO OBJECT

Dad went **to college** on the G.I. Bill.
Sidney went **to Harvard Law School**.
Our family goes **to church** on Sunday.
Let's go **to a movie** tonight.

PRESENT

I grind	we grind
you grind	you grind
he/she/it grinds	they grind

• *Poverty grinds everyone down.*

PRESENT PROGRESSIVE

I am grinding	we are grinding
you are grinding	you are grinding
he/she/it is grinding	they are grinding

• *They are grinding their rusty swords and spears.*

PAST

I ground	we ground
you ground	you ground
he/she/it ground	they ground

• *We ground some more coffee.*

PAST PROGRESSIVE

I was grinding	we were grinding
you were grinding	you were grinding
he/she/it was grinding	they were grinding

• *I was grinding my teeth in my sleep.*

PRESENT PERFECT ... have | has ground
PAST PERFECT ... had ground

FUTURE ... will grind
FUTURE PROGRESSIVE ... will be grinding
FUTURE PERFECT ... will have ground

PAST PASSIVE

I was ground	we were ground
you were ground	you were ground
he/she/it was ground	they were ground

• *The gear teeth were ground pretty badly.*

COMPLEMENTS

grind *crush, sharpen/smooth/press by rubbing*	The wheels of justice grind slow, but they grind exceeding fine. [PROVERB] The mill grinds continuously when the harvest comes in.
grind *clash/grate noisily*	The gears ground whenever I tried to shift. His teeth were grinding loudly. The axle wheels were grinding and squeaking.
grind _____ *crush into powder / tiny pieces*	
OBJECT	The wheel grinds **the seeds**, separating wheat from chaff. The miller is grinding **the corn** into meal. The editorial ground **the opposition's argument** to shreds.
PASSIVE	The corn is ground into meal.
grind _____ *sharpen/smooth by rubbing*	
OBJECT	We ground **all the edges** until they shone. The lens maker ground **the glass** until it was smooth.
grind _____ *rub together forcefully*	
OBJECT	He grinds **his teeth** when he gets really upset.
grind _____ *press/rub with a circular motion*	
OBJECT	He ground **the black widow spider** under his heel. They ground **the dried herbs** with their hands.
grind _____ *oppress*	
OBJECT	The tyrant ground **the colonists** with excessive taxes.

PHRASAL VERBS

grind away at _____ *work steadily on*	She ground away at her thesis.
grind SEP **down** *reduce and destroy [someone's] enthusiasm*	This job really grinds me down.
grind _____ **into** *rub into*	The workers ground dirt into the carpet.
grind on *continue, seemingly endlessly*	The Vietnam War ground on for six more years.
grind SEP **out** *produce mechanically, churn out*	The novelist grinds out a chapter a day.
grind SEP **up** *reduce to small pieces*	Bill grinds the coffee beans up very fine.

PRESENT

I grow	we grow
you grow	you grow
he/she/it grows	they grow

• He grows wheat and barley on his land.

PRESENT PROGRESSIVE

I am growing	we are growing
you are growing	you are growing
he/she/it is growing	they are growing

• He is growing up.

PAST

I grew	we grew
you grew	you grew
he/she/it grew	they grew

• The kids grew a lot this year.

PAST PROGRESSIVE

I was growing	we were growing
you were growing	you were growing
he/she/it was growing	they were growing

• The passengers were growing angry at the delay.

PRESENT PERFECT ... have | has grown
PAST PERFECT ... had grown

FUTURE ... will grow
FUTURE PROGRESSIVE ... will be growing
FUTURE PERFECT ... will have grown

PAST PASSIVE

—	—
—	—
it was grown	they were grown

• The Fair Trade coffee was grown in Mexico.

COMPLEMENTS

grow develop, mature	Weeds were growing in the driveway.
	Many flowers won't grow in partial shade.
grow become taller	My, how you've grown!
	The kids are sure growing.
grow become longer	Her hair grew two inches over the summer.
grow become bigger, expand	Our investments have grown about eight percent a year.
	His reputation is growing even outside the region.
	The company is growing through mergers with smaller firms.
	The deficit has grown every year.
grow _____ raise [plants, a crop]	
OBJECT	We will grow **more corn** next year.
	We can grow **pansies** in the window boxes.
	It isn't good to grow **the same crop** in a field year after year.
WH-CLAUSE	We will grow **what sells the best.**
	They grow **whatever crops can tolerate the heat.**
grow _____ cause to develop and flourish	
OBJECT	We are trying to grow **the business.**
	The company has grown **its profits** effectively.
	The magazine needs to grow **its circulation.**
grow _____ begin	
INFINITIVE	I have grown **to like broccoli.**
	I had grown **to hate Senator Blather's speeches.**
grow _____ become	
PREDICATE ADJECTIVE	The driver grew **tired** as evening approached.
	Ruby grew **pale** at the sight of the snake.
	They grew **accustomed** to the boss's angry outbursts.

PHRASAL VERBS

grow into _____ become big enough for	She's grown into her sister's winter coat.
grow into _____ develop into	Your son has grown into a fine young man.
	The banking problem has grown into a major crisis.
grow up to be _____ develop into	She has grown up to be a poised and confident woman.

PRESENT

I hamstring   we hamstring
you hamstring   you hamstring
he/she/it hamstrings   they hamstring

• *His opposition hamstrings our reform efforts.*

PAST

I hamstrung   we hamstrung
you hamstrung   you hamstrung
he/she/it hamstrung   they hamstrung

• *She hamstrung the project by cutting staff.*

PRESENT PERFECT ... have | has hamstrung
PAST PERFECT   ... had hamstrung

PRESENT PROGRESSIVE

I am hamstringing   we are hamstringing
you are hamstringing   you are hamstringing
he/she/it is hamstringing   they are hamstringing

• *Endless delay is hamstringing our progress.*

PAST PROGRESSIVE

I was hamstringing   we were hamstringing
you were hamstringing   you were hamstringing
he/she/it was hamstringing   they were hamstringing

• *They were hamstringing attempts to pass the bill.*

FUTURE   ... will hamstring
FUTURE PROGRESSIVE   ... will be hamstringing
FUTURE PERFECT   ... will have hamstrung

PAST PASSIVE

I was hamstrung   we were hamstrung
you were hamstrung   you were hamstrung
he/she/it was hamstrung   they were hamstrung

• *Several cattle were hamstrung by wild wolves.*

COMPLEMENTS

hamstring _____ *cripple by cutting the hamstring muscle*

OBJECT   Ranchers would often hamstring **dangerous animals**.

PASSIVE   Rebellious slaves were sometimes hamstrung to keep them from running away.

hamstring _____ *hinder, make more difficult*

OBJECT   Bad weather hamstrung **the rescue efforts**.
Uncertainty about final approval hamstrings **our planning**.

PASSIVE   Development of the property was hamstrung by local opposition.

WH-CLAUSE   Lack of funding hamstrung **whatever plans we proposed**.
Bureaucratic inertia will always hamstring **whatever we do**.

PASSIVE   What we tried to do was hamstrung by insufficient staffing.

PRESENT

I hang	we hang
you hang	you hang
he/she/it hangs	they hang

• *His picture hangs in the boardroom.*

PRESENT PROGRESSIVE

I am hanging	we are hanging
you are hanging	you are hanging
he/she/it is hanging	they are hanging

• *I'm hanging around until she returns.*

PAST

I hung	we hung
you hung	you hung
he/she/it hung	they hung

• *We hung all the ornaments on the tree.*

PAST PROGRESSIVE

I was hanging	we were hanging
you were hanging	you were hanging
he/she/it was hanging	they were hanging

• *They were hanging out at Tom's house.*

PRESENT PERFECT ... have | has hung
PAST PERFECT ... had hung

FUTURE ... will hang
FUTURE PROGRESSIVE ... will be hanging
FUTURE PERFECT ... will have hung

PAST PASSIVE

I was hung	we were hung
you were hung	you were hung
he/she/it was hung	they were hung

• *The stockings were hung by the chimney.*

COMPLEMENTS

NOTE: The past tense and past participle form is *hung* for all meanings of *hang* except one: The form *hanged* is used for the meanings "be suspended by the neck until dead" and "suspend by the neck until dead."

hang *be suspended by the neck until dead*

He will hang for his crimes.
Black Bart was finally hanged.

hang _____ *be suspended, droop*

ADVERB OF PLACE

The gulls hung **above the fishing boats.**
The smoke from the forest fire hung **in the still air.**
Wet laundry hung **everywhere in the small apartment.**

ADVERB OF MANNER

The flag was hanging **limply** from the staff.
His suit hangs **a little too loosely.**
His head hung **in shame** after his arrest.

hang _____ *be prevalent*

ADVERB OF PLACE

Before the battle, tension hung **in the air.**

hang _____ *suspend/fasten without support from below, let droop*

OBJECT (+ ADVERB OF PLACE)

We've already hung **the Christmas wreath.**
We hung **our wet clothing** *on branches.*
I hung **a bird feeder** *in the oak tree.*

PASSIVE

The bridge was hung *from steel cables.*

hang _____ *exhibit [artwork]*

OBJECT

They hung **her paintings** in the main gallery.
I hung **the photograph** in the spring exhibition.

PASSIVE

His pictures have been hung at all the major art shows.

hang _____ *suspend by the neck until dead*

OBJECT

They hanged **the convict** at dawn.

PASSIVE

He was hanged for his many crimes.

PHRASAL VERBS

hang around/out *loiter, linger*
hang on *wait*
hang on to _____ *keep*

Leo hung around, waiting for Josh.
Can you hang on while I take another call?
Hang on to the baby clothes; you may need them again.

have _____ *experience, undergo*
　OBJECT

He had **chicken pox** when he was a child.
Did you have **a good time** at the party?
California had **drought conditions** for several years.
They are having **an argument about visitation rights**.

have _____ *keep in one's mind*
　OBJECT

Senator Blather has **an opinion about everything**.
We have **doubts about the new employee**.
I have **an idea for earning extra money**.

have _____ *host*
　OBJECT

The restaurant is having **a grand opening** this Saturday.

have _____ *eat, drink*
　OBJECT

Dan is having **blackberry pie** for dessert.
Tim had **a refill** on his soft drink.

have _____ *be the parent(s) of*
　OBJECT

We have **two sons and a daughter**.

have _____ *study*
　OBJECT

Terry had **three years of Spanish** in high school.

have _____ *position*
　OBJECT + ADVERB OF PLACE

Mark had **his hands** *on the steering wheel*.
The graduate had **a parent** *on either side of him*.

PHRASAL VERBS

have _____ **back/down/over/up**/etc.
*invite and host [someone] at a specified
location*

We had the Smiths over for dinner.

have _____ **against** *have as a reason
to dislike*

She has a grudge against her ex-boyfriend.

have _____ **on** *be operating*

She has the radio on when she's at home.

have ᔆᴱᴾ **on** *be wearing*

He had on a turtleneck sweater and baggy trousers.

have ᔆᴱᴾ **out** *have removed*

I had one of my upper molars out.

EXPRESSIONS

have had it *have done/endured all
that one can*

I have had it with tax auditors.

have a big mouth *gossip a lot,
reveal secrets a lot*

Don't tell Joanie your troubles; she has a big mouth.

have a bone to pick (with _____**)** *have
something to argue about (with [someone])*

I have a bone to pick with the editor about his changes.

**have [one's] cake and eat it too / have
it both ways** *have the advantages of
something without its disadvantages*

Denny wants to live in the country, but he wants a
grocery store next door. He can't have his cake and
eat it too.

have it good *be rich*

The bank executive really has it good—a Mercedes,
a mansion, and a vacation home in California.

have it out (with _____**)**
*settle an argument (with
[someone])*

The teacher had it out with the principal.

have it that _____
claim/say that

Rumor has it that Glenda is getting married.

have to do with _____
concern, involve

The article has to do with child labor laws.

PRESENT

I have	we have
you have	you have
he/she/it has	they have

 • *November only has 30 days.*

PAST

I had	we had
you had	you had
he/she/it had	they had

 • *We had a really great time.*

PRESENT PERFECT ... have | has had
PAST PERFECT   ... had had

PRESENT PROGRESSIVE

I am having	we are having
you are having	you are having
he/she/it is having	they are having

 • *I'm having some people over.*

PAST PROGRESSIVE

I was having	we were having
you were having	you were having
he/she/it was having	they were having

 • *We were having a lot of problems then.*

FUTURE   ... will have
FUTURE PROGRESSIVE   ... will be having
FUTURE PERFECT   ... will have had

PAST PASSIVE

 Have is not used in the passive voice except
 in idiomatic expressions.

(**COMPLEMENTS**)

NOTE: *Have* is also used as a helping verb to form the perfect tenses.

     have + PAST PARTICIPLE   She has read all six of Jane Austen's novels.

have _____ *possess, own, contain, include*

     OBJECT

Do you have **a car?**
I have **enough food for everyone.**
Ted has **an interesting news item for us.**
Do you have **a minute?**
We have **an office in Tokyo.**
Does the meeting room have **a projection screen?**
The department store has **mattresses on sale.**
A week has **seven days.**
The knitters' club has **525 members.**

have _____ *be characterized by*

     OBJECT

She has **red hair.**
He has **a quick temper.**
My car has **a tendency to stall at stop signs.**

have _____ *must*

     INFINITIVE

I have **to be at the office by 8 o'clock.**
We have **to stop for gas at the next exit.**
You will have **to make up your minds soon.**

NOTE: When the information in the infinitive is clear from context, *have* + INFINITIVE
is often contracted to *have* + to. For example, *Do you have to go now?* may be contracted
to *Do you have to? Have to* is sometimes pronounced /hafta/.

have _____ *cause [to do]*

     OBJECT + BASE-FORM INFINITIVE

I had **the kids** *put away their toys.*
He had **me** *reprint the document.*
We will have **the builder** *modify the deck.*

     OBJECT + PRESENT PARTICIPLE

He had **his crew** *working on the addition.*
The comedian really had **us** *laughing.*
The coach had **the team** *running wind
     sprints.*

     OBJECT + PAST PARTICIPLE

I had **my watch** *repaired.*
Aunt Jenny had **her hip** *replaced this fall.*
They had **the wedding reception** *catered.*

PRESENT

I hear   we hear
you hear   you hear
he/she/it hears   they hear

• *He only hears what he wants to.*

PAST

I heard   we heard
you heard   you heard
he/she/it heard   they heard

• *I heard that there was a problem.*

PRESENT PERFECT ... have | has heard
PAST PERFECT ... had heard

PRESENT PROGRESSIVE

I am hearing   we are hearing
you are hearing   you are hearing
he/she/it is hearing   they are hearing

• *I'm not hearing anything.*

PAST PROGRESSIVE

I was hearing   we were hearing
you were hearing   you were hearing
he/she/it was hearing   they were hearing

• *They were hearing some surprising reports.*

FUTURE ... will hear
FUTURE PROGRESSIVE ... will be hearing
FUTURE PERFECT ... will have heard

PAST PASSIVE

I was heard   we were heard
you were heard   you were heard
he/she/it was heard   they were heard

• *All witnesses were heard in one afternoon.*

COMPLEMENTS

hear *perceive sound by ear*

She can only hear in the middle frequencies.
Sam hears pretty well for someone his age.

hear *make out words/music*

Can everybody hear, or should I turn the radio up?
No one could hear while the band was playing.

hear _____ *perceive by ear*

OBJECT

I just heard **the telephone**.
We could hear **the surf** from our room.

PASSIVE

The dog's barking was heard by everyone in the building.

OBJECT + INFINITIVE [USED ONLY
IN THE PASSIVE]

He was heard *to make threats*.
The senator was heard *to make promises he couldn't keep*.

OBJECT + BASE-FORM INFINITIVE

I heard **him** *start the car*.
We heard **the kids** *turn on the TV*.
I heard **her** *play a Mozart piano concerto*.

OBJECT + PRESENT PARTICIPLE

I heard **him** *starting the car*.
We heard **the kids** *playing in the backyard*.
He heard **someone** *talking on the phone*.

hear _____ *be told, learn*

OBJECT

Did you hear **the news**?
I heard **the final score**.
John has just heard **the results of his test**.

THAT-CLAUSE

I heard **that Jim is leaving the company**.
Did you hear **that they are going to have a baby**?

WH-CLAUSE

Have you heard **who won the game**?
I heard **what you said**.

hear _____ *listen to the two sides in [a court case]*

OBJECT

The judge heard **three divorce cases** this morning.

PHRASAL VERBS

hear from _____ *receive a message from*

We heard from the Ellners last week.

hear of _____ *learn of the existence of*

I've heard of hedgehogs, but I've never seen one.

hear _____ **out** *listen to everything
[someone] has to say*

Simon heard her out, but he didn't change his mind.

PRESENT

I hew	we hew
you hew	you hew
he/she/it hews	they hew

• *The gardener hews the hedges back too far.*

PRESENT PROGRESSIVE

I am hewing	we are hewing
you are hewing	you are hewing
he/she/it is hewing	they are hewing

• *We are hewing wood to make the fence posts.*

PAST

I hewed	we hewed
you hewed	you hewed
he/she/it hewed	they hewed

• *Settlers hewed a clearing in the woods.*

PAST PROGRESSIVE

I was hewing	we were hewing
you were hewing	you were hewing
he/she/it was hewing	they were hewing

• *The farmers were all hewing their winter firewood.*

PRESENT PERFECT ... have | has hewn
PAST PERFECT ... had hewn

FUTURE ... will hew
FUTURE PROGRESSIVE ... will be hewing
FUTURE PERFECT ... will have hewn

PAST PASSIVE

—	—
—	—
it was hewn	they were hewn

• *The stools were hewn out of solid pieces of wood.*

(**COMPLEMENTS**)

hew _____ *chop off / cut down / hack through with a sharp tool*
[OFTEN WITH *down*]

OBJECT
Crews hewed down **hundreds of trees** for the new roadway.
Have you hewn **all the branches you need**?

PASSIVE
The saplings along the path had all been hewn and stacked.

hew _____ *make/shape by cutting/chopping*

OBJECT
We hewed **a narrow trail** along the side of the mountain.
The initial attackers had hewn **an opening** in the enemy line.

PASSIVE
A path had been hewn through the jungle.
The totem pole was hewn from cedar.

hew _____ *adhere/conform strictly*

to OBJECT
Candidates must hew **to the party line**.
Most religions demand that you hew **to certain forms of behavior**.
Many artists do not hew **to traditional forms**.

(**EXPRESSIONS**)

rough-hewn *with a rough surface/quality*
I like the rough-hewn furniture in the camp dining hall.
These rough-hewn alphabets are from the 19th century.

rough-hewn *unrefined*
My neighbors are rough-hewn in appearance and speech.

PRESENT

I hide	we hide
you hide	you hide
he/she/it hides	they hide

• *Our cat always hides in the closet.*

PAST

I hid	we hid
you hid	you hid
he/she/it hid	they hid

• *I hid a house key outside.*

PRESENT PERFECT ... have | has hidden
PAST PERFECT ... had hidden

PRESENT PROGRESSIVE

I am hiding	we are hiding
you are hiding	you are hiding
he/she/it is hiding	they are hiding

• *I'm hiding from Todd.*

PAST PROGRESSIVE

I was hiding	we were hiding
you were hiding	you were hiding
he/she/it was hiding	they were hiding

• *They were hiding the money in offshore accounts.*

FUTURE ... will hide
FUTURE PROGRESSIVE ... will be hiding
FUTURE PERFECT ... will have hidden

PAST PASSIVE

I was hidden	we were hidden
you were hidden	you were hidden
he/she/it was hidden	they were hidden

• *The photos were hidden in a closet.*

COMPLEMENTS

hide *keep oneself out of sight, conceal oneself*

The dog hides whenever we get his cage.
The birds hide in the trees if there is a hawk nearby.
The kids were hiding behind the tree.
The thief hid in an abandoned warehouse.

hide ____ *put out of sight, conceal*

OBJECT

The cat had hidden **her kittens** in the attic.
The burglars hid **themselves** carefully.
The old lady hid **her money** under her mattress.
He hid **the stolen property** in the basement.
Janet hid **her face** behind the newspaper.
They hid **their business losses** by altering the records.

hide ____ *keep secret*

OBJECT

WH-CLAUSE

I tried to hide **my confusion** by changing the subject.
The senator hid **who had actually made the campaign contribution**.
They wanted to hide **what they had done**.
Allison never hid **what she was going to do**.
We all want to hide **whatever makes us look foolish**.

hide ____ *keep from being seen*

OBJECT

PASSIVE

A sign hid **the entrance to his office**.
My iPod had been hidden by a stack of books.

PHRASAL VERBS

hide out *conceal oneself for a period of time*

Jesse and Frank James hid out in
    Meramec Caverns.

EXPRESSIONS

hide [one's] head in the sand *ignore signs of danger*

We hid our heads in the sand when Hitler
    seized control of the government.

hide [one's] light under a bushel *conceal one's talents/ideas*

Share your suggestions, Donna. Don't hide your light
    under a bushel.

PRESENT		PRESENT PROGRESSIVE	
I hit	we hit	I am hitting	we are hitting
you hit	you hit	you are hitting	you are hitting
he/she/it hits	they hit	he/she/it is hitting	they are hitting

 • *He always hits his target.*

 • *I'm hitting a lot of resistance.*

PAST		PAST PROGRESSIVE	
I hit	we hit	I was hitting	we were hitting
you hit	you hit	you were hitting	you were hitting
he/she/it hit	they hit	he/she/it was hitting	they were hitting

 • *The storm hit us pretty hard.*

 • *Prices were hitting all-time highs.*

PRESENT PERFECT	... have | has hit
PAST PERFECT	... had hit

FUTURE	... will hit
FUTURE PROGRESSIVE	... will be hitting
FUTURE PERFECT	... will have hit

PAST PASSIVE	
I was hit	we were hit
you were hit	you were hit
he/she/it was hit	they were hit

 • *Our car was hit by a pickup truck.*

COMPLEMENTS

hit *deliver a blow/setback*

Depression can hit at any time.
The storm will hit sometime tomorrow morning.
The shells and bombs were hitting everywhere.

hit _____ *strike, deliver a blow to*
OBJECT

The batter hit **the pitch** sharply.
I hit **the target** with the first shot.
The bullet hit **him** in the left shoulder.

PASSIVE

Our oak tree was hit by lightning.

hit _____ *cause to suffer, distress*
OBJECT

A terrible drought has hit **the entire Midwest**.
A sharp sell-off hit **the market** today.

hit _____ *activate, turn on/off*
OBJECT

He hit **the brakes** in a panic.
Hit **the light switch**, will you?
They always want to hit **the panic button** right away.

hit _____ *reach [a level/goal]*
OBJECT

Do you think oil will hit **$100 a barrel**?
Sales could hit **our goal of 2,000 units** this week.

PASSIVE

A new record was hit on Wall Street today.

hit _____ *arrive/appear at*
OBJECT

We should hit **Kansas City** around noon.
The tourists hit **all the souvenir shops**.

hit _____ *encounter*
OBJECT

The pilot hit **a headwind** 120 miles from Singapore.
The research was going well, then we hit **a snag**.

hit _____ *become clear to*
OBJECT

The smell of garlic hit **me** as soon as I entered the house.
The solution hit **Johanna** right after lunch.

PHRASAL VERBS

hit on/upon _____ *discover*

She hit upon the idea of extending
     Medicare to people 55 and over.

hold _____ *consider, believe*

OBJECT + (*to be*) PREDICATE ADJECTIVE

The judge held **the defendant** *(to be) blameless.*
I hold **him** *(to be) fully responsible for the accident.*
"We hold **these truths** *to be self-evident* …"
[DECLARATION OF INDEPENDENCE]

THAT-CLAUSE

The court held **that citizens have a right to privacy.**
For years, the tobacco industry held **that cigarettes
    didn't cause cancer.**

hold _____ *conduct*

OBJECT

The seniors held **a bake sale** for their class trip.
We held **a seminar** for the interns.
The neighbors held **a lively conversation** on the porch.
They will hold **a special exhibit on pre-Columbian art.**
The president will hold **a press conference** on Tuesday.

hold _____ *have as one's own*

OBJECT

Amelia Earhart holds **the title of first woman to fly
    solo across the Atlantic Ocean.**
My wife holds **the office of County Clerk.**

hold _____ *keep in one's mind, maintain*

OBJECT

They held **the belief that the earth is flat.**
We will hold **the memory of her** in our hearts forever.

(PHRASAL VERBS)

hold _SEP_ **back/down/in/out/up/etc.**
keep in a specified position

A police barricade held the crowd back.
The auctioneer held up an antique butter churn.

hold _____ **against [someone]** *have as
a reason to think poorly of [someone]*

She still holds it against him that he has never opened
    the door for her.

hold _SEP_ **back** *keep secret, withhold*

The juror held back the fact that he knew the defendant.

hold _SEP_ **down** *have and keep [a job]*

Jake holds down two jobs and takes college classes too.

hold _SEP_ **in** *suppress*

The candidate is good at holding his emotions in.

hold off (on) _____ *delay, postpone*

She held off asking her parents for more money.

hold _SEP_ **off** *keep away, resist*

The old woman held the robber off until police arrived.

hold on *wait*

Hold on while I dry my hands.

hold on *manage to keep one's position*

Although our team was outscored in the final period,
    we held on and won the game.

hold _SEP_ **on** *secure*

A clasp holds the lid on.

hold out *last, endure*

How long will our food hold out?
The settlers held out until the cavalry arrived.

hold out for _____ *insist on getting*

I don't want a cookie; I'm holding out for a cupcake.
The union held out for better working conditions.

hold _SEP_ **over** *keep for more
performances*

The theater held the movie over for six more weeks.

hold _____ **together** *keep united*

It was Mom who held the family together.

hold up *remain in the
same condition*

This old house is holding up pretty well.
Sales of soccer balls are holding up in spite of the
    economy.

hold _SEP_ **up** *delay,
stop*

The discovery of human remains held up construction
for two weeks.

hold _SEP_ **up** *rob*

Three teenagers held the store up in broad daylight.

hold _SEP_ **up** *support*

Special bolts hold up the roof of a coal mine.

I hold	we hold
you hold	you hold
he/she/it holds	they hold

• *A barrel holds 55 U.S. gallons.*

PRESENT PROGRESSIVE

I am holding	we are holding
you are holding	you are holding
he/she/it is holding	they are holding

• *Come on, I'm holding the door.*

PAST

I held	we held
you held	you held
he/she/it held	they held

• *She held that position for years.*

PAST PROGRESSIVE

I was holding	we were holding
you were holding	you were holding
he/she/it was holding	they were holding

• *Susan was holding the baby.*

PRESENT PERFECT ... have | has held
PAST PERFECT ... had held

FUTURE ... will hold
FUTURE PROGRESSIVE ... will be holding
FUTURE PERFECT ... will have held

PAST PASSIVE

I was held	we were held
you were held	you were held
he/she/it was held	they were held

• *The plane was held for transfer passengers.*

(**COMPLEMENTS**)

hold *keep one's position*	So far, our defensive line is holding.
	We hope the tent holds in this wind.
	The beautiful weather will hold through the weekend.
	Our market share is still holding.
	The senator's lead in the polls has held steady.
	Please hold still.
	Please hold. Your call is important to us.
hold *stay together / in one piece*	I hope this rope holds.
hold _____ *grasp*	
OBJECT	I held **the hammer** in my right hand.
	Please hold **the ladder** while I change the lightbulb.
	Hold **my hand** while we cross the street.
hold _____ *keep steady, maintain, keep control of*	
OBJECT	They will hold **their prices** at the current level.
	The runners held **a five-mile-per-hour pace**.
	The house had held **its value** over the years.
	Will you hold **the elevator** for a minute?
	The framework holds **the entire structure** together.
	He needs to hold **his temper** better.
	How long can you hold **your breath**?
	The movie completely held **my attention**.
OBJECT + PREDICATE ADJECTIVE	The senator held **his audience** *spellbound*.
	The scream held **everyone** *frozen in place*.
	The cables hold **the tower** *rigid*.
hold _____ *keep for later use*	
OBJECT	The hotel will hold **the room** for us until 10 P.M.
	Hold **my calls**, please.
PASSIVE	The troops were held in reserve.
hold _____ *contain, have room for*	
OBJECT	The safe deposit box holds **the deed to our house**.
	The tank holds **1,000 gallons**.
	The auditorium can hold **400 people**.

PRESENT

I hurt	we hurt
you hurt	you hurt
he/she/it hurts	they hurt

• *The scandal hurts his re-election chances.*

PRESENT PROGRESSIVE

I am hurting	we are hurting
you are hurting	you are hurting
he/she/it is hurting	they are hurting

• *The auto industry is really hurting.*

PAST

I hurt	we hurt
you hurt	you hurt
he/she/it hurt	they hurt

• *I hurt my knee yesterday.*

PAST PROGRESSIVE

I was hurting	we were hurting
you were hurting	you were hurting
he/she/it was hurting	they were hurting

• *Lack of money was hurting our program.*

PRESENT PERFECT ... have | has hurt
PAST PERFECT ... had hurt

FUTURE ... will hurt
FUTURE PROGRESSIVE ... will be hurting
FUTURE PERFECT ... will have hurt

PAST PASSIVE

I was hurt	we were hurt
you were hurt	you were hurt
he/she/it was hurt	they were hurt

• *He was hurt playing football.*

---(**COMPLEMENTS**)------

hurt *be a source of pain*	Mommy, my stomach hurts.
	My shoulder was hurting again.
	This injection may hurt a little.
	The loss of so many jobs has got to hurt.
hurt *be in a bad situation*	The entire economy is hurting.
hurt _____ *injure, cause pain/harm to*	
OBJECT	He hurt **his back** trying to move the refrigerator.
	Listening to such loud music hurts **my ears**.
	The new shoes are hurting **my feet**.
	Would it hurt **you** to wash the dishes once in a while?
PASSIVE	Her feelings were hurt by what they said.
hurt _____ *damage, harm*	
OBJECT	A high interest rate will hurt **car sales**.
	The unusually cold summer has hurt **vacation rentals**.
	Injuries have hurt **our team's chances**.
	The recession is hurting **sales**.
	Such negative criticism would hurt **anyone's self-image**.
PASSIVE	The dollar has been hurt by high oil prices.

PRESENT

I keep	we keep
you keep	you keep
he/she/it keeps	they keep

• He keeps his keys in the top drawer.

PRESENT PROGRESSIVE

I am keeping	we are keeping
you are keeping	you are keeping
he/she/it is keeping	they are keeping

• I am keeping his letters.

PAST

I kept	we kept
you kept	you kept
he/she/it kept	they kept

• I kept careful records of all the expenses.

PAST PROGRESSIVE

I was keeping	we were keeping
you were keeping	you were keeping
he/she/it was keeping	they were keeping

• We were keeping the grandchildren for the week.

PRESENT PERFECT ... have | has kept
PAST PERFECT ... had kept

FUTURE ... will keep
FUTURE PROGRESSIVE ... will be keeping
FUTURE PERFECT ... will have kept

PAST PASSIVE

I was kept	we were kept
you were kept	you were kept
he/she/it was kept	they were kept

• His antique autos were kept in immaculate condition.

(COMPLEMENTS)

keep *remain in good condition, remain the same*	The yogurt will keep for days.
	How long will meat keep in the freezer?
	No secret keeps for very long.
	Will the work keep until tomorrow?
keep _____ *hold in one's possession, retain*	
OBJECT	We kept **all of our children's letters**.
	Keep **the change**.
	The quarterback kept **the ball**.
keep _____ *store*	
OBJECT + ADVERB OF PLACE	We keep **all of our cash** *in a safe*.
	Where do you keep **the potato chips**?
	We're keeping **the extra envelopes** *in this drawer*.
keep _____ *maintain, take care of*	
OBJECT	Everyone used to keep **a garden**.
	Are you going to keep **your subscription to the magazine**?
	You need to keep **good records**.
keep _____ *continue in an activity/position/condition*	
PREDICATE ADJECTIVE	The soldiers kept **ready**.
	Keep **warm**!
	Amazingly, the children kept **quiet**.
PRESENT PARTICIPLE	Keep **working**!
	The people behind us kept **talking throughout the concert**.
	The company kept **losing money**.
keep _____ *cause to continue in an activity/position/condition*	
OBJECT + ADVERB OF PLACE	Keep **your hands** *over your head*!
	I kept **my eyes** *on the road*.
	Kids! Keep **your hands** *to yourselves*.
	The doctor kept **Alice** *in the hospital* two days longer.
OBJECT + *as* PREDICATE NOUN	The president kept **Wilson** *as ambassador to Great Britain*.
	The team kept **Charlie** *as captain*.
	The new company kept **Chris** *as custodian*.

keep _____ *cause to continue in an activity/position/condition* [continued]

    OBJECT + PREDICATE ADJECTIVE

The soldiers kept **their weapons** *ready*.
Keep **your feet** *dry*!
Please try to keep **the room** *clean*.
The secretary kept **the file** *secret*.

    OBJECT + PRESENT PARTICIPLE

The sergeant kept **the men** *digging trenches*.
Keep **them** *talking*!
He always kept **us** *laughing at his silly jokes*.

    OBJECT + PAST PARTICIPLE

Keep **me** *informed* about the merger.

keep _____ *employ, have in one's service*

    OBJECT

The hotel keeps **a large housekeeping staff**.

keep _____ *adhere to, fulfill*

    OBJECT

John always keeps **his word**.

PHRASAL VERBS

keep away/back/down/in/off/out/etc.
remain in a specified location

Keep away from the edge
   of the bluff.
My parents are coming—keep down!

keep <u>SEP</u> **away/back/down/in/off/out**/etc.
cause to remain in a specified location

Can you keep the squirrels away from the corn?
It's raining; keep the children in.

keep after/at _____ *nag, harass*

The teacher keeps after us about our homework.

keep at/on/up _____ *continue [doing]*

You're doing a great job. Keep at it!
Keep on writing—the paper's due tomorrow.
It kept on snowing for two days.
This report is wonderful. Keep up the good work.

keep <u>SEP</u> **down** *limit*

We're trying to keep our grocery bill down.

keep <u>SEP</u> **down** *not vomit*

When I had the flu, I couldn't keep food down.

keep ([oneself]) from _____ *prevent oneself*
from [doing something]

I could hardly keep from laughing at his costume.
I tried to keep myself from screaming at him.

keep [someone] from _____ *prevent [someone]*
from [doing something]

His counselor kept him from using drugs.

keep <u>SEP</u> **in/inside** *suppress*

She kept her anger inside until he left.

keep _____ **on** *continue to employ*

The boss hopes to keep all the systems analysts on.

keep _____ **on** *continue to operate*

Derek keeps the radio on all night long.

keep <u>SEP</u> **on** *continue to wear [clothing]*

It's cold in here; I'll keep my coat on.

keep <u>SEP</u> **out** *provide protection from*

This jacket should keep out the rain and wind.

keep out of _____ *not become involved in*

My sisters are arguing, and I'm keeping out of it.

keep to [oneself] *avoid being with other people*

The author keeps to himself.

keep _____ **to [oneself]** *not tell*

Be sure to keep this to yourself.

keep <u>SEP</u> **up** *maintain*

It's not easy for Grandpa to keep up a large house.
We have managed to keep up our family traditions.
Keep your spirits up.

    keep up (with _____ **)**
    stay even (with
    [someone/something])

It's hard to keep up with our rich neighbors.

PRESENT

I kneel	we kneel
you kneel	you kneel
he/she/it kneels	they kneel

• *The priest always kneels before the altar.*

PAST

I knelt	we knelt
you knelt	you knelt
he/she/it knelt	they knelt

• *The clergy all knelt in prayer.*

PRESENT PERFECT ... have | has knelt
PAST PERFECT ... had knelt

PRESENT PROGRESSIVE

I am kneeling	we are kneeling
you are kneeling	you are kneeling
he/she/it is kneeling	they are kneeling

• *He is kneeling to reach something under the bed.*

PAST PROGRESSIVE

I was kneeling	we were kneeling
you were kneeling	you were kneeling
he/she/it was kneeling	they were kneeling

• *The soldiers were kneeling behind the wall.*

FUTURE ... will kneel
FUTURE PROGRESSIVE ... will be kneeling
FUTURE PERFECT ... will have knelt

PAST PASSIVE

Kneel is never used in the passive voice.

COMPLEMENTS

kneel *be/rest on one's knee(s)*

Laying floor tiles kept me kneeling
 all afternoon.
The policeman was kneeling on one knee when he fired
 his pistol.

kneel *show respect/submission by being/
resting on one's knee(s)*

The king forced the rebels to kneel.
The nuns knelt before the cross.
He knelt before the king to be knighted.
They all knelt in prayer.

PHRASAL VERBS

kneel down *go down on one's knee(s)*

I knelt down to pick up the kids' toys.
We all had to kneel down to get through the low doorway.

knit

knit | knits · knit · have knit
knit | knits · knitted · have knitted

☑ IRREGULAR
☑ REGULAR

PRESENT

I knit	we knit
you knit	you knit
he/she/it knits	they knit

• *She knits one sweater every year.*

PRESENT PROGRESSIVE

I am knitting	we are knitting
you are knitting	you are knitting
he/she/it is knitting	they are knitting

• *I am knitting a wool baby blanket.*

PAST

I knit	we knit
you knit	you knit
he/she/it knit	they knit

• *The bones knit nicely.*

PAST PROGRESSIVE

I was knitting	we were knitting
you were knitting	you were knitting
he/she/it was knitting	they were knitting

• *He was knitting his hands together.*

PRESENT PERFECT ... have | has knit
PAST PERFECT ... had knit

FUTURE ... will knit
FUTURE PROGRESSIVE ... will be knitting
FUTURE PERFECT ... will have knit

PAST PASSIVE

—	—
—	—
it was knit	they were knit

• *The wall hanging was knit in Scotland.*

COMPLEMENTS

knit *create fabric/clothing by interlocking loops of yarn/thread together with needles*

She knits as a full-time occupation.
A lot of people knit for charity organizations.
My mother knits when she watches TV.

knit *join, grow together*

The broken bone will eventually knit and become strong.
Our neighborhood gradually knit into a close community.

knit _____ *create by interlocking loops of yarn/thread together with needles*

OBJECT

I am knitting **a wool sweater** for a child in Kazakhstan.
Could you knit **a pair of socks** for me?

PASSIVE

The afghan was knit by my grandmother.

knit _____ *cause to join / grow together*

OBJECT

The tree had knit **its roots** into a solid mass.
I knit **my fingers** to form a shallow bowl.
A cast may be required to knit **the broken bone** together.
The major had knit **the unit** into an effective force.

PHRASAL VERBS

knit up *make a knitted item, repair by knitting*

This yarn knits up well.
That scarf pattern knits up quickly.
"Sleep that knits up **the ravell'd sleeve of care**."
[SHAKESPEARE]

EXPRESSIONS

knit [one's] brow(s) *wrinkle one's eyebrows*

Colin knits his brow when he's thinking.

PRESENT

I know	we know
you know	you know
he/she/it knows	they know

• *He always knows what to say.*

PRESENT PROGRESSIVE

Know is never used in the progressive tenses.

PAST

I knew	we knew
you knew	you knew
he/she/it knew	they knew

• *I knew Ben in graduate school.*

PAST PROGRESSIVE

Know is never used in the progressive tenses.

PRESENT PERFECT ... have | has known
PAST PERFECT ... had known

FUTURE ... will know
FUTURE PROGRESSIVE —
FUTURE PERFECT ... will have known

PAST PASSIVE

I was known	we were known
you were known	you were known
he/she/it was known	they were known

• *The problem was known years ago.*

(**COMPLEMENTS**)

know *be aware / have knowledge of something*

"How old is she?" "I don't know."
"Do you think he knows?" "I am sure he doesn't know."

know _____ *be aware*

about/of OBJECT (+ INFINITIVE)

We have known **about his cancer** for several months.
Do you know **about his refusal** *to sell the house*?
I don't know **of another doctor** *to call*.

know _____ *be aware of, realize, have information about*

OBJECT

I know **the answer.**
Tracy knows **a lot about my personal history.**
We know **the place you mean.**

PASSIVE

His password was known only by his wife.

OBJECT + INFINITIVE

I know **him** *to be an honest person.*
We have known **the senator** *to give better speeches.*

PASSIVE

The company has been known *to take big risks before.*

THAT-CLAUSE

We knew **that it was going to be bad.**
They should have known **that we were leaving early.**
Does he know **that we are waiting?**

WH-CLAUSE

I know **what you mean.**
Do the tourists know **where they are going?**
Do you know **why he lied to you?**
I don't know **how much it costs.**

WH-INFINITIVE

He knows **whom to ask.**
Do you know **where to go?**
I know **how to do it.**

know _____ *have in one's memory*

OBJECT

Most of the actors know **their lines** well.

know _____ *be acquainted/familiar with*

OBJECT

I knew **your father** in college.
She knows **everybody in the organization.**

OBJECT + *as* OBJECT

We knew **her** *as Liddy* when we were kids.

know _____ *recognize*

OBJECT

I'd know **his voice** anywhere.

PRESENT

I lead	we lead
you lead	you lead
he/she/it leads	they lead

• *He leads the accounting department.*

PRESENT PROGRESSIVE

I am leading	we are leading
you are leading	you are leading
he/she/it is leading	they are leading

• *He is leading the investigation.*

PAST

I led	we led
you led	you led
he/she/it led	they led

• *Our policy led to considerable success.*

PAST PROGRESSIVE

I was leading	we were leading
you were leading	you were leading
he/she/it was leading	they were leading

• *We were leading until the last minute.*

PRESENT PERFECT ... have | has led
PAST PERFECT ... had led

FUTURE ... will lead
FUTURE PROGRESSIVE ... will be leading
FUTURE PERFECT ... will have led

PAST PASSIVE

I was led	we were led
you were led	you were led
he/she/it was led	they were led

• *The orchestra was led by a young German conductor.*

COMPLEMENTS

lead *guide*

I have never led before.
I can't lead until I know where we are going.
In a formal dance, it is customary for the gentleman to lead.

lead *be first/ahead (in a competition)*

The Giants are leading for the first time.
He has led in every tournament he has played in this year.

lead _____ *be ahead of, be at the head of*
OBJECT

He leads **the league** in goals scored.
Senator Blather will lead **the parade**.

lead _____ *be in charge of*
OBJECT

Admiral Butler is leading **the task force**.
She was leading **the company** at the time.

lead _____ *go [in a direction, to a place]*
ADVERB OF PLACE

This road leads **to my Uncle's farm**.
The path leads **back home**.
His proposal will lead **to disaster**.

lead _____ *guide, conduct*
OBJECT + ADVERB OF PLACE TO/FROM

A guide led **us** *to the monument*.
He will lead **you** *wherever you want to go*.

PASSIVE

The animals were led *back inside the barn*.

lead _____ *cause, influence*
OBJECT + INFINITIVE

The weather forecast led **them** *to cancel their trip*.
The slow sales led **us** *to drop the entire product line*.

PASSIVE

We were led *to believe that we could get dinner here*.

lead _____ *result in*
to OBJECT

A viral infection can lead **to pneumonia**.
Four years of college leads **to a bachelor's degree**.

lead _____ *live, spend [time]*
OBJECT

Our cats led **pampered lives**.

PHRASAL VERBS

lead SEP **away/back/down/in/on/
out**/etc. *guide in a specified direction*

The police led the suspect away.
The sergeant led the soldiers out.

PRESENT

I leap	we leap
you leap	you leap
he/she/it leaps	they leap

• *Superman leaps tall buildings with ease.*

PRESENT PROGRESSIVE

I am leaping	we are leaping
you are leaping	you are leaping
he/she/it is leaping	they are leaping

• *The frogs are leaping all over the place.*

PAST

I leapt	we leapt
you leapt	you leapt
he/she/it leapt	they leapt

• *He leapt at every opportunity he got.*

PAST PROGRESSIVE

I was leaping	we were leaping
you were leaping	you were leaping
he/she/it was leaping	they were leaping

• *They were leaping out of the basket.*

PRESENT PERFECT ... have | has leapt
PAST PERFECT ... had leapt

FUTURE ... will leap
FUTURE PROGRESSIVE ... will be leaping
FUTURE PERFECT ... will have leapt

PAST PASSIVE

I was leapt	we were leapt
you were leapt	you were leapt
he/she/it was leapt	they were leapt

• *The wall was leapt over without any difficulty.*

COMPLEMENTS

leap *jump, spring*

He leaps whenever anybody says "Boo!"
The kids were all leaping with excitement.
Antelope were leaping across the savannah.
The fish were leaping like crazy.
Our Siamese cat leapt onto Grandmother's lap.
He hurt his leg. He can't leap.
The defensive player leapt and intercepted the ball.
The player leapt and slammed the ball into the net.
I leapt as high as I could.

leap _____ *jump over*
  OBJECT

We had to leap **the ditch**.
The horses leapt **the fence** easily.
He leapt **every obstacle his opponents put in his way**.

PHRASAL VERBS

leap down/in/off/on/out/over/up/
etc. *jump in a specified direction*

The wagon slowed down, and the boys
  leapt off.
We were leaping up and down, trying to get their attention.

leap at _____ *accept eagerly*

Max leapt at the chance to be his own boss.
The club leapt at Kyle's offer to bring cupcakes.

leap out at _____ *get the*
immediate attention of

The misspelled word leapt out at the proofreader.

EXPRESSIONS

leap for joy *be extremely happy*

Tad won the spelling bee, and his parents
  leapt for joy.

leap off the page (at _____**)** *be quickly*
noticed (by [someone])

The typographical error leapt off the page at me.
The unemployment statistics leapt off the page at her.

leap to mind *suddenly be thought of*

The author that leaps to mind is William Faulkner.

leap to [one's] feet *jump up excitedly*

The audience leapt to its feet and shouted, "Encore!"

leap to conclusions *make a hasty*
judgment without knowing the facts

Until you have read the entire article, don't leap to
  conclusions.

leave ____ *deliver/provide before going away*

INDIRECT OBJECT + DIRECT OBJECT	They left *you* **a message**.
	I am leaving *the waiter* **a big tip**.
	We left *the kids* **some cookies**.
for PARAPHRASE	They left **a message** *for you*.
	I am leaving **a big tip** *for the waiter*.
	We left **some cookies** *for the kids*.

leave ____ *allow/give [someone] to do*

OBJECT + *for* OBJECT	My older sister left **the dishes** *for me*.
OBJECT + *to* OBJECT	The boss will leave **the decision** *to his assistant*.
OBJECT + *with* OBJECT	While I'm in Toronto, I'm going to leave **the project** *with you*.

leave ____ *give at one's death (often by a will)*

| OBJECT + *to* OBJECT | Grandfather left **his stamp collection** *to his granddaughter*. |
| | Mr. Plavsik left **all his money** *to charity*. |

<hr>

 (**PHRASAL VERBS**)

leave ____ **down/out/up/etc.** *allow to remain in a specified position*	Please leave the window up when you're finished in the room.
leave for ____ *depart in the direction of*	We will be leaving for the airport in 10 minutes.
leave off (____**)** *stop temporarily*	Now, where did we leave off at yesterday's meeting?
	The staff left off trying to organize a company picnic.
leave SEP **off/on** *not put off/on*	He left his jacket off in the classroom.
	She left her coat on because it was chilly inside.
leave SEP **out (of** ____**)** *omit, exclude (from [something])*	Harry left out all references to World War Two.
	Mrs. Crabtree left Norman out of her will.
leave SEP **on** *not switch off*	Leave the light on when you leave the room.

<hr>

 (**EXPRESSIONS**)

leave ____ **open** *not schedule another activity on [a day/date]*	Leave next Saturday open for the bake sale.
leave a bad taste in [one's] mouth *cause one to have a lingering bad impression*	The argument over immigration left a bad taste in my mouth.
leave no stone unturned *search everywhere, do everything possible*	The police left no stone unturned in looking for the murderer.
leave ____ **alone/be** *not disturb*	Leave me alone—I'm trying to study.
	We should leave the matter be for the moment.
leave ____ **out in the cold** *not keep [someone] informed*	The rest of the staff left her out in the cold with regard to the new project.
leave (some) loose ends *not finish a project, not solve a problem*	The movie rushed the ending and left some loose ends.
be left (over) *remain*	Is there any chocolate cake left?
	Some potato salad is left over from the picnic.
	Half a skein of yarn is left over from my sweater project.

PRESENT

I leave	we leave
you leave	you leave
he/she/it leaves	they leave

• *He always leaves home by eight.*

PRESENT PROGRESSIVE

I am leaving	we are leaving
you are leaving	you are leaving
he/she/it is leaving	they are leaving

• *I'm leaving the porch light on.*

PAST

I left	we left
you left	you left
he/she/it left	they left

• *I left you a little surprise.*

PAST PROGRESSIVE

I was leaving	we were leaving
you were leaving	you were leaving
he/she/it was leaving	they were leaving

• *We were just leaving the garage when they called.*

PRESENT PERFECT	... have | has left
PAST PERFECT	... had left

FUTURE	... will leave
FUTURE PROGRESSIVE	... will be leaving
FUTURE PERFECT	... will have left

PAST PASSIVE

I was left	we were left
you were left	you were left
he/she/it was left	they were left

• *Water stains were left all over the ground floor.*

(COMPLEMENTS)

leave *go away, depart*	We are leaving soon. When can you leave? I am not leaving until this is settled.
leave _____ *go away from, depart* OBJECT	Elvis has left **the building**. The train will leave **the station** at 10:13 A.M. I left **the office** early that day.
leave _____ *abandon, quit* OBJECT	He left **the university** in his junior year. Ray has just left **his wife**. I left **the law firm** some time ago.
leave _____ *cause/allow to remain behind* OBJECT	Red wine always leaves **a stain**. He left **a fortune** after his death. The surgery will leave **a little scar**.
OBJECT + ADVERB OF PLACE	I left **my coat** *with the concierge*. The kids left **footprints** *on the tile floor*. She left **her purse** *on the park bench*.
PASSIVE	Somebody's tickets were left *on the counter*.
leave _____ *cause/allow to remain/be in a certain state* OBJECT + PREDICATE NOUN	The accident left **him** *a broken man*. The fire left **the building** *a ruined shell*. The training left **the division** *a formidable fighting force*.
OBJECT + PREDICATE ADJECTIVE	The movie left **me** *confused*. We had to leave **the children** *alone* for a few hours. The incident left **us** *speechless*. Please leave **the door** *open*. Riding a bicycle leaves **Bill** *out of breath*.
OBJECT + PRESENT PARTICIPLE	I left **the kids** *finishing up their homework*. The comedian left **the audience** *roaring with laughter*. We left **the plumber** *ripping out the old sink*. Leave **the engine** *running*.

lend lend | lends · lent · have lent ☑ IRREGULAR

PRESENT

I lend	we lend
you lend	you lend
he/she/it lends	they lend

• *The bank lends money for new cars.*

PAST

I lent	we lent
you lent	you lent
he/she/it lent	they lent

• *The bank lent them the money.*

PRESENT PERFECT ... have | has lent
PAST PERFECT ... had lent

PRESENT PROGRESSIVE

I am lending	we are lending
you are lending	you are lending
he/she/it is lending	they are lending

• *I am lending the truck to Anne for the weekend.*

PAST PROGRESSIVE

I was lending	we were lending
you were lending	you were lending
he/she/it was lending	they were lending

• *The banks were not lending at that time.*

FUTURE ... will lend
FUTURE PROGRESSIVE ... will be lending
FUTURE PERFECT ... will have lent

PAST PASSIVE

I was lent	we were lent
you were lent	you were lent
he/she/it was lent	they were lent

• *The book was lent to me by a friend.*

COMPLEMENTS

lend *give money on condition of repayment (plus interest)*

Banks are not lending now.
Who can afford to lend?
Who is still lending these days?

lend _____ *allow temporary use of on condition of return/payment*

INDIRECT OBJECT + DIRECT OBJECT

I lent *Peter* **my lawnmower**.
I can lend *you* **$25**.
Could I have lent *someone* **the library book**?

to PARAPHRASE

I lent **my lawnmower** *to Peter*.
I can lend **$25** *to you*.
Could I have lent **the library book** *to someone*?

NOTE: Many speakers prefer to use the verb *loan* (rather than *lend*) when referring to money. For example, they would say "The bank will *loan* you the money" rather than "The bank will *lend* you the money." Both are grammatically correct.

lend _____ *make available to*

INDIRECT OBJECT + DIRECT OBJECT

The Red Cross lent *the flood relief effort* its services.

to PARAPHRASE

The Red Cross lent **its services** *to the flood relief effort*.

lend _____ *add*

OBJECT + to OBJECT

The confetti and beads lend **gaiety** *to the Mardi Gras parade*.
The bowl of fruit lends **color** *to an otherwise dull painting*.

PHRASAL VERBS

lend itself to _____ *be suitable for*

The gathering room lends itself to intimate conversation.

lend _SEP_ **out** *allow temporary use of on condition of return*

We lent out our copy of Jane Austen's *Pride and Prejudice*.

EXPRESSIONS

lend an/[one's] ear (to _____ **)** *listen (to [someone])*

The president is speaking; lend an ear.
"Friends, Romans, countrymen, lend me your ears."
[SHAKESPEARE]

PRESENT		PRESENT PROGRESSIVE	
I let	we let	I am letting	we are letting
you let	you let	you are letting	you are letting
he/she/it lets	they let	he/she/it is letting	they are letting

• *He lets us know if there is a problem.*

• *The coach is letting them try again.*

PAST		PAST PROGRESSIVE	
I let	we let	I was letting	we were letting
you let	you let	you were letting	you were letting
he/she/it let	they let	he/she/it was letting	they were letting

• *I let the dogs run in the backyard.*

• *We were letting too many mistakes get through.*

PRESENT PERFECT ... have | has let
PAST PERFECT ... had let

FUTURE ... will let
FUTURE PROGRESSIVE ... will be letting
FUTURE PERFECT ... will have let

PAST PASSIVE	
I was let	we were let
you were let	you were let
he/she/it was let	they were let

• *Several staff members were let go recently.*

COMPLEMENTS

let _____ *allow, permit*
    OBJECT + BASE-FORM INFINITIVE

The referee let **the game** *continue.*
We let **the kids** *watch TV for a while after dinner.*
Don't let **them** *leave without me.*
Let **me** *go!*

let's _____ [CONTRACTION OF **let us**; A WAY TO SUGGEST DOING SOMETHING]
    BASE-FORM INFINITIVE

Let's **go home now.**
Let's **find out what happened.**
Let's **not do that.**

PHRASAL VERBS

let <u>SEP</u> **by/down/in/off/on/out/through/ up/etc.** *allow to come/go in a specified direction*

Let the children in.
The bus stopped and let off two passengers.
Let the dog out.
Stop wrestling and let your brother up.

let <u>SEP</u> **down** *disappoint*

Son, you've let your parents down again.

let <u>SEP</u> **off (easy) (with _____)** *forgive/ release (with [little/no punishment])*

The policeman let the boys off with a warning.
The teacher let me off easy.

let off/out _____ *release, emit*

The teakettle let off a loud whistle.

let on _____ *pretend*

Barry is letting on that he knows about the crisis.

let on _____ *admit*

Charlotte never let on that she was my sister.

let out *end*

When does the movie let out?

let up *slow down, diminish*

The rain appears to be letting up.

EXPRESSIONS

let alone _____ *not to mention, much less*

The patient can't walk, let alone run.
I don't have time to read a chapter, let alone the whole book.

let _____ **alone/be** *not disturb*

Let your sister alone. Let her be.

let _____ **go** *fire, lay off*

The company let four mechanics go last Friday.

let **go/loose of** _____ *release, stop gripping*

If we let go of the rope, we'll fall into the river.

I lie	we lie
you lie	you lie
he/she/it lies	they lie

• *The responsibility lies with all of us.*

I am lying	we are lying
you are lying	you are lying
he/she/it is lying	they are lying

• *The cat is lying asleep on the couch.*

I lay	we lay
you lay	you lay
he/she/it lay	they lay

• *The ship lay at anchor for a week.*

I was lying	we were lying
you were lying	you were lying
he/she/it was lying	they were lying

• *The book was lying on your desk.*

PRESENT PERFECT	... have | has lain
PAST PERFECT	... had lain

FUTURE	... will lie
FUTURE PROGRESSIVE	... will be lying
FUTURE PERFECT	... will have lain

Lie is never used in the passive voice.

NOTE: The irregular verb *lie* is presented here. The regular verb *lie* (*lie* | *lies* · *lied* · *have lied*) means "say something that isn't true"; it may be used without an object (*The suspect is lying*) or with a THAT-CLAUSE (*She lied that her husband was home all evening*).

―― **(COMPLEMENTS)** ―

NOTE: The verbs *lie* and *lay* are often confused, in part because the past tense form of *lie* (*lay*) is the same as the present tense form of *lay*.

INFINITIVE	PRESENT	PAST	PAST PARTICIPLE	BASIC MEANING
lie	lie	**lay**	have lain	"be in a horizontal position"
lay	**lay**	laid	have laid	"put in a horizontal position"

The two verbs are historically related in an odd way: *To lay* means "to cause something *to lie*." In other words, *lay* always requires a direct object, while *lie* is never used with a direct object.

lie *be buried*

Here lie the bones of the city's founder.

lie ____ *be located*
    ADVERB OF PLACE

The report is lying **right in front of you.**
The town lies **in the Thames valley.**
His few hairs lay **across his bald head.**
The ocean lies **to the west.**

lie ____ *be/stay in a horizontal position*
    PREDICATE ADJECTIVE

The ocean lay **flat** as far as we could see.
The tablecloth lay **perfectly smooth.**

lie ____ *be/stay in a certain state/condition*
    PREDICATE ADJECTIVE

The cat lay **motionless,** watching the bird.
The town lay **helpless** in front of the invading army.
The nurse told him to lie **still** while she examined him.
The paintings had lain **hidden** in a barn for 50 years.

lie ____ *be, exist*
    in OBJECT
    with OBJECT

The confusion lies **in our conflicting goals.**
The problem lies **with senior management.**

lie ____ *affect*
    on OBJECT

The wrongful conviction lies heavily **on the prosecutors.**
His extramarital affair lies heavily **on his conscience.**

―― **(PHRASAL VERBS)** ―

**lie ahead/around/back/behind/below/
down/**etc. *be/rest in a specified position*

She lay back and relaxed in the afternoon sun.
I'll lie down for an hour.

PRESENT

I light	we light
you light	you light
he/she/it lights	they light

• Her face lights up when she smiles.

PAST

I lit	we lit
you lit	you lit
he/she/it lit	they lit

• I lit the candles on the birthday cake.

PRESENT PERFECT ... have | has lit
PAST PERFECT ... had lit

PRESENT PROGRESSIVE

I am lighting	we are lighting
you are lighting	you are lighting
he/she/it is lighting	they are lighting

• I am lighting a fire.

PAST PROGRESSIVE

I was lighting	we were lighting
you were lighting	you were lighting
he/she/it was lighting	they were lighting

• Only candles were lighting the dining room.

FUTURE ... will light
FUTURE PROGRESSIVE ... will be lighting
FUTURE PERFECT ... will have lit

PAST PASSIVE

—	—
—	—
it was lit	they were lit

• The room was lit only by the fireplace.

COMPLEMENTS

light *catch fire*

The pile of dry leaves and twigs finally lit.
The smoldering coals lit with a whoosh.
The damp wood never lit.

light _____ *ignite, set fire to, cause to burn*

OBJECT

Sparks from the train lit **trash along the track**.
We should light **the lantern** before it gets dark.

PASSIVE

The fire was lit by an electrical short circuit in the wall.

INDIRECT OBJECT + DIRECT OBJECT

I lit *them* a candle.
We will light *them* a fire.

for PARAPHRASE

I lit **a candle** *for them*.
We will light **a fire** *for them*.

light _____ *illuminate*

OBJECT

We used torches to light **the path**.
The campfire lit **the boys' faces**.
The golden moon lit **the southern sky**.

PASSIVE

The street was lit by the burning buildings.

light _____ *guide with a light*

OBJECT + ADVERB OF PLACE TO/FROM

We lit **the children** *to their rooms* with the lantern.
"And all our yesterdays have lighted **fools** *the way to dusty death*." [SHAKESPEARE]

PHRASAL VERBS

light up *brighten*

The black night lit up with occasional flashes of lightning.
Her face lit up when she heard the news.

EXPRESSIONS

light a fire under _____ *cause to move/work faster/harder*

The coach's tirade lit a fire under his sluggish team.

PRESENT

I lose	we lose
you lose	you lose
he/she/it loses	they lose

• *My team always loses.*

PRESENT PROGRESSIVE

I am losing	we are losing
you are losing	you are losing
he/she/it is losing	they are losing

• *I am losing patience with them.*

PAST

I lost	we lost
you lost	you lost
he/she/it lost	they lost

• *I lost my glasses again.*

PAST PROGRESSIVE

I was losing	we were losing
you were losing	you were losing
he/she/it was losing	they were losing

• *We were losing money on every transaction.*

PRESENT PERFECT … have | has lost
PAST PERFECT … had lost

FUTURE … will lose
FUTURE PROGRESSIVE … will be losing
FUTURE PERFECT … will have lost

PAST PASSIVE

I was lost	we were lost
you were lost	you were lost
he/she/it was lost	they were lost

• *The battle was lost in the first few minutes.*

COMPLEMENTS

lose *not win, be defeated*

The team has never lost this season.
The longer you gamble, the more certain you are to lose.
The Patriots lost by 14 points.

lose _____ *not win, be defeated in*
    OBJECT

Napoleon never lost **a battle**—except the last one.
You can win a battle, but still lose **the war**.
I lost **my bet with Sam**.

lose _____ *be deprived of*
    OBJECT

We lost **some dear friends** in the war.
He has lost **the use of his left hand**.
The senator has lost **their support**.

lose _____ *misplace, be unable to find*
    OBJECT

I lost **the key to my desk**.
The guide lost **his way** in the woods.
I lost **my place in the book**.

    PASSIVE
lose _____ *fail to keep/maintain*

The mountain climbers were lost in the avalanche.

    OBJECT

The cat is losing **its hair**.
My watch is losing **time**.
The sink has been losing **water** for days.
The boat was losing **speed**.
I lost **control of the motorcycle**.

lose _____ *get rid of*
    OBJECT

I finally lost **some weight**.

lose _____ *fail to make use of*
    OBJECT

The company lost **a great opportunity to expand**.
Don't lose **any time** getting to the bookstore.

lose _____ *cause to be deprived of*
    INDIRECT OBJECT + OBJECT

His position on immigration lost **him a lot of votes**.

PHRASAL VERBS

lose out (to _____ **)** *be unsuccessful*
[in a competition (with [someone])]

I applied for the job, but I lost out
to a younger applicant.

PRESENT

I make	we make
you make	you make
he/she/it makes	they make

• *She makes an excellent salary.*

PRESENT PROGRESSIVE

I am making	we are making
you are making	you are making
he/she/it is making	they are making

• *I'm making some coffee.*

PAST

I made	we made
you made	you made
he/she/it made	they made

• *I made lunch for my in-laws.*

PAST PROGRESSIVE

I was making	we were making
you were making	you were making
he/she/it was making	they were making

• *We were making pretty good time.*

PRESENT PERFECT ... have | has made
PAST PERFECT ... had made

FUTURE ... will make
FUTURE PROGRESSIVE ... will be making
FUTURE PERFECT ... will have made

PAST PASSIVE

I was made	we were made
you were made	you were made
he/she/it was made	they were made

• *Mistakes were made at every level.*

—(COMPLEMENTS)—

make _____ *prepare, build, create, produce*

OBJECT
I am going to make **a tuna salad.**
We made **a little shed for the bicycles.**
I made **a bookcase** out of mahogany.
My wife made **a sweater** out of merino wool.
I can make **a booklet of your favorite quotations.**
It's chilly in here; would you make **a fire?**
We're making **plans for spring break.**
The president's children make **their own beds.**
Carpenters made **a hole in the wall** for a window.

PASSIVE
His masterpiece was made in 1683.

INDIRECT OBJECT + DIRECT OBJECT
We will make *Thomas* **a Halloween costume.**
The florist made *Ruth* **a terrific centerpiece.**
His company made *us* **some custom cabinets.**

for PARAPHRASE
His company made **some custom cabinets** *for us.*

WH-CLAUSE
I can only make **what I have supplies for.**
I will make **whatever you want** for your birthday.

make _____ *do, perform*

OBJECT
Senator Blather made **a speech** at the YMCA.
Make **a left turn** at the second traffic light.

make _____ *cause to happen/exist*

OBJECT
The dog made **a terrible mess** again.
The two parties made **a deal.**

PASSIVE
Decisions have to be made quickly.

make _____ *cause to be, appoint, give a job/position to*

OBJECT + PREDICATE NOUN
He made **the company** *a household name.*
The company made **her** *vice president.*
The board made **Boyd** *the CEO.*

PASSIVE
Tom was made *a captain* in 2005.

OBJECT + PREDICATE ADJECTIVE
The new job made **Janet** *very happy.*
These paintings make the **living room** *cheerful.*
Long meetings after lunch make **me** *sleepy.*

make ——— _force, cause_	
OBJECT + BASE-FORM INFINITIVE	They made **me _do it_**!
	The earthquake made **the windows _rattle_**.
	The officials made **the teams _replay the game_**.

make ——— _be used to produce_	
OBJECT	Cotton rags make **the best paper**.
PASSIVE	The sculpture was made entirely of driftwood.

make ——— _earn, succeed in achieving_	
OBJECT	You could make **a lot of money** doing that.
	We made **about 500 miles** driving today.

make ——— _amount to, total_	
OBJECT	Four quarts make **a gallon**.
	Three feet make **a yard**.

| make ——— _arrive at_ | |
| OBJECT | Glen will make **Phoenix** by tomorrow afternoon. |

make ——— _be on time for_	
OBJECT	Do you think we can make **the 2 o'clock flight**?
	Three students didn't make **the deadline for submitting papers**.

————————————————————————————————————(PHRASAL VERBS)———

make away/off with ——— _steal_	The robbers made away with $3,500.
	They made off with my briefcase too.
make for ——— _go toward_	The soldier made for the nearest foxhole.
make for ——— _result in_	Good pitching and hitting make for a successful team.
make like ——— _pretend to be, imitate_	Dad made like a dinosaur and tromped around the room.
make out _succeed_	Gavin made out very well during the dot-com bubble.
make _SEP_ out _distinguish, decipher_	I can barely make out the road in the snowstorm.
	The bank teller couldn't make out the signature on the check.
make _SEP_ out _fill out_	Make the check out to the agency for $25.
make _SEP_ out _understand_	We couldn't make out what the professor was saying.
make _SEP_ over _change the appearance of_	The programmer made over his cubicle with movie posters.
make [someone] out ——— _describe [someone], usually falsely_	Dixie's parents made her out to be a perfect student.
make up _become friendly after a quarrel_	Luke and Lana finally made up after two weeks of not speaking to one another.
make up ——— _form, be the parts of_	These servers make up the backbone of our network.
	The task force was made up of cruisers and destroyers.
make _SEP_ up _put together, prepare_	I made up a pot of chili in 30 minutes.
make _SEP_ up _invent_	Gary made up a story about a dog stealing his homework.
make _SEP_ up _apply cosmetics to_	The artist made her up to look like a witch.
	I have to make myself up before going out.
make _SEP_ up _do [something] that one has missed_	Jan was sick and has to make up the test on Monday.
make up for ——— _compensate for_	How can I make up for the trouble I've caused you?

PRESENT

I mean	we mean
you mean	you mean
he/she/it means	they mean

• *A warm wind means that it will rain.*

PRESENT PROGRESSIVE

I am meaning	we are meaning
you are meaning	you are meaning
he/she/it is meaning	they are meaning

• *We are meaning to go to town tomorrow.*

PAST

I meant	we meant
you meant	you meant
he/she/it meant	they meant

• *I always meant to try skydiving.*

PAST PROGRESSIVE

I was meaning	we were meaning
you were meaning	you were meaning
he/she/it was meaning	they were meaning

• *I was meaning to fix that.*

PRESENT PERFECT   ... have | has meant
PAST PERFECT   ... had meant

FUTURE   ... will mean
FUTURE PROGRESSIVE   ... will be meaning
FUTURE PERFECT   ... will have meant

PAST PASSIVE

I was meant	we were meant
you were meant	you were meant
he/she/it was meant	they were meant

• *No harm was meant.*

COMPLEMENTS

NOTE: The verb *mean* is used in the progressive tenses only in the sense "intend, plan."

mean _____ *signify, indicate*

OBJECT

"Aloha" means **both "hello" and "goodbye"** in Hawaiian.
A rainbow means **good luck**.
It doesn't mean **anything**.
Thanks. That meant **a lot to me**.
This means **war**!

THAT-CLAUSE

The flare means **that there has been an accident**.
The whistle means **that it is time to quit**.
A heavy snowfall means **that there will be no school**.

WH-CLAUSE

It can't mean **what I think it means**.
It means **whatever you want it to mean**.

mean _____ *intend, plan*

(*for*) OBJECT + INFINITIVE

I meant **(for) you** *to do that*.
He was meaning **(for) us** *to finish up here*.

PASSIVE

The truck was meant *to stay with the crew*.

INFINITIVE

We meant **to stop off and do some shopping**.
They didn't mean **to do anything wrong**.
I was meaning **to tell you about that**.

mean _____ *intend* [TO EXPLAIN A PREVIOUS STATEMENT]

THAT-CLAUSE

I meant **that you should wait in my office**.
He meant **that he might have made a mistake**.

EXPRESSIONS

mean business *be serious*

He jokes with reporters, but he means business.

mean everything / the world to _____
be very important to

Jeanine's fiancé means everything to her.
My environmental work means the world to me.

mean nothing to _____ *not be very important to*

Her criticism means nothing to me.

mean nothing to _____ *not make sense to*

This paragraph will mean nothing to the reader.

mean well *have good intentions*

Ed is a little eccentric, but he means well.

PRESENT

I meet	we meet
you meet	you meet
he/she/it meets	they meet

• *The stationmaster meets every train.*

PRESENT PROGRESSIVE

I am meeting	we are meeting
you are meeting	you are meeting
he/she/it is meeting	they are meeting

• *Excuse me, I am meeting someone.*

PAST

I met	we met
you met	you met
he/she/it met	they met

• *I never met your brother.*

PAST PROGRESSIVE

I was meeting	we were meeting
you were meeting	you were meeting
he/she/it was meeting	they were meeting

• *We were meeting in the conference room.*

PRESENT PERFECT ... have | has met
PAST PERFECT ... had met

FUTURE ... will meet
FUTURE PROGRESSIVE ... will be meeting
FUTURE PERFECT ... will have met

PAST PASSIVE

I was met	we were met
you were met	you were met
he/she/it was met	they were met

• *We were met at the airport by the tour guide.*

(COMPLEMENTS)

meet *come together for a particular purpose*	We will meet next Tuesday.
	"When shall we three meet again?" [SHAKESPEARE]
	Can we meet for lunch tomorrow?
	These same two teams will meet in the playoffs.
meet *be joined*	The hiking paths meet at the top of the hill.
meet *become acquainted, be introduced*	Our in-laws will meet in person for the first time.
	It is amazing that we never met before.
meet *come into contact*	The gates have never met properly because they sag.
	Their lips met tenderly.
	The sliding doors met with a thud.
meet _____ *come together by arrangement*	
OBJECT	I met **Carrie** for lunch today.
	I can't meet **them** until next week.
with OBJECT	You will meet **with the search committee** this afternoon.
meet _____ *become acquainted with*	
OBJECT	When did you first meet **your husband**?
	Guess **whom** I met today!
meet _____ *fulfill, satisfy, pay*	
OBJECT	I still have to meet **my undergraduate science requirement**.
	Can he meet **the deadline for the grant application**?
	Her organization works to meet **the needs of the homeless**.
	If you meet **our demands**, no one will get hurt.
	They might not be able to meet **their mortgage payment**.
PASSIVE	The terms of the agreement have not been met.
meet _____ *be present at the arrival of*	
OBJECT	Someone needs to meet **the train**.
	We should meet **their plane** tomorrow.
	Everyone will meet **the boats** when they cross the finish line.
meet _____ *encounter, experience*	
OBJECT	Our plans really met **an obstacle** today.
	My great-great-grandfather met **his death** in the Great War.
	The proposal met **a stone wall** in the committee hearing.

PRESENT

I mistake	we mistake
you mistake	you mistake
he/she/it mistakes	they mistake

• *He always mistakes peoples' names.*

PRESENT PROGRESSIVE

I am mistaking	we are mistaking
you are mistaking	you are mistaking
he/she/it is mistaking	they are mistaking

• *You are mistaking me for somebody else.*

PAST

I mistook	we mistook
you mistook	you mistook
he/she/it mistook	they mistook

• *I mistook what he said.*

PAST PROGRESSIVE

I was mistaking	we were mistaking
you were mistaking	you were mistaking
he/she/it was mistaking	they were mistaking

• *People were always mistaking his car for a taxi.*

PRESENT PERFECT ... have | has mistaken
PAST PERFECT ... had mistaken

FUTURE ... will mistake
FUTURE PROGRESSIVE ... will be mistaking
FUTURE PERFECT ... will have mistaken

PAST PASSIVE

I was mistaken	we were mistaken
you were mistaken	you were mistaken
he/she/it was mistaken	they were mistaken

• *They were mistaken for spies.*

─────────────────────────────────(**COMPLEMENTS**)──

mistake _____ *identify incorrectly*

OBJECT + *for* OBJECT

I'm sorry, I mistook **you** *for an employee.*
Everyone mistakes **him** *for his brother.*
I must have mistaken **the olive oil** *for the vinegar.*

PASSIVE

We were mistaken *for another couple.*

mistake _____ *misunderstand, misjudge*

OBJECT

I totally mistook **the situation.**
Did you mistake **the answer?**
I badly mistook **the nature of their relationship.**

WH-CLAUSE

No one could mistake **what the candidate stood for.**
I mistook **what was going on.**
We must have mistaken **where they said they were going.**

mow | mows · mowed · have mowed
mow | mows · mowed · have mown

☑ REGULAR
☑ IRREGULAR

PRESENT

I mow	we mow
you mow	you mow
he/she/it mows	they mow

• *He mows the lawn on the weekends.*

PRESENT PROGRESSIVE

I am mowing	we are mowing
you are mowing	you are mowing
he/she/it is mowing	they are mowing

• *I'll call you back later; I'm mowing the lawn now.*

PAST

I mowed	we mowed
you mowed	you mowed
he/she/it mowed	they mowed

• *I mowed the grass before it rained.*

PAST PROGRESSIVE

I was mowing	we were mowing
you were mowing	you were mowing
he/she/it was mowing	they were mowing

• *She was mowing the backyard for her allowance.*

PRESENT PERFECT ... have | has mown
PAST PERFECT ... had mown

FUTURE ... will mow
FUTURE PROGRESSIVE ... will be mowing
FUTURE PERFECT ... will have mown

PAST PASSIVE

I was mown	we were mown
you were mown	you were mown
he/she/it was mown	they were mown

• *The lawn was mown just yesterday.*

COMPLEMENTS

mow *cut grass with a machine*

Someone is mowing in back of the house.
How often do you have to mow?
My neighbor can't get his lawn tractor to mow evenly.

mow _____ *cut down [grass, grain, etc.] with a machine*

OBJECT

The city hired me to mow **all of the playing fields**.
A highway crew was mowing **the roadside**.
I can't mow **the lawn** until it gets dry.
They really need to mow **their yard** more often.
In the fields, farmers were mowing, raking, and bundling **hay**.

PASSIVE

The lawn will be mown as soon as we can get to it.

PHRASAL VERBS

mow _SEP_ **down** *knock/shoot down*

An SUV swerved onto the sidewalk
and mowed three pedestrians down.
Enemy snipers mowed down the entire platoon
with machine guns.

PRESENT

I overcome	we overcome
you overcome	you overcome
he/she/it overcomes	they overcome

* *He always overcomes his problems.*

PRESENT PROGRESSIVE

I am overcoming	we are overcoming
you are overcoming	you are overcoming
he/she/it is overcoming	they are overcoming

* *He is overcoming a serious injury.*

PAST

I overcame	we overcame
you overcame	you overcame
he/she/it overcame	they overcame

* *She always overcame obstacles.*

PAST PROGRESSIVE

I was overcoming	we were overcoming
you were overcoming	you were overcoming
he/she/it was overcoming	they were overcoming

* *They were gradually overcoming their opposition.*

PRESENT PERFECT ... have | has overcome
PAST PERFECT ... had overcome

FUTURE ... will overcome
FUTURE PROGRESSIVE ... will be overcoming
FUTURE PERFECT ... will have overcome

PAST PASSIVE

I was overcome	we were overcome
you were overcome	you were overcome
he/she/it was overcome	they were overcome

* *He was overcome with emotion.*

COMPLEMENTS

overcome *prevail, fight and win*

"We shall overcome." [GOSPEL SONG]
They have finally overcome.

overcome *be strongly affected*
[USED ONLY IN THE PASSIVE]

They were overcome with emotion.
The children were overcome with excitement.
Mr. Darcy was overcome by Elizabeth's goodness.
Three firemen were overcome by smoke.

overcome ____ *prevail over, defeat, get control of*

OBJECT

The prisoners overcame **their guards.**
He overcame **all of his personal problems.**
She overcame **her addiction to cigarette smoking.**
The revised proposal overcame **the board's initial resistance.**
Mr. Knightley eventually overcomes **his concerns about Emma's foolishness.**

PASSIVE

The guards were overcome by the prisoners.

overtake

overtake | overtakes · overtook · have overtaken

☑ IRREGULAR

PRESENT

I overtake	we overtake
you overtake	you overtake
he/she/it overtakes	they overtake

• *She overtakes her opponents one by one.*

PRESENT PROGRESSIVE

I am overtaking	we are overtaking
you are overtaking	you are overtaking
he/she/it is overtaking	they are overtaking

• *Laptops are overtaking desktops.*

PAST

I overtook	we overtook
you overtook	you overtook
he/she/it overtook	they overtook

• *He overtook the leader with three laps left.*

PAST PROGRESSIVE

I was overtaking	we were overtaking
you were overtaking	you were overtaking
he/she/it was overtaking	they were overtaking

• *A motorcycle was overtaking the convoy.*

PRESENT PERFECT ... have | has overtaken
PAST PERFECT ... had overtaken

FUTURE ... will overtake
FUTURE PROGRESSIVE ... will be overtaking
FUTURE PERFECT ... will have overtaken

PAST PASSIVE

I was overtaken	we were overtaken
you were overtaken	you were overtaken
he/she/it was overtaken	they were overtaken

• *I was overtaken by sleep on the bus ride to the airport.*

COMPLEMENTS

overtake _____ *catch up with and pass*

OBJECT
The police overtook **the speeding car** at the next exit.
China will overtake **Japan** as the world's second-largest economy.
Do you think that digital books will overtake **traditional books?**
Internet advertising has already overtaken **TV advertising.**

overtake _____ *happen to unexpectedly*

OBJECT
A feeling of peace and contentment was overtaking **me** as I lay on the sofa.
Cancer overtook **my boss** when he was only 53 years old.

PRESENT

I plead	we plead
you plead	you plead
he/she/it pleads	they plead

• *The defendant pleads innocent.*

PRESENT PROGRESSIVE

I am pleading	we are pleading
you are pleading	you are pleading
he/she/it is pleading	they are pleading

• *I am pleading innocent, Your Honor.*

PAST

I pled	we pled
you pled	you pled
he/she/it pled	they pled

• *He already pled his case.*

PAST PROGRESSIVE

I was pleading	we were pleading
you were pleading	you were pleading
he/she/it was pleading	they were pleading

• *The prisoners were pleading with the guards.*

PRESENT PERFECT ... have | has pled
PAST PERFECT ... had pled

FUTURE ... will plead
FUTURE PROGRESSIVE ... will be pleading
FUTURE PERFECT ... will have pled

PAST PASSIVE

—	—
—	—
it was pled	they were pled

• *The case was pled before the district court.*

(COMPLEMENTS)

NOTE: The past tense and past participle form is ordinarily *pleaded* for all meanings of *plead* except "formally declare oneself [innocent/guilty] in court."

plead *make an emotional appeal, beg*

The women and children were pleading.
Standing proudly, the men refused to plead.
The convicts were pleading on their knees.

plead _____ *present/argue [a law case, one's position]*

OBJECT

The lawyer will plead **your case.**
You shouldn't plead **your own case.**
The state's attorney will plead **the government's case.**

plead _____ *formally declare oneself [innocent/guilty] in court*

PREDICATE ADJECTIVE

He pled **guilty on all charges.**
The gang members will plead **innocent.**
How do you plead?

plead _____ *ask/beg*

for OBJECT
for OBJECT + INFINITIVE
with OBJECT (+ INFINITIVE)

The condemned man was pleading **for his life.**
We pleaded **for them** *to be careful.*
I'm pleading **with you!** Let me go to the concert.
They pleaded **with the manager** *to reconsider his decision.*
I have pleaded **with Bob** *to look for a better job.*

INFINITIVE

He pleaded **to come with us.**
The children pleaded **to get a dog.**
I pleaded **to get a bigger budget.**

plead _____ *give as an excuse*

OBJECT

Tanya pleaded **ignorance of the law,** but got a ticket anyway.
The tobacco company heads pleaded **ignorance of the addictive properties of cigarette smoking.**

THAT-CLAUSE

Scott pleaded **that he didn't have enough time to complete the assignment.**
Brandon pleaded **that he didn't see the speed limit sign.**

prove

prove | proves · proved · have proven
prove | proves · proved · have proved

☑ IRREGULAR
☑ REGULAR

PRESENT

I prove	we prove
you prove	you prove
he/she/it proves	they prove

• *His experiment proves that we are right.*

PRESENT PROGRESSIVE

I am proving	we are proving
you are proving	you are proving
he/she/it is proving	they are proving

• *Cal is proving to be a bit of a problem.*

PAST

I proved	we proved
you proved	you proved
he/she/it proved	they proved

• *It proved to be much more difficult.*

PAST PROGRESSIVE

I was proving	we were proving
you were proving	you were proving
he/she/it was proving	they were proving

• *Francine was proving to be a great success.*

PRESENT PERFECT ... have | has proven
PAST PERFECT ... had proven

FUTURE ... will prove
FUTURE PROGRESSIVE ... will be proving
FUTURE PERFECT ... will have proven

PAST PASSIVE

I was proven	we were proven
you were proven	you were proven
he/she/it was proven	they were proven

• *His guilt was never proven.*

COMPLEMENTS

prove _____ *demonstrate that something is true/correct*

OBJECT	For homework, Johanna told the students to prove **the theorem.** I can prove **my claim.**
PASSIVE	The validity of the will was proven in court.
REFLEXIVE PRONOUN + *as* PREDICATE NOUN	Sandra has proven **herself** *as an astronaut.* Emily has proven **herself** *as a teacher.*
OBJECT + (*to be*) PREDICATE NOUN	The lawyer proved **the defendant** *(to be) an innocent bystander.* Her boyfriend's subsequent behavior proved **him** *(to be) a complete loser.* Placido has proven **himself** *(to be) an excellent shortstop.*
OBJECT + (*to be*) PREDICATE ADJECTIVE	Our analysis proved **the plan** *(to be) feasible.* Madeline has proven **herself** *(to be) fearless.*
to OBJECT + THAT-CLAUSE	He proved **to us** *that he had been right all along.* Can they prove **to the police** *that they were not involved in the crime?*
THAT-CLAUSE	In 1616, William Harvey proved **that blood circulates.** The police proved **that the driver was lying.**
WH-CLAUSE	Can they prove **who caused the accident?** I can prove **what I am saying.**

prove _____ *turn out [to be]*

(*to be*) PREDICATE NOUN	Our guide proved **(to be) a stranger to the region.** Our hotel proved **(to be) a dumpy guest house.** Her suggestion proved **(to be) a stroke of pure genius.**
(*to be*) PREDICATE ADJECTIVE	The guide proved **(to be) quite unreliable.** Their claim proved **(to be) false.** Our best guess proved **(to be) totally wrong.**

PRESENT

I put	we put
you put	you put
he/she/it puts	they put

• *He always puts his car in the garage.*

PRESENT PROGRESSIVE

I am putting	we are putting
you are putting	you are putting
he/she/it is putting	they are putting

• *I am putting the dishes into the dishwasher.*

PAST

I put	we put
you put	you put
he/she/it put	they put

• *I put the package on his desk.*

PAST PROGRESSIVE

I was putting	we were putting
you were putting	you were putting
he/she/it was putting	they were putting

• *The kids were putting peanut butter on their fruit.*

PRESENT PERFECT ... have | has put
PAST PERFECT ... had put

FUTURE ... will put
FUTURE PROGRESSIVE ... will be putting
FUTURE PERFECT ... will have put

PAST PASSIVE

I was put	we were put
you were put	you were put
he/she/it was put	they were put

• *The documents were put into the safe.*

(COMPLEMENTS)

put _____ *place, set*

OBJECT + ADVERB OF PLACE

I always put **my keys** *on the dresser*.
We put **the new rug** *in the living room*.
The guards put **a barricade** *across the road*.
She put **her hand** *under the kitten* to lift it.
Terry put **her knitting** *aside* and picked up a book.
The clerk put **a price of $49.99** *on the dress*.
The coach put **pressure** *on the team*.

PASSIVE

The picture was put *above the fireplace*.

put _____ *insert*

OBJECT + ADVERB OF PLACE TO/FROM

I put **the key** *into the lock* and turned it.
We put **the note** *under his door*.
The telephone company will put **a new satellite** *into orbit*.
You will need to put **your car** *into the garage*.

PASSIVE

The suitcases were put *into the closet*.

put _____ *cause to be in a certain condition/state*

OBJECT + ADVERB OF MANNER

His lectures put **me** *to sleep* sometimes.
The CEO's decision put **3,000 people** *out of work*.
Don't put **yourself** *in danger*.
He always puts **me** *in a good mood*.
I'd like to put **the old lawn mower** *to good use*.

put _____ *express, say*

OBJECT + ADVERB OF MANNER

I thought he put **it** *very well*.
You will need to put **your ideas** *in a simpler form*.
I put **my comments** *in writing*.

PASSIVE

His complaints were put *rather rudely*,
    I thought.

---

put _SEP_ **across** _communicate successfully_	He managed to put across the complexity of the plan.
put _SEP_ **aside** _save_	We put aside the income tax refund for our retirement.
put _SEP_ **away** _store_	We need to put away the good silverware. Would you put the ketchup away, please?
put _SEP_ **away** _eat/drink a lot of_	Steve can really put away the potato chips.
put _SEP_ **down** _overcome with force, suppress_	The government put down a rebellion in the provinces.
put _SEP_ **down** _write down_	It's important to put everything down on paper.
put _SEP_ **down** _include on a list_	The campaign volunteer put me down as a "maybe."
put _SEP_ **down** _find fault with, insult_	She put him down in front of all their friends.
put _SEP_ **down** _pay as the first installment_	You can put 10% down and pay the rest in 90 days.
put forth _____ _grow_ [PLANTS]	The daffodils are putting forth their blooms early.
put _SEP_ **forth/forward** _propose, suggest_	She put forward her plan to save endangered species.
put _SEP_ **in** _add_	Could you put in a paragraph about offshore drilling?
put _SEP_ **in** _install_	We put in more shelves for our books.
put in for _____ _formally request_	The defendant put in for a change of venue. Drake put in for the vacant Senate seat.
put _SEP_ **off** _repel_	Bubba's vulgar language really puts me off.
put _SEP_ **off** _postpone_	We'll have to put the meeting off until next week.
put on _____ _pretend_	Ron put on his fake French accent, and we all laughed.
put _____ **on** _deceive_ [someone]	Don't believe him; he's just putting you on.
put _SEP_ **on** _dress in_ [clothing]	Will I need to put my coat on?
put _SEP_ **on** _add_	Uncle Nelson has put on quite a bit of weight.
put _SEP_ **on** _present_ [entertainment]	The senior class put on a musical.
put _SEP_ **on** _apply_ [cosmetics]	She puts lipstick on in the morning and after lunch.
put _SEP_ **on** _start_ [something] _playing/working_	We put on some rock music for Dad. Mom put a pot of coffee on for us.
put _SEP_ **out** _extinguish_	The campers put the fire out with water from the pond.
put _SEP_ **out** _publish, issue_	They put out 40 titles a year. The Beatles put "The White Album" out in 1968.
put out _____ _generate a lot of_	Your laptop puts out a lot of heat.
put _SEP_ **out** _make unconscious_	The anesthesia will put you out, and you won't remember the surgery.
put _SEP_ **through** _succeed in doing_	The new CEO put the merger through.
put _____ **through** _pay for_ [someone's] _attendance at_	Laurie put herself through law school at Georgetown.
put _SEP_ **up** _give lodging to_	We can put your parents up for one night. The airline put the stranded passengers up at a hotel.
put _SEP_ **up** _offer_	Our neighbors put their house up for sale.
put _SEP_ **up** _provide_	John put up $2,000 for the new playground.
put _SEP_ **up** _build_	They put up a new drugstore in just four months.
put _SEP_ **up** _nominate_	They put Renni up for a three-year term.
put up with _____ _tolerate_	Martha couldn't put up with the noise anymore.
put upon _____ _take advantage of_	I don't like to be put upon by my friends.

top **30** verb

PRESENT		**PRESENT PROGRESSIVE**	
I quit	we quit	I am quitting	we are quitting
you quit	you quit	you are quitting	you are quitting
he/she/it quits	they quit	he/she/it is quitting	they are quitting

   ° *He usually quits around 5 o'clock.*   ° *I am quitting next week.*

PAST		**PAST PROGRESSIVE**	
I quit	we quit	I was quitting	we were quitting
you quit	you quit	you were quitting	you were quitting
he/she/it quit	they quit	he/she/it was quitting	they were quitting

   ° *I quit my job last year.*   ° *He was quitting because he needed a full-time job.*

PRESENT PERFECT	... have	has quit
PAST PERFECT	... had quit

FUTURE	... will quit
FUTURE PROGRESSIVE	... will be quitting
FUTURE PERFECT	... will have quit

PAST PASSIVE

     Quit is never used in the passive voice.

                                                         (**COMPLEMENTS**)

quit *stop functioning*

My cell phone just quit.
The engine quits if you give it too much gas.
His poor old heart finally quit.

quit *stop working at the end of a work period*

When do they quit for the day?
I am getting tired. How soon can we quit?
We can't quit until the next shift comes in.

quit *resign from a job*

That's it. I quit!
How many people quit in the course of a month?
We are moving to a new town, so I will have to quit.

quit *admit defeat, give up*

You beat me again. I quit.
No matter how bad things look, we will never quit.
They quit before the game was half over.

quit _____ *voluntarily stop doing [a job, school, activity]*

     OBJECT

I am going to quit **my job** at the end of the year.
Tom quit **the police force** and went to law school.
Mike quit **college** to join the Marines.
He quit **the team** because he injured his knee.

     WH-CLAUSE

You need to quit **what you are doing** and get a better job.
Quit **whatever you are doing** and listen to this!

     PRESENT PARTICIPLE

I have to quit **smoking so much**.
The company is going to quit **paying overtime**.
He can't quit **worrying about what is going to happen**.

quit _____ *leave, move away from*

     OBJECT

They quit **the suburbs** and moved into the city.

                                                        (**PHRASAL VERBS**)

quit on _____ *leave one's job without warning [someone]*

The carpenters quit on us in the middle
   of the renovation.

quit on _____ *stop functioning while [someone] is using it*

The lawn mower quits on me when I get into the tall grass.
The furnace quit on us again.

read _____ *learn from printed/on-screen material*

THAT-CLAUSE

I read **that the company may be up for sale.**
The coach read **that we are favored to win.**
We read **that the parade may be cancelled.**

read _____ *learn/interpret the meaning of*

OBJECT

I couldn't read **her face** at all.
He is very good at reading **people's body language.**
Economists don't always read **inflationary signals** correctly.
Diplomatic experts read **the implications of every government action.**

OBJECT + *as* OBJECT

I read **his note** *as an apology.*
Everyone read **his press release** *as an announcement of his candidacy.*

read _____ *measure and show*

OBJECT

The speedometer reads **55 miles per hour.**
The thermometer reads **32 degrees Celsius.**

read _____ *state*

DIRECT QUOTATION

The sign reads, **"No shirt, no shoes, no service."**

(PHRASAL VERBS)

read _____ **in/into** *infer [additional ideas/ messages] from reading*

What did you read into Senator Blather's remarks?

read ^SEP^ **off** *read aloud [a list]*

The teacher read off the names of students who had won awards.

read ^SEP^ **over/through** *read completely*

Would you read over my paper before I turn it in?

read up on _____ *study/learn by reading*

We have to read up on the current drug laws before the conference next week.

(EXPRESSIONS)

read between the lines *understand the intended but not explicit meaning of something said/written*

She is good at reading between the lines of politicians' speeches.

read lips *determine the words that someone is saying by watching him/her speak*

When talking to someone who reads lips, you should talk normally.

Read my lips. *Believe what I am about to tell you.*

"Read my lips: No new taxes." [PRESIDENT GEORGE H.W. BUSH]

read [someone] his/her rights *state [someone's] legal rights to [someone who has been arrested]*

The arresting officer read the suspect his rights.

read [someone] like a book *understand [someone] well*

His calm manner doesn't fool me; I can read him like a book.

read [someone] the riot act *scold severely*

When Ed came home late, his father read him the riot act.

read [someone's] mind/thoughts *understand what [someone] is thinking*

How did you know I wanted pizza for dinner? You must have read my mind.

PRESENT

I read	we read
you read	you read
he/she/it reads	they read

• *He never reads his e-mail.*

PRESENT PROGRESSIVE

I am reading	we are reading
you are reading	you are reading
he/she/it is reading	they are reading

• *Be quiet! I'm reading.*

PAST

I read	we read
you read	you read
he/she/it read	they read

• *She read nothing but short stories.*

PAST PROGRESSIVE

I was reading	we were reading
you were reading	you were reading
he/she/it was reading	they were reading

• *I was just reading your note.*

PRESENT PERFECT ... have | has read
PAST PERFECT ... had read

FUTURE ... will read
FUTURE PROGRESSIVE ... will be reading
FUTURE PERFECT ... will have read

PAST PASSIVE

—	—
—	—
it was read	they were read

• *The transcript was read aloud in court.*

NOTE: The present form of *read* rhymes with *seed*; the past forms of *read* rhyme with *bed*.

───────────────(**COMPLEMENTS**)───────────────

read *understand writing/printing*   Can any of the children read yet?

read *look at and understand the content*   I love to read.
of printed material   I always read on the airplane.

read _____ *speak [written/printed/on-screen words] aloud*

ADVERB OF MANNER	She reads **beautifully**.
	DJ reads **with a different voice for each character**.
	He reads **too softly for everyone to hear**.
OBJECT	Thank you. You read **that** beautifully.
	Paul read **the memo** in a perfect imitation of the boss's voice.
INDIRECT OBJECT + DIRECT OBJECT	Can you read *me a story*?
	The teacher reads *the class a book* for the last 15 minutes.
to PARAPHRASE	Can you read *a story to me*?
	The teacher reads *a book to the class* for the last 15 minutes.
PASSIVE	We were read a story every night.

read _____ *decode and get information from [a set of letters/numbers/symbols]*

OBJECT	I can't read **her handwriting**.
	He taught himself to read **Old Icelandic**.
	The gas man came to read **the meter** this morning.
	Yvonne can't read **music**, but she plays beautifully.
	Will my computer be able to read **this file**?

read _____ *look at and understand the content of [written/printed/on-screen material]*

OBJECT	I read **the newspaper** every morning at breakfast.
	He read **your e-mail** and will get back to you.
PASSIVE	*Julius Caesar* was read in every tenth-grade classroom.
WH-CLAUSE	I read **what you said about me**.
	You need to read **what is in the fine print** very carefully.
	He will read **whatever he can get his hands on**.

rend

rend | rends · rent · have rent
rend | rends · rended · have rended

☑ IRREGULAR
☑ REGULAR

PRESENT

I rend	we rend
you rend	you rend
he/she/it rends	they rend

• *It rends my heart to see her so unhappy.*

PAST

I rent	we rent
you rent	you rent
he/she/it rent	they rent

• *The howling of wolves rent the night air.*

PRESENT PERFECT ... have | has rent
PAST PERFECT ... had rent

PRESENT PROGRESSIVE

I am rending	we are rending
you are rending	you are rending
he/she/it is rending	they are rending

• *We are rending cotton rags to make paper.*

PAST PROGRESSIVE

I was rending	we were rending
you were rending	you were rending
he/she/it was rending	they were rending

• *The grieving mourners were rending their clothes.*

FUTURE ... will rend
FUTURE PROGRESSIVE ... will be rending
FUTURE PERFECT ... will have rent

PAST PASSIVE

—	—
—	—
it was rent	they were rent

• *The quiet was rent by a loud explosion.*

COMPLEMENTS

rend ____ *tear/split forcefully into pieces*

OBJECT	The trap cruelly rent **the animal's skin.**
	The dryer had rent **the delicate fabrics** to shreds.
	Carnivores' teeth are designed to rend **their prey.**
PASSIVE	The drapes were rent from top to bottom.

rend ____ *disturb/pierce with sound*

OBJECT	The wolves' howling rent **the night.**
PASSIVE	The night was rent by the wolves' howling.

rend ____ *distress, cause pain to*

OBJECT	Suspicion and doubt rent **their relationship.**
PASSIVE	Her heart was rent by the dreadful sight.

PRESENT

I rid	we rid
you rid	you rid
he/she/it rids	they rid

• *The cat rids the barn of mice.*

PAST

I rid	we rid
you rid	you rid
he/she/it rid	they rid

• *They rid themselves of all their coats.*

PRESENT PERFECT ... have | has rid
PAST PERFECT ... had rid

PRESENT PROGRESSIVE

I am ridding	we are ridding
you are ridding	you are ridding
he/she/it is ridding	they are ridding

• *The store is ridding itself of unsold merchandise.*

PAST PROGRESSIVE

I was ridding	we were ridding
you were ridding	you were ridding
he/she/it was ridding	they were ridding

• *I was ridding myself of all my junk.*

FUTURE ... will rid
FUTURE PROGRESSIVE ... will be ridding
FUTURE PERFECT ... will have rid

PAST PASSIVE

I was rid	we were rid
you were rid	you were rid
he/she/it was rid	they were rid

• *We were finally rid of unwanted visitors.*

───────────────────────────────(**COMPLEMENTS**)───

rid _____ *free from [someone/something not wanted]*

OBJECT + *of* OBJECT	They hoped to rid **the world** *of nuclear weapons.*
	I can't rid **myself** *of this miserable cold.*
	You must rid **yourself** *of all debt.*
	They were trying to rid **the field** *of all noxious weeds.*
	The alderman wants to rid **the city** *of one-way streets.*
	The sheriff is trying to rid **the county** *of drug dealers.*
	"Will no one rid **me** *of this troublesome priest?*" [HENRY II, LEADING TO THE MURDER OF THOMAS BECKET IN 1170]
PASSIVE	The tent was rid *of all mosquitoes.*

PRESENT

I ride	we ride
you ride	you ride
he/she/it rides	they ride

• *He rides the bus to work every day.*

PRESENT PROGRESSIVE

I am riding	we are riding
you are riding	you are riding
he/she/it is riding	they are riding

• *Our hopes are riding on the new government.*

PAST

I rode	we rode
you rode	you rode
he/she/it rode	they rode

• *I rode my bicycle to the store yesterday.*

PAST PROGRESSIVE

I was riding	we were riding
you were riding	you were riding
he/she/it was riding	they were riding

• *He was riding in the first race.*

PRESENT PERFECT ... have | has ridden
PAST PERFECT ... had ridden

FUTURE ... will ride
FUTURE PROGRESSIVE ... will be riding
FUTURE PERFECT ... will have ridden

PAST PASSIVE

— —
— —
it was ridden   they were ridden

• *That horse was last ridden a week ago.*

COMPLEMENTS

ride *sit on a horse/bicycle/motorcycle/ etc. and make it move along*

Do you know how to ride?
She rides quite well.
You never forget how to ride.
The cowboys rode 70 miles the first day.

ride *move along in a vehicle*

He never rides when he can walk.
I rode to work that day.
They rode in a school bus to the meeting.

ride _____ *sit on and make move along*
    OBJECT

The kids were riding **their bicycles** in the park.
We rented horses and rode **them** all afternoon.

ride _____ *move along in/on*
    OBJECT

We rode **the train** when we were in Germany.
I usually ride **the bus** to work.
They rode **every ride** at Disneyland.

ride _____ *be carried along on/by*
    OBJECT

The surfers were riding **the waves**.
Investors rode **the boom in housing** for 20 years.
The TV networks were still riding **the fad of reality TV**.

ride _____ *tease, nag*
    OBJECT

The girls are constantly riding **each other** about music.
I had better get back to work. The boss is really riding **us**.

PHRASAL VERBS

ride away/down/off/out/up/etc. *move along in a specified direction*

Marvin stopped by to talk, then rode off.
We rode out to the ferry landing this morning.

ride on _____ *depend on*

The company's reputation is riding on these negotiations.
All his hopes are riding on being promoted to news anchor.

ride _SEP_ **out** *survive in safety*

We rode out the storm in the basement.
Can our company ride out these perilous economic times?

ride up *move upward out of place*

His jeans rode up as he jogged across the parking lot.

PRESENT

I ring	we ring
you ring	you ring
he/she/it rings	they ring

• *The bell rings on the quarter hour.*

PRESENT PROGRESSIVE

I am ringing	we are ringing
you are ringing	you are ringing
he/she/it is ringing	they are ringing

• *Your alarm clock is ringing.*

PAST

I rang	we rang
you rang	you rang
he/she/it rang	they rang

• *The phone rang as I was doing dishes.*

PAST PROGRESSIVE

I was ringing	we were ringing
you were ringing	you were ringing
he/she/it was ringing	they were ringing

• *The phone was ringing all morning.*

PRESENT PERFECT ... have | has rung
PAST PERFECT ... had rung

FUTURE ... will ring
FUTURE PROGRESSIVE ... will be ringing
FUTURE PERFECT ... will have rung

PAST PASSIVE

I was rung	we were rung
you were rung	you were rung
he/she/it was rung	they were rung

• *The church bell was rung every Sunday for years.*

NOTE: The irregular verb *ring* is presented here. The regular verb *ring* (*ring* | *rings* · *ringed* · *have ringed*) means "surround, form a circle around," as in *Cypress trees ring the lake.*

― COMPLEMENTS ―

ring *make the sound of a bell*
All of the church bells were ringing.
Good wine glasses will ring if you tap them.

ring *call for service by telephone/bell*
If you need help, just ring.
We rang, but nobody came.
Please ring for service.

ring *fill a place with sound*
The sound of cannons rang through the air.

ring *be filled with sound*
The halls rang with laughter as the students left for the holiday.
After the explosion, my ears rang for half an hour.

ring _____ *cause [a bell/alarm] to sound*

OBJECT
I knocked and rang **the doorbell**.
It takes a lot of practice to ring **the big church bells**.

PASSIVE
The bells are always rung on Easter.

ring _____ *seem to be*

PREDICATE ADJECTIVE
The immigrant's story rings **true**.
Harry's apology rang **hollow**.

― PHRASAL VERBS ―

ring out *sound clearly and loudly*
Three shots rang out in the crisp autumn air.

ring SEP **up** *record the price of [something] on a cash register*
The cashier rang up the cauliflower at $1.99 a head.

― EXPRESSIONS ―

ring a bell *seem familiar*
You're right—that name rings a bell.

ring in the new (year), ring out the old *celebrate the beginning of the new year*
We ring in the new year by watching the ball drop at New York's Times Square.

ring off the hook *ring constantly*
I got nothing done this morning—the phone was ringing off the hook.

I rise	we rise
you rise	you rise
he/she/it rises	they rise

• *The land slowly rises toward the hills.*

I am rising	we are rising
you are rising	you are rising
he/she/it is rising	they are rising

• *His temperature is still rising.*

I rose	we rose
you rose	you rose
he/she/it rose	they rose

• *The river rose until the banks overflowed.*

I was rising	we were rising
you were rising	you were rising
he/she/it was rising	they were rising

• *Prices were steadily rising.*

... have | has risen
... had risen

... will rise
... will be rising
... will have risen

Risen is never used in the passive voice.

(COMPLEMENTS)

rise *go to a higher level*

The tide will be rising until four.
The moon was just rising above the trees.
A loud cheer rose from the spectators.
White smoke was rising from the chimney.
The Beatles rose to fame overnight.
Carly rose to be CEO of a Fortune 500 company.
He rose from office boy to company director.

rise *stand/get up*

All rise! [COMMAND ISSUED WHEN A JUDGE ENTERS
     A COURTROOM]
He rose from the couch and turned off the TV.
We usually rise before dawn.

rise *become greater/higher/stronger*

As we start going downhill, our speed will rise rapidly.
The Roman Empire rose and fell.
Stock prices rose two percent today.
My income has not risen as much as inflation has.
During the concert, the noise rose to unbearable levels.
The hills steadily rose as we drove northward.
The bread dough was rising quickly.
His voice rose to a pitiful squeak.
Gas prices have been rising lately.
The wind rose to near gale force.

(PHRASAL VERBS)

rise above _____ *ignore [a bad situation]*

The legislators rose above their
     petty disagreements and passed an excellent bill.

rise up (against _____**)** *rebel/revolt
(against [someone/something])*

The colonists rose up against George III and his army.

(EXPRESSIONS)

rise and shine *get out of bed and be
energetic*

Rise and shine! We've got a big day
     ahead of us.

rise to the occasion *succeed in dealing
with a difficult situation*

The president rose to the occasion and delivered
     a forceful, inspiring speech.

PRESENT

I run	we run
you run	you run
he/she/it runs	they run

　• *The road runs west to the river.*

PRESENT PROGRESSIVE

I am running	we are running
you are running	you are running
he/she/it is running	they are running

　• *He is running in the Boston Marathon.*

PAST

I ran	we ran
you ran	you ran
he/she/it ran	they ran

　• *The children ran through the door.*

PAST PROGRESSIVE

I was running	we were running
you were running	you were running
he/she/it was running	they were running

　• *The program was running a little late.*

PRESENT PERFECT ... have | has run
PAST PERFECT ... had run

FUTURE ... will run
FUTURE PROGRESSIVE ... will be running
FUTURE PERFECT ... will have run

PAST PASSIVE

I was run	we were run
you were run	you were run
he/she/it was run	they were run

　• *The store was run by Harry and his children.*

（ **COMPLEMENTS** ）

run *go by moving one's legs faster than in walking*	The kids never stop running. I try to run two miles every day. The tiger has escaped! Run!
run *flow* [OF LIQUIDS]	The Missouri River runs into the Mississippi River at St. Louis. The paint was too thin. It ran down the wall in streaks.
run *spread, move freely*	A murmur ran through the crowd. A light breeze ran through the tall grass.
run *operate, be in use/action*	The train runs three times a day. The engine is not running very smoothly. The network servers are not running.
run ___ *operate* 　OBJECT	Do you know how to run **this printing press**? She can run **any equipment in the woodworking shop**.
run ___ *manage* 　OBJECT	He runs **the local supermarket**. The church runs **a preschool program**.
run ___ *go* 　ADVERB OF PLACE TO/FROM	I need to run **to the bank**. We've got to run **home** for something. The ferry runs **from Modoc to Ste. Genevieve and back**.
run ___ *transport* 　OBJECT + ADVERB OF PLACE TO/FROM	Can you run **me** *back to the office*? I will run **you** *over to the station*.
run ___ *continue, extend* 　ADVERB OF TIME 　ADVERB OF PLACE TO/FROM	The festival runs **for four weeks in June**. The fiscal year runs **from July 1 to June 30**. The literature class runs **every quarter**. This path runs **up the bluff to Deer Pond**.
run ___ *cause to continue/extend* 　OBJECT + ADVERB OF PLACE TO/FROM	We ran **electrical conduit** *under the floor*. The logging company ran **a gravel road** *out to the camp*.

top 30 verb

run _____ *perform* OBJECT	Can you run **some errands** for me? The doctor will need to run **some tests**.
run _____ *cost* [INFORMAL] (INDIRECT OBJECT +) DIRECT OBJECT	The shipping will run **$8.95**. The trip will run *you* **about $500**.
run _____ *publish* OBJECT	The newspaper ran **several articles on homeless people**. Our company ran **an ad** in the July issue.
run _____ *be [at a certain level]* PREDICATE ADJECTIVE	The store is running **low** on toilet paper. We ran **late** getting to the theater.

—(**PHRASAL VERBS**)—

run across _____ *come upon by chance*	We ran across our cousins at the farmers' market. We ran across old photos of Great-grandfather.
run against _____ *be a candidate opposing*	Senator Blather ran against gun control. She ran against another alderman in the primary.
run along *go away*	Why don't you kids run along? Be back here in two hours.
run (around) with _____ *socialize with*	Tara runs around with her friends from high school.
run _____ **by/past** *seek advice about / approval for [something] from*	Sam ran the speech by Toby.
run SEP **down** *drain all the power from*	Stop trying to start the car; you'll run the battery down.
run SEP **down** *criticize*	Brandi ran down the rest of the group.
run for _____ *be a candidate for*	The governor is running for a fourth term.
run _____ **for** *support [someone] as a candidate for*	The party ran an unknown businessman for mayor.
run into _____ *collide with*	My sister ran into a deer on the highway.
run into _____ *meet by chance*	Janey ran into Hulga at the grocery store.
run SEP **off** *print, make copies of*	I ran off several extra sets for you.
run on _____ *use for power*	Our hybrid car runs on gasoline and an NiMH battery.
run on *continue without stopping*	The presentation of awards ran on forever.
run out *come to an end, be used up*	Time is running out, and I still have an essay to write. Our supply of helium ran out—no more balloons!
run out of _____ *use up*	Mom finally ran out of patience with us kids. They ran out of popcorn before the second show.
run over *overflow*	Quick! The bathtub is running over.
run over _____ *knock down while driving*	Her friend ran over a skunk.
run over _____ *exceed a limit*	The class was supposed to last an hour, but it ran over.
run SEP **over** *bring [something]*	Would you run the latest proposal over to my office?
run through _____ *use up*	Shane ran through his inheritance in a year.
run to _____ *amount to*	The grocery bill runs to $123.44. Homer's *Odyssey* runs to more than 12,000 lines.

run SEP **up** *accumulate [debt]*	George ran up a sizable tab at the luxury hotel.
run SEP **up** *cause to increase*	Technology gains ran stock prices up. The Cobras ran up a big lead, then benched their starters.
run up against _____ *encounter*	He finally ran up against a problem he couldn't solve.

PRESENT		PRESENT PROGRESSIVE	
I saw	we saw	I am sawing	we are sawing
you saw	you saw	you are sawing	you are sawing
he/she/it saws	they saw	he/she/it is sawing	they are sawing

• He saws plywood with a special blade.

• I am sawing fence posts.

PAST		PAST PROGRESSIVE	
I sawed	we sawed	I was sawing	we were sawing
you sawed	you sawed	you were sawing	you were sawing
he/she/it sawed	they sawed	he/she/it was sawing	they were sawing

• I sawed the board in half.

• He was sawing as fast as he could.

PRESENT PERFECT ... have | has sawn
PAST PERFECT ... had sawn

FUTURE ... will saw
FUTURE PROGRESSIVE ... will be sawing
FUTURE PERFECT ... will have sawn

PAST PASSIVE

—   —
—   —
it was sawn   they were sawn

• The beams were sawn nearly through.

COMPLEMENTS

saw *cut using a saw*

We have been sawing all afternoon.
I will have to saw at an angle.
Look out for nails when you saw.
The new blade saws smoothly.

saw *be cut using a saw*

These pine two-by-fours saw very easily.

saw *use a sawing motion*

Holmes was sawing on his violin.
When he jumped off the cliff, his arms sawed up and down.

saw _____ *cut/shape using a saw*

OBJECT

We are sawing **oak planks** for flooring.
I will saw **the sheets of fiberglass** with a special blade.
John sawed **the boards** into two-foot lengths.
They have sawn **a lot of timber** this week.
We were sawing **jigsaw puzzles** out of masonite.

PASSIVE

The lumber had been sawn against the grain.

PHRASAL VERBS

saw at _____ *cut back and forth using a knife/bar/etc.*

The prisoner was sawing at the window
bars with a table knife.

saw _SEP_ **down** *cut down*

The lumberjacks sawed the entire woods down.

saw _SEP_ **off** *cut off*

She sawed off the branches that she could reach.

saw _SEP_ **up** *cut into pieces*

Gerry sawed the board up into seven pieces of equal length.

PRESENT

I say	we say
you say	you say
he/she/it says	they say

• *He always says that he is too busy.*

PRESENT PROGRESSIVE

I am saying	we are saying
you are saying	you are saying
he/she/it is saying	they are saying

• *I am not saying anything.*

PAST

I said	we said
you said	you said
he/she/it said	they said

• *She said something I couldn't understand.*

PAST PROGRESSIVE

I was saying	we were saying
you were saying	you were saying
he/she/it was saying	they were saying

• *We were saying that it wouldn't be a problem.*

PRESENT PERFECT	... have | has said
PAST PERFECT	... had said

FUTURE	... will say
FUTURE PROGRESSIVE	... will be saying
FUTURE PERFECT	... will have said

PAST PASSIVE

I was said	we were said
you were said	you were said
he/she/it was said	they were said

• *They were said to be in the oil business.*

COMPLEMENTS

say _____ *speak, put into words, express*

OBJECT	The teacher said **"hello"** in Latin.
	They said **nothing about it**.
	Would you say **your name** again, slowly?
PASSIVE	His name was said, but I didn't catch it.
INFINITIVE	He said **to go ahead without him**.
	The tour guide says **to be back on the bus in 15 minutes**.
	The recipe said **to use only the egg whites**.
	Her note said **to leave the back door unlocked**.
THAT-CLAUSE	They said **that they would come back later**.
	The law says **that everyone is presumed to be innocent**.
	He said **that we should expect snow**.
WH-CLAUSE	He never said **what he meant to do about the problem**.
	Did he say **when they were coming**?
WH-INFINITIVE	The instructions say **how to attach the handlebars**.
DIRECT QUOTATION	**"Good morning,"** she said. **"We're glad you're here."**

say _____ *show, indicate*

OBJECT	The clock says **2:15**.
	His expression said **it all**.
(to OBJECT +) THAT-CLAUSE	The tone of his voice says **that he's disappointed**.
	My instinct says *to me* that we should really be cautious.
WH-CLAUSE	Their veto says **what they think about the proposal**.

be said _____ *be commonly reported* [USED ONLY IN THE PASSIVE]

INFINITIVE	She was said to be one of the best lawyers around.
	He is said to take forever to make up his mind.

EXPRESSIONS

have _____ **to say for yourself** *be able to say in one's favor/defense*
The defendant had nothing to say for himself.
What do you have to say for yourself, young man?

say the word *give a signal*
When I say the word, jump out and shout "Happy Birthday!"

say yes/no (to _____**)** *agree/disagree (with [someone/something])*
Sarah said yes to Lucas when he proposed to her.
Just say no to drugs.

PRESENT

I see	we see
you see	you see
he/she/it sees	they see

• *He sees a physical therapist once a week.*

PRESENT PROGRESSIVE

I am seeing	we are seeing
you are seeing	you are seeing
he/she/it is seeing	they are seeing

• *I am seeing them at 10 o'clock.*

PAST

I saw	we saw
you saw	you saw
he/she/it saw	they saw

• *I saw Marian yesterday.*

PAST PROGRESSIVE

I was seeing	we were seeing
you were seeing	you were seeing
he/she/it was seeing	they were seeing

• *We were seeing some friends last night.*

PRESENT PERFECT   ... have | has seen
PAST PERFECT   ... had seen

FUTURE   ... will see
FUTURE PROGRESSIVE   ... will be seeing
FUTURE PERFECT   ... will have seen

PAST PASSIVE

I was seen	we were seen
you were seen	you were seen
he/she/it was seen	they were seen

• *The suspect was last seen fleeing the crime scene.*

COMPLEMENTS

see *use the sense of sight*

Ray can't see anymore.
You won't be able to see temporarily.

see *understand [something previously said]*

Oh, I see! [USUALLY SPOKEN EMPHATICALLY]

see *acknowledge [something previously said]*

I see. [USUALLY SPOKEN IN A LEVEL OR FALLING TONE]

see _____ *observe with one's eyes*

  OBJECT

I saw **Tom** at the grocery store.
We saw **the documentary** on TV last night.
What do you see?

    PASSIVE

The star is best seen through a high-powered telescope.

  OBJECT + BASE-FORM INFINITIVE

Sam saw **the wind** *rip the roof off the house.*
Nobody saw **the suspect** *break into the house.*

  OBJECT + PRESENT PARTICIPLE

We saw **Charles** *walking to school.*
I'm sorry. I didn't see **you** *standing there.*

    PASSIVE

Mary was seen *talking to Brett.*

  OBJECT + PAST PARTICIPLE

Someone must have seen **the car** *stolen.*
We saw **the bridge** *swept away in the flood.*

  THAT-CLAUSE

I see **that you bought a new car.**
We saw in the paper **that your son is getting married.**

    EMPHATIC PARAPHRASE

You bought a new car, I see.

  WH-CLAUSE

I saw **what they are making for dinner.**
Did anybody see **where the kids went?**

see _____ *understand*

  OBJECT

I see **your point.**
We all see **the attractions of living in a big city.**
Nobody saw **the magnitude of the risk.**

  OBJECT + INFINITIVE
  [USED ONLY IN THE PASSIVE]

He is widely seen *to be qualified.*
The judge was seen *to favor the prosecution.*

  THAT-CLAUSE

I see **that we are in big trouble.**
Our lawyer saw **that they were on shaky legal ground.**

  WH-CLAUSE

I see **what we should do.**
No one saw **how risky the plan was.**

see _____ *meet with, visit*

    OBJECT   I will see **the reporters** at 2 o'clock.

                       Guess **whom** I saw today?

                       Would you stop by and see **Aunt Tillie**?

    PASSIVE   You will be seen by the next available doctor.

see _____ *seek advice/information/help from*

    OBJECT   You should see **a doctor** about that rash.

                       Steve saw **a cancer specialist** today.

                       Alexander is seeing **his thesis advisor** on Tuesday.

see _____ *find out*

    WH-CLAUSE   See **who's at the door**, please.

                       Kari will see **what the congressman wants**.

see _____ *have a romantic relationship with* [USED ONLY IN THE PROGRESSIVE TENSES]

    OBJECT   Paul is seeing **a friend of mine**.

                       She is finally seeing **someone that we all like**.

                       Are you seeing **anyone**?

see _____ *accompany*

    OBJECT + ADVERB OF PLACE TO/FROM   Louise saw **her guests** *to the door*.

                       Jake saw **Mallory** *home from the party*.

see _____ *consider*

    OBJECT + *as* PREDICATE NOUN   They saw **Laura** *as a threat*.

                       I see **this** *as a golden opportunity*.

    OBJECT + *as* PREDICATE ADJECTIVE   We see **her** *as inexperienced and unreliable*.

                       The manager saw **his staff** *as eager and energetic*.

                       Traders will see **the economic picture** *as unstable*.

see _____ *make sure*

    (*to it*) THAT-CLAUSE   See (**to it**) **that the lights are turned off before you leave**.

                       We asked the janitor to see (**to it**) **that the boxes are removed from the hallway**.

see _____ *experience*

    OBJECT   My hometown has seen **lots of changes**.

                       The price of milk has seen **a large increase**.

                                          (**PHRASAL VERBS**)

see _____ **back/down/in/out/up**/etc.   May I see you back to your office?
accompany in a specified direction   The receptionist will see you out.

see about _____ *take care of*   My secretary will see about ordering new carpet.

see in *look inside*   The neighbors can see in if the drapes are open.

see _____ **off** *accompany [to a place*   I'll see you off at the train station.
of departure]

see out *look outside*   The windows were papered over so we couldn't see out.

see through *look through something*   The windshield is so dirty I can't see through.

see through _____ *understand the*   His wife finally saw through all his lies.
deception in

                see _SEP_ **through**   Glenda saw the project through.
                bring to completion

                see _SEP_ **through**   An extra $100 a week will see us through.
                help in a difficult time

                see to _____   Would you see to the lizard in the kitchen?
                take care of

top 30 verb

PRESENT		PRESENT PROGRESSIVE	
I seek	we seek	I am seeking	we are seeking
you seek	you seek	you are seeking	you are seeking
he/she/it seeks	they seek	he/she/it is seeking	they are seeking

* *France seeks to establish trade relations.*

* *We are only seeking the truth.*

PAST		PAST PROGRESSIVE	
I sought	we sought	I was seeking	we were seeking
you sought	you sought	you were seeking	you were seeking
he/she/it sought	they sought	he/she/it was seeking	they were seeking

* *The hikers sought a safe place to camp.*

* *The birds were seeking suitable nesting places.*

PRESENT PERFECT	... have | has sought
PAST PERFECT	... had sought

FUTURE	... will seek
FUTURE PROGRESSIVE	... will be seeking
FUTURE PERFECT	... will have sought

PAST PASSIVE

I was sought	we were sought
you were sought	you were sought
he/she/it was sought	they were sought

* *Voting rights were sought by women's groups for decades.*

COMPLEMENTS

seek _____ look for

  OBJECT

Ruby was seeking **a good place for the family reunion.**
Seek **shelter** immediately when you hear the tornado siren.
We sought **anybody who could answer our questions.**

  PASSIVE

A suspect in the killing is being sought by the police.

seek _____ ask for

  OBJECT

You need to seek **professional advice.**
I am seeking **information about cell phones.**
We should seek **help on this problem.**

  PASSIVE

Technical information on wind farms is being sought.

seek _____ try, attempt

  INFINITIVE

We sought **to find a better solution to the problem.**
They are seeking **to replace their old computers.**
We never sought **to cause any problems.**
The company has always sought **to have excellent customer relations.**

seek _____ try to get/achieve

  OBJECT

The plaintiff is seeking **damages of $2 million.**
He sought **revenge for his brother's murder.**
She sought **perfection in everything she did.**

PHRASAL VERBS

seek _SEP_ **out** look for and find

The candidate sought out the best pollsters
  in the country.

EXPRESSIONS

Seek and ye shall find. *If you look*
hard enough for something, you will
find it. [BIBLE]

The farmers' market has every kind
  of vegetable and fruit you can think of.
  Just seek and ye shall find.

PRESENT

I sell	we sell
you sell	you sell
he/she/it sells	they sell

• *Our store sells sports equipment.*

PAST

I sold	we sold
you sold	you sold
he/she/it sold	they sold

• *We sold the desk on craigslist.*

PRESENT PERFECT	... have	has sold
PAST PERFECT	... had sold

PRESENT PROGRESSIVE

I am selling	we are selling
you are selling	you are selling
he/she/it is selling	they are selling

• *These gadgets are selling like crazy.*

PAST PROGRESSIVE

I was selling	we were selling
you were selling	you were selling
he/she/it was selling	they were selling

• *We were selling children's clothing at half price.*

FUTURE	... will sell
FUTURE PROGRESSIVE	... will be selling
FUTURE PERFECT	... will have sold

PAST PASSIVE

I was sold	we were sold
you were sold	you were sold
he/she/it was sold	they were sold

• *That house was sold last week.*

(**COMPLEMENTS**)

sell *be a successful product/idea*

I think that his new CD will really sell.
His proposal will never sell.

sell _____ *exchange for money*

OBJECT

I want to sell **my old computer**.
He finally sold **his jewelry business**.
Should we sell **the rocking chair** or give it away?

OBJECT + *for* OBJECT

She sold **the lamp** *for $10*.
How much did you sell **the table** *for*?

INDIRECT OBJECT + DIRECT OBJECT

We sold *them* **some lawn furniture**.
Jay sold *the dealer* **his coin collection**.

to PARAPHRASE

We sold **some lawn furniture** *to them*.
Jay sold **his coin collection** *to the dealer*.

OBJECT + WH-CLAUSE

He sold **us** *just what we had in mind*.
We sell **people** *whatever kind of car they want*.

sell _____ *be given in exchange [for money]*

for OBJECT

The Picasso painting sold **for $104 million**.
The antique rolling pin sold **for $25**.

sell _____ *offer for purchase*

OBJECT

The hardware store sells **electrical and plumbing supplies**.
Our group is selling **raffle tickets**.
They sell **fish sandwiches** on Friday.

PASSIVE

Gym memberships are sold by the month.

OBJECT + *for* OBJECT

The boutique is selling **scarves** *for as little as $7*.

sell _____ *be offered for purchase*

for OBJECT

Milk is selling **for $3.50 a gallon**.

sell _____ *successfully promote*

OBJECT

John really knows how to sell **his vision for the company**.

(**PHRASAL VERBS**)

sell SEP **off** *liquidate*

We sold off our clothing division two years ago.

sell out of _____ *sell all of*

We sold out of French Roast coffee yesterday.
We are sold out of chocolate ice cream.

PRESENT

I send	we send
you send	you send
he/she/it sends	they send

- *The firm sends letters by registered mail.*

PAST

I sent	we sent
you sent	you sent
he/she/it sent	they sent

- *They sent us a nice note.*

PRESENT PERFECT   ... have | has sent
PAST PERFECT   ... had sent

PRESENT PROGRESSIVE

I am sending	we are sending
you are sending	you are sending
he/she/it is sending	they are sending

- *I am sending you an e-mail.*

PAST PROGRESSIVE

I was sending	we were sending
you were sending	you were sending
he/she/it was sending	they were sending

- *She was sending her children to a private school.*

FUTURE   ... will send
FUTURE PROGRESSIVE   ... will be sending
FUTURE PERFECT   ... will have sent

PAST PASSIVE

I was sent	we were sent
you were sent	you were sent
he/she/it was sent	they were sent

- *The letter was sent to the wrong address.*

COMPLEMENTS

send _____ *mail, dispatch*

   OBJECT

They forgot to send **the letter.**
We will send **a car** to pick them up.

send _____ *cause to go / be carried*

   OBJECT + ADVERB OF PLACE TO/FROM

We sent **our luggage** *on ahead.*
I sent **the children** *to bed* early.
The wizard sent **Dorothy** *back to Kansas.*
The accident sent **a cloud of dust** *into the air.*

   PASSIVE

The package was sent *to the wrong office.*

   INDIRECT OBJECT + DIRECT OBJECT

Send *me* **your ideas.**
We sent *them* **a wedding present.**

   to PARAPHRASE

Send **your ideas** *to me.*
We sent **a wedding present** *to them.*

PHRASAL VERBS

send __SEP__ **away/back/by/down/in/out/
over/etc.** *cause to go in a specified direction*

The publisher sent my manuscript back unread.
You may send the ambassador in now.

send **(away/back/down/off/out/up)
for** _____ *summon, request*

Send for the school nurse immediately.
Abby sent away for extra copies of the report.
Let's send out for pizza.

send __SEP__ **in** *submit*

Please send your application in by December 31.

send _____ **in for** *put [someone] into a
contest as a replacement for*

The coach sent Hopkins in for Busam.

send __SEP__ **off** *mail*

We sent off a present to our granddaughter.

send __SEP__ **off** *cause to go away*

Send the children off so that we can talk privately.

send __SEP__ **off** *say farewell to [someone
leaving on a trip]*

The town sent the soldiers off with a parade.

send __SEP__ **out** *issue, distribute*

The company sent a press release out this morning.

send _____ **out for** *cause [someone] to go
on an errand to get*

I sent Billie out for some more ice cream.

send __SEP__ **up/down** *cause to go up/down*

Good economic news sent the stock market up.

(**PHRASAL VERBS**)

set ___SEP___ aside/down/forward/out/ up/etc. *put in a specified position*	The logician set the problem aside and went to lunch. Our neighbors set scraps out for our dog.
set about _____ *begin*	The Scouts set about repairing the holes in the tent.
set _____ against *cause to disagree with*	His budget policies set the president against Congress.
set _____ apart *make distinctive*	His honesty and sense of justice set him apart.
set ___SEP___ aside *keep apart*	We set aside $200 a month for the kids' education.
set ___SEP___ aside *reject, nullify*	They set their differences aside and became close friends. Congress set the issue aside for the time being. The Supreme Court set aside the appellate court ruling.
set ___SEP___ back *delay*	The bad economy will set back our plans to expand. The president's order set genetic research back six years.
set ___SEP___ back *cost [someone]* [INFORMAL]	How much did the new lawn tractor set you back?
set ___SEP___ down *put in writing*	The secretary has set down what was said at the executive meeting.
set _____ down to *blame [something] on*	The boss set Hank's mistake down to inexperience and naïveté.
set ___SEP___ forth *announce, make known*	The church set forth its principles of equality and inclusion.
set in *begin*	Decay has already set in. With all the political commercials on TV, voter fatigue has set in.
set off/out *depart, start out*	Three hundred pioneers set off from St. Joseph, Missouri. Refugees set out in overcrowded boats for the mainland.
set ___SEP___ off *make distinctive*	The designer set the title off from the text below.
set ___SEP___ off *cause to be very emotional*	Be careful not to set Dolores off; she's already angry.
set ___SEP___ off *trigger, cause to make a noise*	My son set the metal detector off with his belt buckle.
set ___SEP___ off *cause to explode*	Quarrymen set off 150 pounds of dynamite.
set on/upon _____ *attack*	The citizens set upon the soldiers and beat them badly.
set ___SEP___ out *display*	The store sets out its Christmas items right after Halloween.
set ___SEP___ out *plant*	Don't set your tomatoes out before the last frost.
set to _____ *begin*	Farmers set to plugging the hole in the dike. Engineers set to work on the project.
set _____ to *order to*	My parents set me to vacuuming the dining room.
set ___SEP___ up *arrange*	Let's set a meeting up with the committee chairpersons.
set ___SEP___ up *build, erect*	Gerry set up a miniature railroad in the living room.
set ___SEP___ up *found, establish*	Our group set up a web-based discussion forum.
set ___SEP___ up *raise to power / a higher position / etc.*	Adolf Hitler set himself up as dictator.
set ___SEP___ up *prepare for use*	She set her mom's computer up to do e-mail.
set ___SEP___ up *make [someone] the target of a joke/deception*	They set me up on April Fool's Day, and I fell for it.
set ___SEP___ up with *arrange a date for [someone] with*	Would you set me up with your roommate?

PRESENT

I set	we set
you set	you set
he/she/it sets	they set

• *The auctioneer sets a minimum bid.*

PAST

I set	we set
you set	you set
he/she/it set	they set

• *I set my chair next to the window.*

PRESENT PERFECT ... have | has set
PAST PERFECT ... had set

PRESENT PROGRESSIVE

I am setting	we are setting
you are setting	you are setting
he/she/it is setting	they are setting

• *I am setting the alarm for 6 A.M.*

PAST PROGRESSIVE

I was setting	we were setting
you were setting	you were setting
he/she/it was setting	they were setting

• *We were setting a new direction for the company.*

FUTURE ... will set
FUTURE PROGRESSIVE ... will be setting
FUTURE PERFECT ... will have set

PAST PASSIVE

I was set	we were set
you were set	you were set
he/she/it was set	they were set

• *The couch was set in front of the TV screen.*

COMPLEMENTS

set *sink below the horizon*	The sun will set at 6:43 tonight. The moon was just setting below the trees in the west. Orion was setting behind the snowy hills.
set *become solid/rigid*	The chocolate mousse never set properly. The cement in the patio was setting nicely. Be careful. The glue sets in just a few seconds.
set _____ *put, lay* OBJECT + ADVERB OF PLACE	The hunters set **their guns** *against the fence.* I set **my foot** *on the bottom rung of the ladder.* She set **the novel** *in postwar Canada.*
PASSIVE	The house was set *well back from the road.* The movie was set *in Los Angeles.* The album had been set *on a shelf in the living room.*
set _____ *arrange, adjust* OBJECT	The doctor set **my dislocated shoulder.** I have set **the clock** for daylight saving time. I set **the volume on the radio** way too high. Last winter, we set **the thermostat** at 62 degrees.
PASSIVE	His face was set in a permanent scowl.
set _____ *establish, fix* OBJECT	The track team set **a record for the 400-meter relay.** The Hunt brothers tried to set **the price of silver.** Sarah and Lucas have set **the date of their wedding.** Graham sets **a good example for the other children.** The real estate agent set **the price of our house** at $235,000. We set **a fund-raising goal of $200.**
set _____ *cause to be in a certain state/condition* OBJECT + PREDICATE ADJECTIVE	Lincoln set **the slaves** *free.* Grandpa always set **the dogs** *loose* after breakfast.
OBJECT + *to* PRESENT PARTICIPLE	The speech set **us** *to thinking about harnessing the sun's energy.*

PRESENT

I sew	we sew
you sew	you sew
he/she/it sews	they sew

• *We sew only sports jerseys here.*

PAST

I sewed	we sewed
you sewed	you sewed
he/she/it sewed	they sewed

• *You sewed the pocket on upside down!*

PRESENT PERFECT ... have | has sewn
PAST PERFECT ... had sewn

PRESENT PROGRESSIVE

I am sewing	we are sewing
you are sewing	you are sewing
he/she/it is sewing	they are sewing

• *He is sewing his own Halloween costume.*

PAST PROGRESSIVE

I was sewing	we were sewing
you were sewing	you were sewing
he/she/it was sewing	they were sewing

• *I was sewing a baby blanket for charity.*

FUTURE ... will sew
FUTURE PROGRESSIVE ... will be sewing
FUTURE PERFECT ... will have sewn

PAST PASSIVE

— —
— —
it was sewn they were sewn

• *All clothes by this company were sewn in the United States.*

___

COMPLEMENTS

sew *stitch together a garment, etc.*

Don't bother Mom—she's sewing.
Aunt Rosie sews in her spare time.

sew _____ *stitch together, fasten with stitches*

OBJECT

The seamstress can sew **a jacket** in a single day.
Our neighbor sews **quilts** for a living.

PASSIVE

The costumes have already been sewn for the play.

OBJECT + PAST PARTICIPLE

An assistant will sew **the incision** *closed*.

PASSIVE

The pockets were sewn *shut*.

INDIRECT OBJECT + DIRECT OBJECT

My sister is sewing *me* **a pair of pajamas**.
Birds sewed *Cinderella* **a gown to wear to the ball**.

for PARAPHRASE

My sister is sewing **a pair of pajamas** *for me*.
Birds sewed **a gown** *for Cinderella* to wear to the ball.

___

PHRASAL VERBS

sew <u>SEP</u> **on** *attach with stitches*

Will you please sew this button on?
I sewed the merit badges on for you.

sew <u>SEP</u> **up** *stitch together*

The intern sewed the surgical patient up.

sew <u>SEP</u> **up** *conclude [a deal, a discussion]*

Players sewed contract talks up with owners on Friday.
We can sew up the entire deal by noon.

I shake   we shake
you shake   you shake
he/she/it shakes   they shake

• *The windows shake when it's windy.*

PAST

I shook   we shook
you shook   you shook
he/she/it shook   they shook

• *I shook the umbrella before I closed it.*

PRESENT PERFECT ... have | has shaken
PAST PERFECT   ... had shaken

PRESENT PROGRESSIVE

I am shaking   we are shaking
you are shaking   you are shaking
he/she/it is shaking   they are shaking

• *My hands are shaking.*

PAST PROGRESSIVE

I was shaking   we were shaking
you were shaking   you were shaking
he/she/it was shaking   they were shaking

• *He was shaking his head in disbelief.*

FUTURE   ... will shake
FUTURE PROGRESSIVE ... will be shaking
FUTURE PERFECT   ... will have shaken

PAST PASSIVE

I was shaken   we were shaken
you were shaken   you were shaken
he/she/it was shaken   they were shaken

• *Everyone was badly shaken by the earthquake.*

COMPLEMENTS

shake *tremble, vibrate*

His voice shakes whenever he gets excited.
The floor shakes whenever a train goes by.
My legs were beginning to shake from the strain of lifting
the box.

shake _____ *cause to move quickly up and down / back and forth / from side to side*

OBJECT

The cat is shaking **its toy mouse** furiously.
I shook **David** by the shoulder to wake him up.
I shook **my head** vigorously, trying to get him to stop talking.
We shook **the rugs** and put them back on the floor.
They shook **hands** and smiled for the camera.
Shake **the dressing** well before using.

shake _____ *shock, surprise, upset*

OBJECT

The news about the accident shook **us all** badly.
The sudden increase in oil prices shook **the financial markets**.
Her daughter's death shook **her religious faith**.

PASSIVE

She was visibly shaken when she returned.

PHRASAL VERBS

shake _SEP_ **down/off/out/up/etc.**
*cause to move quickly in a specified
direction*

The gardener shook the apples down.
Tip Top stood up and shook the dust off.

shake _SEP_ **down** *get money from
by using threats*

The politician shook down corporations for campaign
contributions.

shake _SEP_ **off** *get away from*

The car thief was unable to shake the police off.

shake _SEP_ **off** *get rid of*

It took me a week to shake off a cold.

shake _SEP_ **out** *clean by shaking*

We put fresh sheets on the bed and shook out the blankets.

shake _SEP_ **out** *straighten by
shaking*

Lydia shook the shirts out before hanging them up.

shake _SEP_ **up** *mix by shaking*

I shook the salad dressing up before opening the bottle.

shake _SEP_ **up** *change greatly*

The new department head shook up the staff with a round
of hiring and firing.

shave

shave | shaves · shaved · have shaved
shave | shaves · shaved · have shaven

☑ REGULAR
☑ IRREGULAR

PRESENT

I shave	we shave
you shave	you shave
he/she/it shaves	they shave

• *He shaves every morning.*

PRESENT PROGRESSIVE

I am shaving	we are shaving
you are shaving	you are shaving
he/she/it is shaving	they are shaving

• *Can you get the phone? I'm shaving.*

PAST

I shaved	we shaved
you shaved	you shaved
he/she/it shaved	they shaved

• *We shaved some soap to get thin flakes.*

PAST PROGRESSIVE

I was shaving	we were shaving
you were shaving	you were shaving
he/she/it was shaving	they were shaving

• *He was shaving by the time he was 16.*

PRESENT PERFECT ... have | has shaven
PAST PERFECT ... had shaven

FUTURE ... will shave
FUTURE PROGRESSIVE ... will be shaving
FUTURE PERFECT ... will have shaven

PAST PASSIVE

I was shaven	we were shaven
you were shaven	you were shaven
he/she/it was shaven	they were shaven

• *His head was shaven every few days.*

COMPLEMENTS

shave cut off one's beard

I need to shave.
Richard Nixon had such a heavy beard that he shaved twice a day.
When was the last time you shaved?

shave _____ cut off the hair of with a razor

OBJECT

Before the surgery, a nurse shaved **my back**.
Most women shave **their legs**.
Competitive swimmers shave **their whole bodies**.

PASSIVE

Before the makeup could be applied, his head was shaven.

shave _____ cut a thin slice from

OBJECT

We shaved **dark chocolate** to get chocolate curls.
Shave **the cheese** as thin as you can.

PASSIVE

Thin slices of prosciutto were shaven for the appetizers.

shave _____ reduce slightly

OBJECT

We have to shave **our prices** to remain competitive.
The factory shaved **costs** by turning the heat down five degrees.
The store shaved **ten cents** off the regular price.
The injury shaved **the odds of our winning**.

PASSIVE

A few seconds were shaven from the old record.

PHRASAL VERBS

shave _SEP_ **off** cut [from]

He shaved off a little sliver from the edge
of the table with a plane.

PRESENT

I shear	we shear
you shear	you shear
he/she/it shears	they shear

• *He always shears the sheep himself.*

PRESENT PROGRESSIVE

I am shearing	we are shearing
you are shearing	you are shearing
he/she/it is shearing	they are shearing

• *We are shearing all this week.*

PAST

I sheared	we sheared
you sheared	you sheared
he/she/it sheared	they sheared

• *He sheared the rough edges off.*

PAST PROGRESSIVE

I was shearing	we were shearing
you were shearing	you were shearing
he/she/it was shearing	they were shearing

• *She was shearing the plants almost to the ground.*

PRESENT PERFECT   ... have | has shorn
PAST PERFECT   ... had shorn

FUTURE   ... will shear
FUTURE PROGRESSIVE   ... will be shearing
FUTURE PERFECT   ... will have shorn

PAST PASSIVE

I was shorn	we were shorn
you were shorn	you were shorn
he/she/it was shorn	they were shorn

• *The sheep were shorn last week.*

COMPLEMENTS

shear *remove fleece from sheep*

Nobody can shear all day long without getting exhausted.
Are we going to shear tomorrow?
We will shear until it gets too dark.

shear *break off under stress*
[OFTEN WITH *off*]

The wing sheared off in the crash.
A bolt sheared when we put too much weight on the press.

shear _____ *remove [hair, wool, grass, etc.] by cutting/chopping*

OBJECT

An army barber sheared **my hair** the day I was inducted.
Very few ranches shear **their own sheep** these days.
They shear **the putting greens** to about half an inch.

PASSIVE

After the sheep have been shorn, the wool is weighed.

shear _____ *break off by cutting through* [OFTEN WITH *off*]

OBJECT

The SUV swerved and sheared **a utility pole** off.

PASSIVE

The roof of the truck was shorn off in the collision.

shear _____ *deprive*

OBJECT + *of* OBJECT

Rebels have shorn **the dictator** *of power*.
A hospital gown sheared **me** *of all dignity*.

PASSIVE

I was shorn *of all my money* in the poker game.

PRESENT

PRESENT

I shed	we shed
you shed	you shed
he/she/it sheds	they shed

• *The tree sheds its leaves all over the patio.*

PAST

I shed	we shed
you shed	you shed
he/she/it shed	they shed

• *The cats shed all over my black sweater.*

PRESENT PERFECT ... have | has shed
PAST PERFECT ... had shed

PRESENT PROGRESSIVE

I am shedding	we are shedding
you are shedding	you are shedding
he/she/it is shedding	they are shedding

• *They are shedding their distrust of modern ways.*

PAST PROGRESSIVE

I was shedding	we were shedding
you were shedding	you were shedding
he/she/it was shedding	they were shedding

• *The dogs were shedding as the days grew longer.*

FUTURE ... will shed
FUTURE PROGRESSIVE ... will be shedding
FUTURE PERFECT ... will have shed

PAST PASSIVE

I was shed	we were shed
you were shed	you were shed
he/she/it was shed	they were shed

• *Our coats were shed as soon as we stepped onto the plane.*

COMPLEMENTS

shed *cast off / lose fur/skin/leaves naturally*

My dog sheds in the spring and autumn.
Most reptiles shed whenever they get too big for their old skin.
Most trees in temperate latitudes shed annually.

shed _____ *cast off / lose [fur/skin/leaves] naturally*

OBJECT

Most long-haired dogs shed **a lot of fur** in the spring.
All snakes shed **their skins**.
Most shade trees shed **their leaves**.

PASSIVE

Cat hair had been shed all over the rug.

shed _____ *take off, get rid of*

OBJECT

The kids shed **their clothes** and put on their bathing suits.
I hope to shed **about ten pounds** this year.
Many people never shed **their fear of public speaking**.
You will have to shed **some of your low-performing stocks**.

PASSIVE

Their fear of foreign travel has never really been shed.

shed _____ *cause to flow/drain/slough off*

OBJECT

My new jacket sheds **water** pretty well.
Our tent didn't seem to shed **a drop of water**.
The roof is steep enough to shed **snow**.

shed _____ *let flow*

OBJECT

We shed **many tears** over her death.
The soldier shed **a lot of blood** before a tourniquet was applied.

EXPRESSIONS

shed crocodile tears *pretend that one is crying*

The banks were shedding crocodile tears
for depositors who lost money.

PRESENT

I shine	we shine
you shine	you shine
he/she/it shines	they shine

• *The sun always shines in Arizona.*

PRESENT PROGRESSIVE

I am shining	we are shining
you are shining	you are shining
he/she/it is shining	they are shining

• *A light is shining in the window.*

PAST

I shone	we shone
you shone	you shone
he/she/it shone	they shone

• *He shone the light right into our eyes.*

PAST PROGRESSIVE

I was shining	we were shining
you were shining	you were shining
he/she/it was shining	they were shining

• *Their eyes were shining with excitement.*

PRESENT PERFECT ... have | has shone
PAST PERFECT ... had shone

FUTURE ... will shine
FUTURE PROGRESSIVE ... will be shining
FUTURE PERFECT ... will have shone

PAST PASSIVE

—	—
—	—
it was shone	they were shone

• *The spotlight was shone on the escaping prisoners.*

COMPLEMENTS

NOTE: The irregular form *shone* is used both with and without an object, except in the sense "make bright by polishing"; the regular form *shined* is used only with an object.

shine *give off / reflect light, be bright*

The stars were shining brightly.
The jewels shone in the display case.
The sun, reflecting from the glass building, shone in our eyes.
Their swords and spears shone in the moonlight.
The princess's hair shone like gold.
The lighthouse shone through the mist, guiding us to port.

shine *have a bright appearance*

Fred's face was shining with joy as he ran to meet Rosemary.

shine *do very well*

Melissa shines in social studies.

shine _____ *cause to give off light*

OBJECT + ADVERB OF PLACE TO/FROM

The guide shone **his flashlight** *into the back of the tomb.*
The policeman is shining **his headlights** *on the abandoned car.*
The newspaper shone **light** *on corruption at City Hall.*

PASSIVE

Bright lights were shone *on the prisoners' faces* all night long.

shine _____ *make bright by polishing*

OBJECT

The jeweler shined **the gem** until it sparkled.
I shined **my shoes** carefully before the interview.

PHRASAL VERBS

shine down/in/out/up/etc.
give off light in a specified direction

The sun shone down on us as we walked along the beach.

shine _____ **down/in/out/up**/etc.
cause to give off light in a specified direction

Shine the flashlight up a little higher.

shine through *be clearly shown*

Her personality really shines through in her photography.

shoe   shoe | shoes · shod · have shod
shoe | shoes · shoed · have shoed

☑ IRREGULAR
☑ REGULAR

PRESENT

I shoe	we shoe
you shoe	you shoe
he/she/it shoes	they shoe

• *He only shoes horses on the weekends.*

PAST

I shod	we shod
you shod	you shod
he/she/it shod	they shod

• *I shod their horses last fall.*

PRESENT PERFECT ... have | has shod
PAST PERFECT ... had shod

PRESENT PROGRESSIVE

I am shoeing	we are shoeing
you are shoeing	you are shoeing
he/she/it is shoeing	they are shoeing

• *The blacksmith is shoeing horses this afternoon.*

PAST PROGRESSIVE

I was shoeing	we were shoeing
you were shoeing	you were shoeing
he/she/it was shoeing	they were shoeing

• *People were shoeing horses in the Middle Ages.*

FUTURE ... will shoe
FUTURE PROGRESSIVE ... will be shoeing
FUTURE PERFECT ... will have shod

PAST PASSIVE

—	—
—	—
it was shod	they were shod

• *Racehorses were often shod with aluminum shoes.*

COMPLEMENTS

shoe _____ *attach protective shoes to the hooves of*

OBJECT — Horse owners must shoe **their horses** regularly.
A professional blacksmith usually shoes **horses.**

PASSIVE — Your horses should be shod professionally.

shoe _____ *furnish/fit with footwear* [ONLY IN THE PASSIVE]

PASSIVE — In Hawaii, most kids are shod only in flip-flops.
The peasant children were shod in flimsy leather moccasins.

PRESENT

I shoot	we shoot
you shoot	you shoot
he/she/it shoots	they shoot

• *MacInnis shoots and scores!*

PRESENT PROGRESSIVE

I am shooting	we are shooting
you are shooting	you are shooting
he/she/it is shooting	they are shooting

• *The guards are shooting from the perimeter.*

PAST

I shot	we shot
you shot	you shot
he/she/it shot	they shot

• *They shot several deer this fall.*

PAST PROGRESSIVE

I was shooting	we were shooting
you were shooting	you were shooting
he/she/it was shooting	they were shooting

• *They were shooting the scene in our neighborhood.*

PRESENT PERFECT ... have | has shot
PAST PERFECT ... had shot

FUTURE ... will shoot
FUTURE PROGRESSIVE ... will be shooting
FUTURE PERFECT ... will have shot

PAST PASSIVE

I was shot	we were shot
you were shot	you were shot
he/she/it was shot	they were shot

• Up in the Air *was shot in St. Louis.*

(COMPLEMENTS)

shoot *fire a weapon*	The police were ordered to shoot if necessary.
	I picked up the bow and shot.
shoot *hit/kick/throw/strike a ball/ puck toward a goal*	James shoots from the baseline. [BASKETBALL]
	Beckham shoots from just outside the penalty area. [SOCCER]
	Pronger shoots under the goalie's glove. [HOCKEY]
shoot *make a photograph/film*	Just point the camera and shoot.
	The crew is shooting in Las Vegas.
shoot _____ *fire [a gun]*	
OBJECT	Can you shoot **a rifle**?
	Revelers shot **pistols** into the air on New Year's Eve.
shoot _____ *strike with a bullet/arrow*	
OBJECT	An unknown assailant shot **three people**.
	We were shooting **tin cans** behind the barn.
PASSIVE	Somebody has been shot.
WH-CLAUSE	You can only shoot **what is in season**.
	Shoot **whatever moves**.
shoot _____ *photograph, film*	
OBJECT	We want to shoot **the boats in the harbor**.
	They were shooting **a video of the parade**.
PASSIVE	The dream sequence was shot in black and white.
shoot _____ *move very quickly*	
ADVERB OF PLACE TO/FROM	The car shot **through the intersection**.
	The song shot **straight to the top of the charts**.

(PHRASAL VERBS)

shoot away/down/in/off/out/ over/up/etc. *move very quickly in a specified direction*	The motorcycle shot away when the light turned green.
shoot for _____ *have as a goal*	Eli is shooting for a Ph.D. in environmental sciences.
shoot up *grow quickly*	The daffodils shot up overnight.
	Yu-chan is really shooting up.

128 **show** show | shows · showed · have shown
show | shows · showed · have showed
☑ IRREGULAR
☑ REGULAR

PHRASAL VERBS

show _SEP_ **around/away/down/in/out/up**/etc. _lead/guide in a specified direction_	Sam was showing the White House visitors around.
	A guide showed us down to the cafeteria.
show _SEP_ **off** _display, exhibit_	The bride-to-be showed off her wedding gown.
show off _do something to attract attention_	Ronny was always showing off in front of the girls.
show up _arrive_	Ozzie showed up just in time for dinner.
show up _appear_	The Republican ratings show up as the red line on your screen.
show up _be easily seen_	His thinning hair really shows up in this photo.
show _SEP_ **up** _outmatch, humble_	Fred showed everybody up at the math contest.

EXPRESSIONS

show [one's] face _make an appearance_	I wonder if Todd will show his face at the party tonight.
show [one's] hand _reveal one's intentions_	He never showed his hand while discussing free trade.
show [one's] teeth _act in a threatening manner_	Boyd showed his teeth whenever someone criticized his girlfriend.
show signs of _____ _give indications of_	The patient shows signs of bipolar disorder.
	The student is showing signs of fatigue.
show [someone] the ropes _show [someone] how to do something_	Don't worry; the secretary who's retiring will show you the ropes.
show [one's] true colors _show what one is really like_	The boss showed his true colors when he laughed about firing three employees right before Christmas.

PRESENT

I show	we show
you show	you show
he/she/it shows	they show

• *The picture shows a vase of sunflowers.*

PRESENT PROGRESSIVE

I am showing	we are showing
you are showing	you are showing
he/she/it is showing	they are showing

• *I am showing some friends around the garden.*

PAST

I showed	we showed
you showed	you showed
he/she/it showed	they showed

• *He showed no emotion as he spoke.*

PAST PROGRESSIVE

I was showing	we were showing
you were showing	you were showing
he/she/it was showing	they were showing

• *The movie was showing at a theater downtown.*

PRESENT PERFECT   ... have | has shown
PAST PERFECT   ... had shown

FUTURE   ... will show
FUTURE PROGRESSIVE   ... will be showing
FUTURE PERFECT   ... will have shown

PAST PASSIVE

I was shown	we were shown
you were shown	you were shown
he/she/it was shown	they were shown

• *The theory was shown to be seriously flawed.*

COMPLEMENTS

show *be visible/present/presented/displayed*

The house's age is obviously showing.
The buds are just beginning to show.
Nothing showed on the X-rays.
The wine stain doesn't show.
Our visitors never showed.
When is the movie showing?
He never lets his feelings show.

show ＿＿＿ *lead, guide*

OBJECT + ADVERB OF PLACE TO/FROM

May I show **you** *to your seats*, ladies?
The receptionist will show **us** *to the conference room*.

show ＿＿＿ *display*

OBJECT

You must show **your ID card** before you can enter.
The car showed **signs of having been in an accident**.

PASSIVE

Her paintings have been shown all over the world.

INDIRECT OBJECT + DIRECT OBJECT

Show *me* **the money**.
The realtor showed *some prospective buyers* **the house**.
They always showed *their employees* **real consideration**.

to PARAPHRASE

Show **the money** *to me*.
The realtor showed **the house** *to some prospective buyers*.
They always showed **real consideration** *to their employees*.

show ＿＿＿ *demonstrate*

OBJECT + INFINITIVE

John showed **himself** *to be an excellent landscaper*.
The map showed **the city** *to be smaller than we had been told*.

PASSIVE

The results were shown *to be faked*.

(OBJECT +) THAT-CLAUSE

The concert shows **that Louise has made enormous progress.**
We showed *them* **that we were fully prepared to do the job.**

(OBJECT +) WH-CLAUSE

The X-ray showed **what had happened.**
Janet showed *me* **how much we could save on insurance.**

(OBJECT +) WH-INFINITIVE

The chart showed **how much to invest.**
The manual shows *you* **what to do.**
Lou will show *them* **where to park.**

shrink shrink | shrinks · shrank · have shrunk ☑ IRREGULAR

PRESENT

I shrink	we shrink
you shrink	you shrink
he/she/it shrinks	they shrink

• *Wool shrinks if washed in hot water.*

PRESENT PROGRESSIVE

I am shrinking	we are shrinking
you are shrinking	you are shrinking
he/she/it is shrinking	they are shrinking

• *Our margin of error is shrinking.*

PAST

I shrank	we shrank
you shrank	you shrank
he/she/it shrank	they shrank

• *The architect shrank the house by a third.*

PAST PROGRESSIVE

I was shrinking	we were shrinking
you were shrinking	you were shrinking
he/she/it was shrinking	they were shrinking

• *The laundry was always shrinking my shirts.*

PRESENT PERFECT ... have | has shrunk
PAST PERFECT ... had shrunk

FUTURE ... will shrink
FUTURE PROGRESSIVE ... will be shrinking
FUTURE PERFECT ... will have shrunk

PAST PASSIVE

I was shrunk	we were shrunk
you were shrunk	you were shrunk
he/she/it was shrunk	they were shrunk

• *The deficit was shrunk significantly in the third quarter.*

COMPLEMENTS

shrink *become smaller*

Hot metal shrinks as it cools.
Our budget is shrinking by the minute.
Average take-home pay has shrunk over the last five years.
Arctic sea ice is shrinking more every summer.
My waist has shrunk a bit, thanks to my diet.

shrink ____ *cause to become smaller*

OBJECT

He shrank **the wool sweaters** by using water that was
too hot.
We waterproofed the wet barrels by shrinking **them**
in the sun.
We are trying to shrink **our inventory of unsold goods**.

PASSIVE

Our profits have been shrunk by rising costs.

shrink ____ *try to avoid*

from OBJECT

Most actors don't shrink **from the limelight**.
The president does not shrink **from his role as
commander-in-chief**.

from PRESENT PARTICIPLE

Reggie won't shrink **from telling the truth on the witness
stand**.
Scientists don't shrink **from examining all the data**.

PHRASAL VERBS

shrink away/back (from ____)
draw back (from [someone/something]),
as in fear

The children shrank away from the
homeless man.
The cats shrank back at the sight of the dogs.

PRESENT

I shut	we shut
you shut	you shut
he/she/it shuts	they shut

• *Sandy shuts the store by 8 P.M.*

PRESENT PROGRESSIVE

I am shutting	we are shutting
you are shutting	you are shutting
he/she/it is shutting	they are shutting

• *Hurry! The ushers are shutting the doors.*

PAST

I shut	we shut
you shut	you shut
he/she/it shut	they shut

• *He shut himself in his office.*

PAST PROGRESSIVE

I was shutting	we were shutting
you were shutting	you were shutting
he/she/it was shutting	they were shutting

• *The highway patrol was shutting the roads.*

PRESENT PERFECT ... have | has shut
PAST PERFECT   ... had shut

FUTURE   ... will shut
FUTURE PROGRESSIVE ... will be shutting
FUTURE PERFECT   ... will have shut

PAST PASSIVE

I was shut	we were shut
you were shut	you were shut
he/she/it was shut	they were shut

• *The gates were shut by the guard.*

COMPLEMENTS

shut *close*

The door is shutting behind him.
The gate shut with a loud crash.
My eyes slowly shut and I fell asleep.
The lid shut on my fingers.
We heard the trap shut with a snap.
All government offices shut at five.

shut _____ *cause to close*

OBJECT

I shut **the windows** and drew the curtains.
President Roosevelt shut **all the banks** temporarily to prevent failures.
He shut **the book** and returned it to the shelf.
The Navy is going to shut **the entire shipyard**.
Once inside, I shut **the umbrella**.

PASSIVE

The entrance was shut after the last worker arrived.

shut _____ *confine, pen*

OBJECT + ADVERB OF PLACE

We always shut **the animals** *in the barn* at night.
The blockade shut **the enemy fleet** *inside the port*.

PASSIVE

The prisoners were shut *inside a makeshift jail*.

PHRASAL VERBS

shut _SEP_ **down** *close permanently*

Producers shut the play down after only 10 performances.
The car manufacturer shut down three automotive plants.

shut _SEP_ **in** *surround, enclose*

The cowboys shut the cattle in.

shut off *stop operating*

The motor shut off 15 minutes ago.

shut _SEP_ **off** *turn off*

They shut off the gas before leaving on vacation.

shut _SEP_ **off** *stop movement into and out of*

Police shut the street off during the standoff.
Authorities shut off the downtown area because of a bomb threat.

shut _SEP_ **out** *exclude*

The manager shut us out of the decision making.

shut up *stop talking* [INFORMAL]

Would you shut up and listen to me?

shut _SEP_ **up** *lock up*

Guards shut the prisoners up in their cells.

PRESENT

I sing	we sing
you sing	you sing
he/she/it sings	they sing

• *He sings in the church choir.*

PRESENT PROGRESSIVE

I am singing	we are singing
you are singing	you are singing
he/she/it is singing	they are singing

• *The birds are singing in the trees.*

PAST

I sang	we sang
you sang	you sang
he/she/it sang	they sang

• *She sang several songs by Bellini.*

PAST PROGRESSIVE

I was singing	we were singing
you were singing	you were singing
he/she/it was singing	they were singing

• *The group was singing around the campfire.*

PRESENT PERFECT ... have | has sung
PAST PERFECT ... had sung

FUTURE ... will sing
FUTURE PROGRESSIVE ... will be singing
FUTURE PERFECT ... will have sung

PAST PASSIVE

—	—
—	—
it was sung	they were sung

• *The opera was sung in English.*

(**COMPLEMENTS**)

sing *make musical sounds with one's voice*	Do you like to sing? Everybody can learn to sing. She sings beautifully. Jeff sang at his and Susan's wedding. The birds are already singing by 5:30.
sing *make musical sounds, hum, buzz, whistle*	The engine's vibration was making some metal part sing. The telephone wires were singing in the wind. The teakettle began to sing.
sing _____ *perform [a piece of vocal music]*	
OBJECT	The choir sang **several traditional Christmas carols**. The Beatles sang **their own compositions**. Herbie sang **1960s hits** at the class reunion.
PASSIVE	The national anthem is sung before every baseball game.

(**PHRASAL VERBS**)

sing along *sing together*	Everyone at the party sang along with the music.

(**EXPRESSIONS**)

sing a different tune *have changed one's opinion*	He used to favor the death penalty; now he's singing a different tune.
sing [someone's] praises *say good things about [someone]*	Your English teacher is singing your praises.
sing the praises of _____ *say good things about [someone/something]*	The whole office is singing the praises of the new copier.
sing _____ **to sleep** *put to sleep by singing*	The babysitter was able to sing the baby to sleep.

PRESENT

I sink	we sink
you sink	you sink
he/she/it sinks	they sink

- *Productivity sinks in the summer.*

PRESENT PROGRESSIVE

I am sinking	we are sinking
you are sinking	you are sinking
he/she/it is sinking	they are sinking

- *Oil production is gradually sinking.*

PAST

I sank	we sank
you sank	you sank
he/she/it sank	they sank

- *The stock market sank again today.*

PAST PROGRESSIVE

I was sinking	we were sinking
you were sinking	you were sinking
he/she/it was sinking	they were sinking

- *Our spirits were sinking by the minute.*

PRESENT PERFECT	... have	has sunk
PAST PERFECT	... had sunk

FUTURE	... will sink
FUTURE PROGRESSIVE	... will be sinking
FUTURE PERFECT	... will have sunk

PAST PASSIVE

I was sunk	we were sunk
you were sunk	you were sunk
he/she/it was sunk	they were sunk

- *The boat was sunk in 50 feet of water.*

(**COMPLEMENTS**)

sink *go below the surface*	The ship sank in less than an hour. My boots were sinking in the soft mud. The wheels sank into the snowdrift.
sink *go down gradually*	The hot air balloon was sinking to the earth. Tired and hungry, the travelers sank to their knees. The sun was sinking in the west. The temperature sank as night fell. Senator Blather's poll numbers were steadily sinking. The value of our portfolio has sunk by 20%.
sink *become weaker*	My heart sank when I heard the bad news. The patient in Room 413 is sinking rapidly, Doctor.
sink _____ *cause to go below the surface*	
OBJECT	An explosion in the engine room sank **the fishing boat**. I sank **a shovel** into the wet ground.
PASSIVE	The barges were sunk by the storm.
OBJECT + ADVERB OF PLACE TO/FROM	We sank **the screws** *into the wood*. The dog sank **its teeth** *into my leg*.
PASSIVE	The steel supports were sunk *in five feet of concrete*.
sink _____ *go gradually [into a certain state/condition]*	
into OBJECT	The family sank **into poverty**. The once-proud company sank **into oblivion**. His widow and orphans sank **into despair**.
sink _____ *ruin*	
OBJECT	These awful rumors could sink **the company**. The defeat sank **all our hopes for the championship**.
PASSIVE	The plans for expansion were sunk by the economic downturn.

(**PHRASAL VERBS**)

sink back *lean back and relax*	After work, I poured a drink and sank back on the sofa.
sink in *be understood*	Has Trina's desperate situation sunk in yet? The teacher's explanation will sink in eventually.

PRESENT

I sit	we sit
you sit	you sit
he/she/it sits	they sit

• *The cat always sits by the window.*

PRESENT PROGRESSIVE

I am sitting	we are sitting
you are sitting	you are sitting
he/she/it is sitting	they are sitting

• *I'm just sitting here, waiting for somebody.*

PAST

I sat	we sat
you sat	you sat
he/she/it sat	they sat

• *We sat on a park bench in the sun.*

PAST PROGRESSIVE

I was sitting	we were sitting
you were sitting	you were sitting
he/she/it was sitting	they were sitting

• *We were sitting by the fireplace.*

PRESENT PERFECT ... have | has sat
PAST PERFECT ... had sat

FUTURE ... will sit
FUTURE PROGRESSIVE ... will be sitting
FUTURE PERFECT ... will have sat

PAST PASSIVE

Sit is rarely used in the passive voice.

COMPLEMENTS

sit *be seated*
Never stand when you can sit.
The plane can't take off until you sit and fasten your seat belt.
I can't sit very long before my legs start to hurt.
We trained the dog to sit on command.

sit *be in session, meet*
[OF A GOVERNMENTAL BODY]
By law, the Supreme Court sits on the first Monday in October.
The budget committee is sitting this afternoon.
The state legislature does not normally sit during the summer.

sit ___ *be seated/located*
ADVERB OF PLACE
I sat **next to him** at dinner.
The flock of birds sat **on a telephone wire**.
We are sitting **on the runway**, waiting to take off.
The statue sits **in the center of the town square**.
When I got to the office, a new computer was sitting **on my desk**.
My briefcase was sitting **by the chair**, right where I had left it.

sit ___ *have enough seats for*
OBJECT
Our dining room table sits **eight**.

PHRASAL VERBS

sit around *spend time idly*
We're just sitting around listening to music.

sit back *relax*
We sat back and enjoyed the show.

sit back/by *not be involved*
I refuse to sit back and do nothing when their lives are in danger.

sit SEP **down** *cause to be in a sitting position*
Momma sat us kids down and told us that Grandma had died.

sit in for ___ *replace*
The sports editor sat in for the regular news anchor last night.

sit in (on ___) *attend ([an event])*
The board meeting is tomorrow morning, and I'd like to sit in.
Would it be okay if I sat in on your Language and Culture class?

sit on ___ *be a member of*
She sat on the jury that convicted my neighbor.
Senator Blather sits on the Committee on Appropriations.

sit on ___ *delay in revealing*
The reporter is sitting on a story about the president's health.

sit SEP **out** *not participate in*
I'm going to sit this dance out.

sit through ___ *attend all of*
Do we have to sit through another boring lecture?

sit up *sit upright*
Sit up! Slouching is bad for your posture.

sit up *not go to bed*
Kristen sat up knitting half the night.

sit up *become suddenly alert*
Cassie sat up suddenly and looked at the door.

PRESENT

I slay	we slay
you slay	you slay
he/she/it slays	they slay

• *His jokes always slay me.*

PRESENT PROGRESSIVE

I am slaying	we are slaying
you are slaying	you are slaying
he/she/it is slaying	they are slaying

• *Storm troopers are slaying the town's inhabitants.*

PAST

I slew	we slew
you slew	you slew
he/she/it slew	they slew

• *The killer slew his victim in cold blood.*

PAST PROGRESSIVE

I was slaying	we were slaying
you were slaying	you were slaying
he/she/it was slaying	they were slaying

• *My brother was slaying dragons in a video game.*

PRESENT PERFECT ... have | has slain
PAST PERFECT ... had slain

FUTURE ... will slay
FUTURE PROGRESSIVE ... will be slaying
FUTURE PERFECT ... will have slain

PAST PASSIVE

I was slain	we were slain
you were slain	you were slain
he/she/it was slain	they were slain

• *Hundreds of soldiers were slain in the attack.*

(**COMPLEMENTS**)

NOTE: In the past tense, *slew* is ordinarily used in the sense "kill violently" and *slayed* is ordinarily used in the sense "amuse immensely."

slay _____ *kill violently*

OBJECT   Some meat processing plants slay **a thousand cows** a day.
Serial killers slay **multiple victims** before they are caught.

PASSIVE   How many people are slain by drunk drivers every year?
The victims were slain in their beds.

slay _____ *amuse immensely*

OBJECT   His comedy act slayed **his audiences**.
You slay **me**, you really do!
He can slay **a crowd** just by looking at them.

I sleep	we sleep
you sleep	you sleep
he/she/it sleeps	they sleep

• *He usually sleeps seven hours a night.*

I am sleeping	we are sleeping
you are sleeping	you are sleeping
he/she/it is sleeping	they are sleeping

• *I am not sleeping very well lately.*

I slept	we slept
you slept	you slept
he/she/it slept	they slept

• *The kids slept in a tent in the backyard.*

I was sleeping	we were sleeping
you were sleeping	you were sleeping
he/she/it was sleeping	they were sleeping

• *Our guests were sleeping in the spare bedroom.*

PRESENT PERFECT ... have | has slept
PAST PERFECT ... had slept

FUTURE ... will sleep
FUTURE PROGRESSIVE ... will be sleeping
FUTURE PERFECT ... will have slept

PAST PASSIVE

Sleep is never used in the passive voice.

COMPLEMENTS

sleep *not be awake*

We all need to sleep.
I slept through the storm.
He only slept a few hours last night.
Be quiet; the baby is sleeping.

sleep *be inactive*

New York never sleeps.
The surveillance system never sleeps.
The security force never sleeps.

sleep _____ *take as a place for sleeping*
ADVERB OF PLACE

The children sleep **in their own bedrooms**.
We usually sleep **at a motel** when we visit my grandparents.
When we go camping, we sleep **in an ultralight tent**.
If I get home late, I sleep **downstairs** so I don't wake anybody.

sleep _____ *provide sleeping accommodations for*
OBJECT

The suite sleeps **four adults** comfortably.
The studio apartments only sleep **two people**.
The lodge will be able to sleep **our entire family**.

PHRASAL VERBS

sleep in *sleep after one's normal time to rise*

Sorry, I slept in this morning.
　What's for lunch?

sleep SEP **off** *recover from while sleeping*

Sherri drank too much at the party and had to sleep it off.

sleep on _____ *delay a decision on*

I'll sleep on the matter and give you an answer tomorrow.

sleep through _____ *be asleep and unaware of*

Our neighbors slept through the thunderstorm.

EXPRESSIONS

sleep a wink *sleep briefly*
[USUALLY NEGATIVE]

I didn't sleep a wink last night.

sleep like a baby/log *sleep long and well*

I played two hours of tennis last evening and slept like
　a log.

PRESENT

I slide	we slide
you slide	you slide
he/she/it slides	they slide

• *The glass door slides easily now.*

PAST

I slid	we slid
you slid	you slid
he/she/it slid	they slid

• *The car slid into the ditch.*

PRESENT PERFECT ... have | has slid
PAST PERFECT ... had slid

PRESENT PROGRESSIVE

I am sliding	we are sliding
you are sliding	you are sliding
he/she/it is sliding	they are sliding

• *Look out! The car is sliding.*

PAST PROGRESSIVE

I was sliding	we were sliding
you were sliding	you were sliding
he/she/it was sliding	they were sliding

• *The kids were sliding down Prosser Hill.*

FUTURE ... will slide
FUTURE PROGRESSIVE ... will be sliding
FUTURE PERFECT ... will have slid

PAST PASSIVE

I was slid	we were slid
you were slid	you were slid
he/she/it was slid	they were slid

• *The logs were slid down the hill.*

COMPLEMENTS

slide *slip, shift, drop*	Hang on to me—I'm sliding. The bag of groceries slid from my hand. Make sure the load doesn't slide.
slide *gradually become worse*	His reputation is beginning to slide. Our once-strong financial position was sliding.
slide _____ *move/glide smoothly over a surface* ADVERB OF PLACE TO/FROM	The car slid **into a snowbank**. I slid **behind the wheel**. The canoes slid **into the water**. The truck in front of us was sliding **all over the road**. The drawer slides **on side-mounted tracks**.
slide _____ *gradually go/move [into a worse condition]* ADVERB OF PLACE TO/FROM	The patient was sliding **into a coma**. The company gradually slid **into mediocrity**. The quality of dental care was sliding **downhill**. The temperature slid **into the twenties** overnight.
slide _____ *put/push/move smoothly* OBJECT + ADVERB OF PLACE TO/FROM	She slid the **keys** *into her purse*. I slid **my hands** gently *under the kitten* and lifted it up. Just slide **your paper** *under my office door*.
PASSIVE	The refrigerator was slid *into place*.
INDIRECT OBJECT + DIRECT OBJECT	The suspect slid *the detective* **his driver's license**. The cook slid **me a bowl of soup**.
to PARAPHRASE	The suspect slid **his driver's license** *to the detective*. The cook slid **a bowl of soup** *to me*.

PHRASAL VERBS

slide around/back/down/off/out/under/ up/etc. *slide in a specified direction*	We slid back down several times. The roofer lost his balance and slid off. The window easily slides up and down.
slide ᴽᴇᴾ **around/back/down/in/off/ out/up/**etc. *cause to slide in a specified direction*	The goalie slid the puck back to a defenseman. The locksmith can't slide the bolt in and out.

PRESENT

I sling	we sling
you sling	you sling
he/she/it slings	they sling

• *He slings mud in every campaign he's in.*

PRESENT PROGRESSIVE

I am slinging	we are slinging
you are slinging	you are slinging
he/she/it is slinging	they are slinging

• *We are slinging a hammock between these trees.*

PAST

I slung	we slung
you slung	you slung
he/she/it slung	they slung

• *He slung a rope over a branch for a swing.*

PAST PROGRESSIVE

I was slinging	we were slinging
you were slinging	you were slinging
he/she/it was slinging	they were slinging

• *They were slinging stones at the attackers.*

PRESENT PERFECT ... have | has slung
PAST PERFECT ... had slung

FUTURE ... will sling
FUTURE PROGRESSIVE ... will be slinging
FUTURE PERFECT ... will have slung

PAST PASSIVE

I was slung	we were slung
you were slung	you were slung
he/she/it was slung	they were slung

• *A blanket was carelessly slung across the door opening.*

COMPLEMENTS

sling _____ *hurl with a swinging motion*

OBJECT + ADVERB OF PLACE TO/FROM — The kids were slinging **rocks** *at the crows in the field.*
David slung **a stone** *at Goliath.*
Fishermen slung **their nets** *over the water.*

PASSIVE — A volley of steel balls was slung *at the attackers.*

sling _____ *place/toss carelessly/quickly*

OBJECT + ADVERB OF PLACE TO/FROM — I slung **a sandwich and some fruit** *into my backpack.*
The waiter slung **some food** *on the table* and walked away.
She slung **her long hair** *back from her face.*

PASSIVE — Our supplies were slung *onto the counter* without a glance from the clerk.

sling _____ *suspend loosely*

OBJECT + ADVERB OF PLACE TO/FROM — They had slung **a wire** *from one tower to the other.*

PASSIVE — A bridge had been slung *across the river far below.*

EXPRESSIONS

sling mud (at _____ **)** *insult, discredit* — The candidates were slinging mud at each other throughout the debate.

PRESENT

I slink	we slink
you slink	you slink
he/she/it slinks	they slink

* *The senator always slinks from controversy.*

PRESENT PROGRESSIVE

I am slinking	we are slinking
you are slinking	you are slinking
he/she/it is slinking	they are slinking

* *My dog is slinking around, looking guilty.*

PAST

I slunk	we slunk
you slunk	you slunk
he/she/it slunk	they slunk

* *He slunk back, embarrassed by his error.*

PAST PROGRESSIVE

I was slinking	we were slinking
you were slinking	you were slinking
he/she/it was slinking	they were slinking

* *A line of dancers was slinking across the stage.*

PRESENT PERFECT   ... have | has slunk
PAST PERFECT   ... had slunk

FUTURE   ... will slink
FUTURE PROGRESSIVE   ... will be slinking
FUTURE PERFECT   ... will have slunk

PAST PASSIVE

Slink is never used in the passive voice.

COMPLEMENTS

slink _____ *move furtively*
   ADVERB OF PLACE TO/FROM   The cat was slinking **closer and closer to the bird.**
                                       The homeless man slunk **from alley to alley.**

slink _____ *move sensuously/provocatively*
   ADVERB OF PLACE TO/FROM   Delilah slunk **toward Sampson.**
                                       The dancers were slinking **around the stage** seductively.
                                       The models slunk **down the runway.**

PHRASAL VERBS

slink around/away/off/out/etc.   A small animal was slinking around
slink in a specified direction   in the dark.
                                       The thief slunk away from the sudden light.
                                       My husband slunk off to a bar when my mother arrived.

PRESENT

I slit	we slit
you slit	you slit
he/she/it slits	they slit

• *He slits letters open with a pocketknife.*

PRESENT PROGRESSIVE

I am slitting	we are slitting
you are slitting	you are slitting
he/she/it is slitting	they are slitting

• *We are slitting the material into thin strips.*

PAST

I slit	we slit
you slit	you slit
he/she/it slit	they slit

• *She slit the tape and opened the package.*

PAST PROGRESSIVE

I was slitting	we were slitting
you were slitting	you were slitting
he/she/it was slitting	they were slitting

• *The staff was slitting the envelopes open.*

PRESENT PERFECT ... have | has slit
PAST PERFECT ... had slit

FUTURE ... will slit
FUTURE PROGRESSIVE ... will be slitting
FUTURE PERFECT ... will have slit

PAST PASSIVE

—	—
—	—
it was slit	they were slit

• *The victim's throat was slit.*

(**COMPLEMENTS**)

slit _____ make a long narrow cut in

OBJECT

Tommy slit **his thumb** on a piece of glass.
A friend of mine slit **her wrists,** but we got her to the emergency room in time.
The workers are slitting **a shallow trench** to lay the cable.

PASSIVE

The birds' throats are slit and then the feathers are removed.

slit _____ cut lengthwise [into strips]

OBJECT + into OBJECT

We slit **the paper** *into two-inch strips* and wrote a name on each.
The prisoner slit **the sheet** *into strips to be fashioned into a rope.*
I slit **the cardboard** *into pieces to be used as spacers.*

PASSIVE

The banana leaves had been slit *into strips.*

PRESENT

I sneak	we sneak
you sneak	you sneak
he/she/it sneaks	they sneak

• *He sneaks a candy bar at bedtime.*

PRESENT PROGRESSIVE

I am sneaking	we are sneaking
you are sneaking	you are sneaking
he/she/it is sneaking	they are sneaking

• *The prisoners are sneaking past the guards.*

PAST

I snuck	we snuck
you snuck	you snuck
he/she/it snuck	they snuck

• *We snuck out of the meeting early.*

PAST PROGRESSIVE

I was sneaking	we were sneaking
you were sneaking	you were sneaking
he/she/it was sneaking	they were sneaking

• *I was sneaking a quick snack in the kitchen.*

PRESENT PERFECT	... have | has snuck
PAST PERFECT	... had snuck

FUTURE	... will sneak
FUTURE PROGRESSIVE	... will be sneaking
FUTURE PERFECT	... will have snuck

PAST PASSIVE

I was snuck	we were snuck
you were snuck	you were snuck
he/she/it was snuck	they were snuck

• *Food was snuck out of the cafeteria.*

COMPLEMENTS

sneak _____ *move quietly and secretly in order not to be noticed*

ADVERB OF PLACE TO/FROM

They were trying to sneak **into the game.**
We had to sneak **back into the dorms** after curfew.
Apparently, the prisoners had snuck **over the wall.**
Someone had snuck **into the coffee room** and eaten
  all the donuts.

sneak _____ *take/bring quietly and secretly in order not to be noticed*

OBJECT + ADVERB OF PLACE TO/FROM

I snuck **a recorder** *into the meeting.*
The kids had snuck **some cookies** *out of the kitchen.*
They had snuck **some friends** *into the hotel pool.*

PASSIVE

Something had been snuck *out of the secure area.*

PHRASAL VERBS

**sneak along/around/away/in/out/
up/etc.** *sneak in a specified direction*

Nobody likes people who sneak around.
The kids snuck away with a bag of candy.

sneak _____ **along/away/in/out/
up/etc.** *sneak [someone/something]
in a specified direction*

I wasn't invited, but my friends snuck me in.

sneak up on _____ *approach quietly
and secretly*

We snuck up on Dad while he was working the crossword
  puzzle.
Sandy snuck up on me and tapped me on the shoulder.

sow | sows · sowed · have sown
sow | sows · sowed · have sowed

☑ IRREGULAR
☑ REGULAR

PRESENT

I sow	we sow
you sow	you sow
he/she/it sows	they sow

• *Few people sow by hand anymore.*

PAST

I sowed	we sowed
you sowed	you sowed
he/she/it sowed	they sowed

• *We sowed wheat and barley this year.*

PRESENT PERFECT ... have | has sown
PAST PERFECT ... had sown

PRESENT PROGRESSIVE

I am sowing	we are sowing
you are sowing	you are sowing
he/she/it is sowing	they are sowing

• *They are sowing rumors about our candidate.*

PAST PROGRESSIVE

I was sowing	we were sowing
you were sowing	you were sowing
he/she/it was sowing	they were sowing

• *The farmers were sowing their fields this week.*

FUTURE ... will sow
FUTURE PROGRESSIVE ... will be sowing
FUTURE PERFECT ... will have sown

PAST PASSIVE

—	—
—	—
it was sown	they were sown

• *Nothing but confusion was sown by the new policy.*

(COMPLEMENTS)

sow *plant seeds to produce a crop*

Farmers sow in straight lines so they can weed between the rows.

sow _____ *plant/scatter (seeds)*

OBJECT

When we sow **seeds** by hand, it is called "broadcasting."
Many farmers in the United States only sow **genetically engineered seeds.**
"A man reaps **what** he sows." [BIBLE]

PASSIVE

When seeds were sown by hand, birds ate half of them.

sow _____ *cause*

OBJECT

Their rigid rules have sown **resentment.**
Agitators sowed **fear** among the townspeople.

PASSIVE

Doubts about his leadership had been sown.

(EXPRESSIONS)

sow [one's] (wild) oats *behave wildly/recklessly in one's youth*

Gary was sowing his wild oats the summer before he started college.

sow the seeds of _____ *set in motion*

Thomas Paine sowed the seeds of the American Revolution.

sow the wind and reap the whirlwind *start trouble that becomes worse than one expected*

"They sow the wind and reap the whirlwind." [BIBLE]

PRESENT

I speak	we speak
you speak	you speak
he/she/it speaks	they speak

• *He speaks really well.*

PRESENT PROGRESSIVE

I am speaking	we are speaking
you are speaking	you are speaking
he/she/it is speaking	they are speaking

• *I am speaking at the luncheon this afternoon.*

PAST

I spoke	we spoke
you spoke	you spoke
he/she/it spoke	they spoke

• *They spoke about website design.*

PAST PROGRESSIVE

I was speaking	we were speaking
you were speaking	you were speaking
he/she/it was speaking	they were speaking

• *They were speaking French at the time.*

PRESENT PERFECT ... have | has spoken
PAST PERFECT ... had spoken

FUTURE ... will speak
FUTURE PROGRESSIVE ... will be speaking
FUTURE PERFECT ... will have spoken

PAST PASSIVE

—	—
—	—
it was spoken	they were spoken

• *English was spoken everywhere they traveled.*

(COMPLEMENTS)

speak *talk, say words*	Are you hurt? Can you speak? Most children start speaking before their second birthday. He was so upset he couldn't speak.
speak *have a conversation*	They need to find a place where they can speak privately. They were speaking in whispers. After their argument, they weren't speaking for months.
speak *make a public presentation*	Everybody at the conference wants to hear her speak. It takes a lot of practice to speak in public. I am not used to speaking without notes.
speak _____ *say, express* OBJECT	They are speaking **the truth about what happened.** He spoke **gentle words of wisdom.**
speak _____ *have a conversation with* *to* OBJECT	We spoke **to the police** about the break-in. Have you spoken **to your mother?** May I speak **to Mr. Huntleigh?**

speak _____ *talk in [a specific language]*
   OBJECT
   PASSIVE
	She can speak **German and Dutch** pretty well.
	How many languages do you speak?
	Both English and French were spoken at the conference.

(PHRASAL VERBS)

speak for _____ *say something on behalf of*	I am speaking only for myself. The candidate spoke for lowering taxes. "I speak for the trees, for the trees have no tongues." [DR. SEUSS]
speak for _____ *ask for*	I'd like to speak for the last slice of cheesecake. The last copy of the book is already spoken for.
speak of _____ *speak about*	Grandpa spoke of hardships during the Great Depression.
speak out *express one's opinion*	Thomas speaks out at every meeting he attends.
speak up *speak more loudly*	Speak up! We can't hear you in the back row.
speak up for _____ *speak in support of*	She always speaks up for military families.

PRESENT

I speed	we speed
you speed	you speed
he/she/it speeds	they speed

• *He speeds when he gets on the freeway.*

PRESENT PROGRESSIVE

I am speeding	we are speeding
you are speeding	you are speeding
he/she/it is speeding	they are speeding

• *She is already speeding away.*

PAST

I sped	we sped
you sped	you sped
he/she/it sped	they sped

• *The sailboat sped before the wind.*

PAST PROGRESSIVE

I was speeding	we were speeding
you were speeding	you were speeding
he/she/it was speeding	they were speeding

• *We got pulled over because we were speeding.*

PRESENT PERFECT ... have | has sped
PAST PERFECT ... had sped

FUTURE ... will speed
FUTURE PROGRESSIVE ... will be speeding
FUTURE PERFECT ... will have sped

PAST PASSIVE

Speed is rarely used in the passive voice.

COMPLEMENTS

speed *go/move fast*

The dogs sped across the roadway.
The skiers sped down the slope toward the lodge.
The horses are speeding around the final turn.
The rescuers were speeding to the scene of the accident.

speed *drive faster than the legal limit*

If you speed, you could lose your driver's license.
He was speeding in a construction zone and had to pay
a huge fine.

speed _____ *cause to go/move faster*
    OBJECT

We changed the rules to speed **the approval process**.
Some men will try anything to speed **hair growth**.
Trying to speed **an entrenched bureaucracy** is next
to impossible.

PHRASAL VERBS

**speed along/away/down/over/past/
up/etc.** *go fast in a specified direction*

An ambulance sped past with its siren
blaring.
Teens were speeding up and down Main Street.

speed _____ **along/away/down/over/
past/up/etc.** *cause to go faster in a
specified direction*

The manager tried to speed the process along.
The delivery service sped the package over.

speed up *go/move faster*

Ricky sped up when he saw the police car.
We tend to speed up going downhill.

speed ⎡SEP⎤ **up** *cause to go/move faster*

We really need to speed up the production line.

PRESENT		PRESENT PROGRESSIVE	
I spend	we spend	I am spending	we are spending
you spend	you spend	you are spending	you are spending
he/she/it spends	they spend	he/she/it is spending	they are spending

• *He spends too much when he eats out.*   • *We are spending too much time on this project.*

PAST		PAST PROGRESSIVE	
I spent	we spent	I was spending	we were spending
you spent	you spent	you were spending	you were spending
he/she/it spent	they spent	he/she/it was spending	they were spending

• *We spent some time with my parents.*   • *We were spending a week in Phoenix.*

PRESENT PERFECT ... have | has spent
PAST PERFECT ... had spent

FUTURE ... will spend
FUTURE PROGRESSIVE ... will be spending
FUTURE PERFECT ... will have spent

PAST PASSIVE

I was spent	we were spent
you were spent	you were spent
he/she/it was spent	they were spent

• *A fortune was spent trying to fix the problem.*

(COMPLEMENTS)

spend *pay out money*

They just love to spend.
We can't keep spending at this rate.
They spend and spend until they are broke.

spend _____ *pay [money]*

    OBJECT

We will spend **a lot** fixing our roof.
They spend **over half their income** on housing.
You have to spend **money** to make money.

    PASSIVE

The insurance settlement had already been spent.

spend _____ *be occupied for [a period of time]*

    OBJECT + ADVERB OF PLACE

I will spend **all of next week** *in Chicago.*
The kids spent **half the summer** *at camp.*

    OBJECT + PRESENT PARTICIPLE

We spent **all week** *working on the budget.*
A horse spends **three hours a day** *sleeping.*

    PASSIVE

Last weekend was spent *cleaning out the garage.*

spend _____ *exhaust, use up*

    OBJECT

The storm finally spent **itself** during the night.
General Lee had already spent **all his reserves.**

    PASSIVE

Your talent would be better spent writing textbooks.

PRESENT

I spin	we spin
you spin	you spin
he/she/it spins	they spin

• *The disk spins at a high speed.*

PRESENT PROGRESSIVE

I am spinning	we are spinning
you are spinning	you are spinning
he/she/it is spinning	they are spinning

• *The senator's office is spinning the story.*

PAST

I spun	we spun
you spun	you spun
he/she/it spun	they spun

• *I spun the wool to make yarn.*

PAST PROGRESSIVE

I was spinning	we were spinning
you were spinning	you were spinning
he/she/it was spinning	they were spinning

• *Our wheels were spinning on the ice.*

PRESENT PERFECT ... have | has spun
PAST PERFECT ... had spun

FUTURE ... will spin
FUTURE PROGRESSIVE ... will be spinning
FUTURE PERFECT ... will have spun

PAST PASSIVE

I was spun	we were spun
you were spun	you were spun
he/she/it was spun	they were spun

• *The bets were placed and the roulette wheel was spun.*

COMPLEMENTS

spin *whirl around quickly*	The altimeter was spinning fast.
	The dryer is still spinning.
	Your wheels will spin in this slush.
	The earth spins on a 23.4-degree axis.
	The policeman spun when he heard the shot.
spin *seem to be whirling around quickly, as if to make someone dizzy*	I have to sit down; my head is spinning.
	The news was enough to make your head spin.
spin _____ *cause to whirl around quickly*	
OBJECT	I spun **the propeller** to get the engine started.
	The drivers were spinning **their wheels** in the soft ground.
	I showed the kids how to spin **their new top**.
	The server spun **the ball** so that it bounced at an odd angle.
PASSIVE	The wheel was spun by the next contestant.
spin _____ *draw out and twist into yarn*	
OBJECT	My daughter spins **wool fleece** into yarn.
PASSIVE	The cashmere yarn had been spun by hand.
spin _____ *make a web* [OF SPIDERS]	
OBJECT	Spiders had spun **webs** in every corner.
spin _____ *interpret in a way favorable to oneself*	
OBJECT	The aides were busily spinning **the election results**.
	He was trying to spin **the news** to minimize the damage.
PASSIVE	The story was spun until it was unrecognizable.

PHRASAL VERBS

spin away/off/out/etc. *spin in a specified direction*	The Frisbee is spinning away toward TipTop.
spin ⎡SEP⎤ **away/off/out**/etc. *cause to spin in a specified direction*	He spun himself away from the computer.
spin off *separate and fly away from something that is spinning*	The fan blade may spin off if you don't tighten it.
spin ⎡SEP⎤ **off** *create a separate company from part of an existing one*	The chemical company spun off its herbicide division.

PRESENT

I spit	we spit
you spit	you spit
he/she/it spits	they spit

• *Our cat spits when she sees a dog.*

PRESENT PROGRESSIVE

I am spitting	we are spitting
you are spitting	you are spitting
he/she/it is spitting	they are spitting

• *The victim is spitting blood.*

PAST

I spit/spat	we spit/spat
you spit/spat	you spit/spat
he/she/it spit/spat	they spit/spat

• *He coughed and spit into his handkerchief.*

PAST PROGRESSIVE

I was spitting	we were spitting
you were spitting	you were spitting
he/she/it was spitting	they were spitting

• *They were spitting watermelon seeds.*

PRESENT PERFECT ... have | has spit/spat
PAST PERFECT ... had spit/spat

FUTURE ... will spit
FUTURE PROGRESSIVE ... will be spitting
FUTURE PERFECT ... will have spit/spat

PAST PASSIVE

I was spit/spat	we were spit/spat
you were spit/spat	you were spit/spat
he/she/it was spit/spat	they were spit/spat

• *The words were spat in utter contempt.*

(**COMPLEMENTS**)

spit *force something [often, saliva] from one's mouth*

Rinse out your mouth and spit, please.
People who chew tobacco have to spit constantly.
I have such a bad taste in my mouth that I'm spitting all the time.

spit *be very angry*

He was spitting angrily.
The defendant was spitting with sudden rage.

spit *rain/snow lightly*

It's spitting outside; you'd better wear a raincoat.

spit _____ *force from one's mouth*
    OBJECT

The diner spit **a chicken bone** across the table.
Aaron accidentally spit **a mouthful of soda** all over the floor.

spit _____ *throw out [liquid, fire]*
    OBJECT

The engine was spitting **oil**.
The pan was so hot that it spit **cooking oil** on my hand.
The bonfire was spitting **sparks** high into the night air.

spit _____ *say/express angrily*
    OBJECT

The man spit **abuse** at the crowd.
He spat **an oath** and slammed the door.
The man spat **an incoherent warning** at the children.

I split   we split
you split   you split
he/she/it splits   they split

• *Pine always splits along the grain.*

PAST

I split   we split
you split   you split
he/she/it split   they split

• *We split the cost equally.*

PRESENT PERFECT   ... have | has split
PAST PERFECT   ... had split

PRESENT PROGRESSIVE

I am splitting   we are splitting
you are splitting   you are splitting
he/she/it is splitting   they are splitting

• *The couple next door is splitting.*

PAST PROGRESSIVE

I was splitting   we were splitting
you were splitting   you were splitting
he/she/it was splitting   they were splitting

• *I was splitting enough wood to last all winter.*

FUTURE   ... will split
FUTURE PROGRESSIVE   ... will be splitting
FUTURE PERFECT   ... will have split

PAST PASSIVE

I was split   we were split
you were split   you were split
he/she/it was split   they were split

• *The prize was split among the winning contestants.*

COMPLEMENTS

split *separate/divide into parts*	My lips were splitting from the sun.
	The ice was heaving and splitting.
	The trail splits at the top of the ridge.
	The class split into three groups.
split *end a marriage/relationship*	My cousin and his wife are splitting after five years.
	Jayne got into a fight with her boyfriend and they decided to split.
	Do you think they will split after what happened?
	This issue could cause the Republican Party to split.
split _____ *cause to separate/divide into parts*	
OBJECT	We split the **logs** for firewood.
	Would you split **the English muffins** and toast them?
	They split **the searchers** into small groups so they could cover more ground.
PASSIVE	Diamonds are still split by hand.
	The atom was first split in 1932.
split _____ *share/divide among participants*	
OBJECT	We need to split **the workload** more fairly.
	Investors will split **the profits** in proportion to the size of their investment.
	Rhonda split **a pizza** with Stan.
	If we get the winning ticket, we will split **the prize** equally.
PASSIVE	Overtime hours must be split among all workers.
WH-CLAUSE	The group split **what they had earned**.
	We will split **whatever we win**.
	They decided to split **however much money they get**.

PHRASAL VERBS

split _SEP_ **up (into** _____ **)** *divide (into [groups, etc.])*	He split the class up into three groups according to height.
split _SEP_ **off** *separate*	The forum moderator split the topic off from the main thread.
split off (from _____ **)** *separate (from [someone/something])*	Icebergs are splitting off from glaciers at an alarming rate.

PRESENT

I spread	we spread
you spread	you spread
he/she/it spreads	they spread

• *He spreads peanut butter on his bagels.*

PRESENT PROGRESSIVE

I am spreading	we are spreading
you are spreading	you are spreading
he/she/it is spreading	they are spreading

• *The city is spreading into the valley.*

PAST

I spread	we spread
you spread	you spread
he/she/it spread	they spread

• *We spread a blanket on the grass.*

PAST PROGRESSIVE

I was spreading	we were spreading
you were spreading	you were spreading
he/she/it was spreading	they were spreading

• *They were spreading rumors about the senator.*

PRESENT PERFECT ... have | has spread
PAST PERFECT ... had spread

FUTURE ... will spread
FUTURE PROGRESSIVE ... will be spreading
FUTURE PERFECT ... will have spread

PAST PASSIVE

I was spread	we were spread
you were spread	you were spread
he/she/it was spread	they were spread

• *The seeds were spread by a mechanical applicator.*

COMPLEMENTS

spread *move/extend outward*
Bad news spreads like wildfire.
The floodwater was spreading by the minute.
Violence is spreading in much of the world.

spread _____ *extend [over/to an area]*
  ADVERB OF PLACE TO/FROM
The ripples spread **across the pond.**
Elm disease has spread **through the upper Midwest.**
The impact of deflation spread **throughout the economy.**
The city is spreading **in all directions.**
The forest fire spread **to several hilltop villages.**

spread _____ *cause to move/expand outward*
  OBJECT
He is always spreading **rumors.**
The senator hopes to spread **the blame for the mistake.**
  PASSIVE
Malaria is spread by one type of mosquito.

spread _____ *open/stretch out*
  OBJECT
The bird spread **its wings.**

spread _____ *distribute*
  OBJECT + ADVERB OF PLACE TO/FROM
He spread **the map** *across the hood of the car.*
Spread **the jam** *on every corner of the bread.*
The eruption spread **dust** *over hundreds of square miles.*
They spread **the payments** *over five years.*
  PASSIVE
Protective cloths had been spread *across the floor.*

PHRASAL VERBS

spread _SEP_ **around** *publicize*
They spread the news around that
  her campaign staff had been fired.

spread out *scatter*
The rescuers spread out to search the mountainside.

EXPRESSIONS

spread it on thick *exaggerate praise/blame*
The car salesman was really spreading
  it on thick.

spread [oneself] too thin *do too many things at once*
Between work and volunteer activities, Emma has spread
  herself too thin.

PRESENT

I spring	we spring
you spring	you spring
he/she/it springs	they spring

• He springs out of bed in the morning.

PRESENT PROGRESSIVE

I am springing	we are springing
you are springing	you are springing
he/she/it is springing	they are springing

• Crocuses are springing up everywhere.

PAST

I sprang/sprung	we sprang/sprung
you sprang/sprung	you sprang/sprung
he/she/it sprang/sprung	they sprang/sprung

• The door sprang open.

PAST PROGRESSIVE

I was springing	we were springing
you were springing	you were springing
he/she/it was springing	they were springing

• Dolphins were springing out of the water.

PRESENT PERFECT ... have | has sprung
PAST PERFECT ... had sprung

FUTURE ... will spring
FUTURE PROGRESSIVE ... will be springing
FUTURE PERFECT ... will have sprung

PAST PASSIVE

I was sprung	we were sprung
you were sprung	you were sprung
he/she/it was sprung	they were sprung

• The trap was sprung by a raccoon.

COMPLEMENTS

spring _____ jump/move suddenly
ADVERB OF PLACE TO/FROM

I sprang **out of my chair** and ran to the door.
The soldiers sprang **up** when the captain came into the room.
We sprang **to the ropes** before the boat could pull away.
The car sprang **forward**, nearly hitting us.
The car door sprang **open** and Fred jumped out.

spring _____ suddenly appear
ADVERB OF PLACE TO/FROM

A dog suddenly sprang **out of the fog**.
Jack sprang **out the front door** and greeted us warmly.
The robbers sprang **out of nowhere**.
Tears sprang **from his eyes**.
A cry sprang **from her throat**.

spring _____ cause to snap shut
OBJECT

An opossum sprang **the trap**.

PHRASAL VERBS

spring for _____ pay for
I'll spring for a new coat for you.

spring up begin, be started
A wonderful friendship sprang up between us.
A new fast-food restaurant sprang up on the corner.

spring up begin to grow
Flowers and weeds are springing up in the garden.

EXPRESSIONS

spring a leak begin to leak
Our boat sprang a leak in the middle of the lake.

spring into action become suddenly active
After Amber read his letter, she sprang into action.

spring to mind be thought of
Which president springs to mind when I say "father of our country"?

PRESENT

I stand	we stand
you stand	you stand
he/she/it stands	they stand

• *The treasurer stands by the CEO.*

PRESENT PROGRESSIVE

I am standing	we are standing
you are standing	you are standing
he/she/it is standing	they are standing

• *I am standing in the checkout lane.*

PAST

I stood	we stood
you stood	you stood
he/she/it stood	they stood

• *We all stood for the national anthem.*

PAST PROGRESSIVE

I was standing	we were standing
you were standing	you were standing
he/she/it was standing	they were standing

• *We were standing for hours at the reception.*

PRESENT PERFECT … have | has stood
PAST PERFECT   … had stood

FUTURE   … will stand
FUTURE PROGRESSIVE … will be standing
FUTURE PERFECT   … will have stood

PAST PASSIVE

I was stood	we were stood
you were stood	you were stood
he/she/it was stood	they were stood

• *The pictures were all stood along the wall.*

(COMPLEMENTS)

stand *be/get in an upright position*

Please stand.
Everyone stood when the funeral procession went by.
By the end of the game, we were all standing and cheering.

stand *remain undisturbed*
[OF FOOD, LIQUID]

Let the tea leaves stand for a few minutes.
The custard needs to stand until it is at room temperature.
The mixture should stand until all the liquid is absorbed.

stand *remain as is*

The committee's original recommendation stands.
The judge let the lower court's ruling stand.
That tradition has stood since the school began.

stand _____ *cause to be in an upright position*

OBJECT + ADVERB OF PLACE

She stood **the dolls** *against the dresser*.
The librarian stood **the books** *on the shelf*.
Stand **the children** *in front of a mirror*.
Stand **the rugs** *in the corner*, please.
We stood **the flagstaff** *in a big pot*.

PASSIVE

The palm plants were stood *along the garden wall*.

stand _____ *be located*

ADVERB OF PLACE

The church stands **at the corner of Waterman and Kingshighway**.
A rake and hoe stood **against the fence**.
The train is standing **at the station**.
He was standing **just outside the door**, waiting for us.
The town stands **on a little hill overlooking the bay**.

stand _____ *step to and remain [in a certain place]*

ADVERB OF PLACE

Stand **over there**, please.
I stood **to the side** and let them pass.
We all stood **on the grass** so that the ambulance could get by.

stand _____ *be [in a certain condition]*

PREDICATE ADJECTIVE

He stood **firm in his opposition to the plan**.
I stand **ready to help**.
The house stood **empty** for many years.

stand _____ tolerate, endure [USUALLY USED IN QUESTIONS OR NEGATIVE STATEMENTS]

OBJECT	How do you stand **the pressure**?
	I can't stand **the suspense**.
	No one can stand **his superior attitude**.
PRESENT PARTICIPLE	How can you stand **listening to that nonsense**?
	Wine grapes can't stand **being in poorly drained soil**.
	I can't stand **not knowing what happened**.

stand _____ be of a specified height

OBJECT	Tim stands **six foot four**.
	The horse stands **15 hands at the withers**.

—(**PHRASAL VERBS**)—

stand apart/aside/back/off/etc. _stand in a specified position_	Max stood aside and let the medics by. We stood back so that we wouldn't get hurt.
stand around _loiter, be idle_	They stood around with their hands in their pockets.
stand at _____ _be at a specified amount/ number_	The bid stands at $250. Our team's record stands at 11–4.
stand by _be near and ready if needed_	He asked me to stand by in case his car wouldn't start.
stand by _stand near but not involve oneself_	Three people stood by and watched the robbery take place.
stand by _____ _support, defend_	She stood by her husband throughout his illness.
stand for _____ _represent_	"U.S.A." stands for "United States of America."
stand for _____ _tolerate_ [USUALLY NEGATIVE]	We won't stand for your nonsense any longer.
stand in for _____ _take the place of, act for_	Would you stand in for me at next Tuesday's meeting?
stand out _be distinctive_	Because of his height, Don really stands out in a crowd.
stand over _____ _keep close watch on_	I can't get any work done if you're standing over me.
stand up _prove to be true/good_	This idea won't stand up under scrutiny.
stand _SEP_ **up** _fail to keep a date with_	Lori stood him up again.
stand up for _____ _support, defend_	When Nancy was criticized, her coach stood up for her. My parents always stood up for immigrants' rights.
stand up to _____ _resist, refuse to be treated badly by_	The candidate stood up to the lies on talk radio.

—(**EXPRESSIONS**)—

stand a chance (of _____ **)** _have a chance of_	Does your team stand a chance of winning?
stand corrected _admit that one is wrong_	I stand corrected; there are two _m_'s in _recommend_.
stand head and shoulders above _____ _be far superior to_	Their book stood head and shoulders above the competition.
stand in [someone's] way _oppose/obstruct [someone]_	She beat every candidate who stood in her way to the nomination.
stand on [one's] own two feet _be independent, not need anyone's help_	Son, it's time for you to get your own apartment and stand on your own two feet.
stand [one's] ground _maintain one's position while being attacked_	The politician stood his ground in spite of accusations by the opposition party.
stand still for _____ _tolerate_ [USUALLY NEGATIVE]	Senator Blather won't stand still for criticism of his immigration policy.
stand to reason _be sensible/reasonable_	It stands to reason that interest rates are low in a recession.

top 30 verb

PRESENT

I steal	we steal
you steal	you steal
he/she/it steals	they steal

• *Our dog steals food from the cats' dishes.*

PRESENT PROGRESSIVE

I am stealing	we are stealing
you are stealing	you are stealing
he/she/it is stealing	they are stealing

• *I am stealing an idea from you—okay?*

PAST

I stole	we stole
you stole	you stole
he/she/it stole	they stole

• *Someone stole my wallet at the gym.*

PAST PROGRESSIVE

I was stealing	we were stealing
you were stealing	you were stealing
he/she/it was stealing	they were stealing

• *They were stealing into the kitchen for cookies.*

PRESENT PERFECT ... have | has stolen
PAST PERFECT ... had stolen

FUTURE ... will steal
FUTURE PROGRESSIVE ... will be stealing
FUTURE PERFECT ... will have stolen

PAST PASSIVE

I was stolen	we were stolen
you were stolen	you were stolen
he/she/it was stolen	they were stolen

• *The car was stolen right out of the garage.*

―(COMPLEMENTS)―

steal *take something that doesn't belong to one without paying for it / without permission*

"Thou shalt not steal." [BIBLE]
Fagin forced the children to steal.
Even though he was starving, Oliver refused to steal.

steal _____ *take without paying for / without permission*
   OBJECT

Somebody stole **my son's bicycle.**
He claimed that they had stolen **his idea.**

    PASSIVE

iPods are stolen out of backpacks every day.

steal _____ *take/borrow while acknowledging the fact* [OFTEN USED HUMOROUSLY]
   OBJECT

Can I steal **your husband** for a few minutes?
I need to steal **a few minutes of your time.**
Can I steal **your chair?**

steal _____ *move quietly/secretly*
   ADVERB OF PLACE TO/FROM

The thieves stole **into the garage** and took some tools.
We stole **into the boss's office** for a surprise birthday party.
The cavalry stole **behind Union lines** and attacked
    from the rear.

steal _____ *get/win in a tricky manner*
   OBJECT

Sam felt that Bob had stolen **Martha's affections.**

steal _____ *take secretly and slyly*
   OBJECT

He managed to steal **a look at the classified documents.**
I stole **a kiss** when we had driven for a mile.

―(PHRASAL VERBS)―

steal away/down/in/out/up/etc. *move quietly/secretly in a specified direction*

My aunt stole away and cried.

―(EXPRESSIONS)―

steal [someone's] thunder *say/do what [someone else] intended to say/do, thereby lessening his/her impact*

Her opponent stole her thunder by
   appearing on TV an hour before she did.

steal the show *receive more attention than anyone else at an event*

A young tap dancer named Dulé Hill stole the show.

PRESENT		PRESENT PROGRESSIVE	
I stick	we stick	I am sticking	we are sticking
you stick	you stick	you are sticking	you are sticking
he/she/it sticks	they stick	he/she/it is sticking	they are sticking

• *The store sticks labels on fruit.*   • *The glue isn't sticking very well.*

PAST		PAST PROGRESSIVE	
I stuck	we stuck	I was sticking	we were sticking
you stuck	you stuck	you were sticking	you were sticking
he/she/it stuck	they stuck	he/she/it was sticking	they were sticking

• *A nurse stuck a bandage on Lynda's knee.*   • *My shoes were sticking to the floor.*

PRESENT PERFECT	... have	has stuck
PAST PERFECT	... had stuck

FUTURE	... will stick
FUTURE PROGRESSIVE	... will be sticking
FUTURE PERFECT	... will have stuck

PAST PASSIVE	
I was stuck	we were stuck
you were stuck	you were stuck
he/she/it was stuck	they were stuck

• *A note was stuck on my door while I was gone.*

COMPLEMENTS

stick *remain fixed in place*

The drawer is still sticking.
Our wheels stuck in the soft earth.
I'm afraid the proposal is stuck in committee.
The transmission has stuck in first gear.
If you throw enough dirt at somebody, some of it will stick.
Snow was sticking on the ground.
Our pants were sticking to the plastic seats.

stick _____ *attach, fasten, fix*
    OBJECT + ADVERB OF PLACE

We stuck **a patch** *on the tire.*
I stuck **some pictures** *on the wall.*
They stuck **the interns** *in a dingy basement office.*

    PASSIVE

He was stuck *in a dead-end job.*

stick _____ *poke, pierce, thrust*
    OBJECT + ADVERB OF PLACE

The nurse stuck **a thermometer** *in his mouth.*
The cowboy stuck **a cigarette** *behind his ear.*
The little boy stuck **a pin** *into the balloon.*
The workers stuck **their hands** *in their pockets.*

    PASSIVE

Political signs had been stuck *on the lawn.*

PHRASAL VERBS

stick down/in/out/up/etc. *extend in a specified position*

My toes were sticking out from under the quilt.
The lid was sticking up on the jewelry box.

stick SEP **away/back/down/in/on/out/up/etc.** *thrust/attach in a specified location*

Margaret stuck the report back in the drawer.
I'll stick the stamps on at the post office.
He stuck his tongue out at the teacher.

stick around *remain nearby*

I asked Barb to stick around until I started my car.

stick by _____ *remain loyal to*

Sara stuck by him through thick and thin.

stick out *be distinctive*

That lime green shirt of his really sticks out.

stick SEP **out** *endure*

Bob quit his new job after a week; he couldn't stick it out.

stick to _____ *adhere to*

Everyone should stick to the point being discussed.

stick SEP **up** *rob*

Two masked men stuck up a gas station last night.

stick up for _____ *defend*

Mom always stuck up for us kids.

PRESENT

I sting	we sting
you sting	you sting
he/she/it stings	they sting

• *That antiseptic really stings.*

PRESENT PROGRESSIVE

I am stinging	we are stinging
you are stinging	you are stinging
he/she/it is stinging	they are stinging

• *My hands are still stinging.*

PAST

I stung	we stung
you stung	you stung
he/she/it stung	they stung

• *The smoke from the grill stung our eyes.*

PAST PROGRESSIVE

I was stinging	we were stinging
you were stinging	you were stinging
he/she/it was stinging	they were stinging

• *Sweat bees were stinging everyone at the picnic.*

PRESENT PERFECT ... have | has stung
PAST PERFECT ... had stung

FUTURE ... will sting
FUTURE PROGRESSIVE ... will be stinging
FUTURE PERFECT ... will have stung

PAST PASSIVE

I was stung	we were stung
you were stung	you were stung
he/she/it was stung	they were stung

• *The swimmers were stung by jellyfish.*

COMPLEMENTS

sting *hurt by pricking/piercing the skin*	Wasps will sting if you get too close to their nest.
	Careful—those plants sting if you even brush them.
	The insects sting when the wind dies down.
sting *feel a sharp tingling/burning pain*	My skin is stinging.
	Our throats were stinging from the exhaust.
	My hands stung from the vibrations.
sting *cause emotional pain*	His criticisms stung at first.
	Malicious gossip stings terribly.
	Man, what he said really stings!
sting ＿＿＿ *hurt by pricking/piercing the skin of*	
OBJECT	A bee just stung **me**.
PASSIVE	The kids who were playing in the sandbox were stung by ants.
sting ＿＿＿ *cause a sharp tingling/burning pain to*	
OBJECT	The medicine stung **my throat**.
	The sunblock stung **my eyes**.
	The cold stung **my ears and hands**.
PASSIVE	My ears and hands were stung by the cold.
sting ＿＿＿ *cause emotional pain to*	
OBJECT	Unjust criticism stings **a writer**.
	Being ridiculed would sting **anyone**.
PASSIVE	I was stung by her malicious attack.
	We were stung by how quickly they reacted.

PRESENT

I stink	we stink
you stink	you stink
he/she/it stinks	they stink

• *The barn really stinks.*

PRESENT PROGRESSIVE

I am stinking	we are stinking
you are stinking	you are stinking
he/she/it is stinking	they are stinking

• *The durian is stinking up our apartment.*

PAST

I stank/stunk	we stank/stunk
you stank/stunk	you stank/stunk
he/she/it stank/stunk	they stank/stunk

• *The whole economic situation stank.*

PAST PROGRESSIVE

I was stinking	we were stinking
you were stinking	you were stinking
he/she/it was stinking	they were stinking

• *The dead skunk was stinking to high heaven.*

PRESENT PERFECT ... have | has stunk
PAST PERFECT ... had stunk

FUTURE ... will stink
FUTURE PROGRESSIVE ... will be stinking
FUTURE PERFECT ... will have stunk

PAST PASSIVE

Stink is never used in the passive voice.

COMPLEMENTS

stink *give off a strong, unpleasant smell*

The alley stank like an open sewer.
When tissue swells and stinks, it may be a sign of gangrene.
His breath stank from cheap tobacco.
You need to take out the garbage before it starts to stink.

stink *be worthless / very bad*

The movie stinks. No one liked it.
The proposed merger stinks and will probably end up in court.
I think the plan stinks and should be junked.
The company's reputation stinks because of what they did.

PHRASAL VERBS

stink _SEP_ **up** *fill with a strong, unpleasant smell*

Will hamsters stink up the house?

EXPRESSIONS

stink up the joint/place *perform very badly*

Our team really stunk up the joint tonight.

stink to high heaven *give off an extremely unpleasant smell*

When broccoli goes bad, it stinks to high heaven.

PRESENT

I strew	we strew
you strew	you strew
he/she/it strews	they strew

• *A flower girl strews petals down the aisle.*

PRESENT PROGRESSIVE

I am strewing	we are strewing
you are strewing	you are strewing
he/she/it is strewing	they are strewing

• *The wind is strewing leaves on the patio.*

PAST

I strewed	we strewed
you strewed	you strewed
he/she/it strewed	they strewed

• *We strewed the dance floor with chalk.*

PAST PROGRESSIVE

I was strewing	we were strewing
you were strewing	you were strewing
he/she/it was strewing	they were strewing

• *The woman was strewing flowers on his grave.*

PRESENT PERFECT ... have | has strewn
PAST PERFECT ... had strewn

FUTURE ... will strew
FUTURE PROGRESSIVE ... will be strewing
FUTURE PERFECT ... will have strewn

PAST PASSIVE

—	—
—	—
it was strewn	they were strewn

• *The puppy's food was strewn all around the kitchen.*

COMPLEMENTS

strew _____ *scatter, spread untidily*

OBJECT + ADVERB OF PLACE — The storm had strewn **paper and trash** *everywhere.*
The rebels were strewing **mines** *throughout the valley.*
An explosion strew **concrete and metal** *over a four-block area.*

PASSIVE — Newspapers and magazines were strewn *around the living room.*

strew _____ *be scattered/littered over*

OBJECT — A carpet of leaves strewed **the pathway,** making it impossible to see.
Rusting cars and trucks strewed **the front yard.**

strew _____ *cover [a surface] by scattering [with something]*

OBJECT + *with* OBJECT — His parents have strewn **their dining room table** *with potted plants.*
Our neighbors are strewing **their lawn** *with wrought iron furniture.*
The author strewed **her novel** *with clues to the killer's identity.*

PASSIVE — The beach was strewn *with rotting wood.*

PRESENT

I stride	we stride
you stride	you stride
he/she/it strides	they stride

• He strides in like he is on a mission.

PRESENT PROGRESSIVE

I am striding	we are striding
you are striding	you are striding
he/she/it is striding	they are striding

• The horses are striding along at a fast clip now.

PAST

I strode	we strode
you strode	you strode
he/she/it strode	they strode

• The cowboys strode into the town square.

PAST PROGRESSIVE

I was striding	we were striding
you were striding	you were striding
he/she/it was striding	they were striding

• They were striding as though they were on parade.

PRESENT PERFECT ... have | has stridden
PAST PERFECT ... had stridden

FUTURE ... will stride
FUTURE PROGRESSIVE ... will be striding
FUTURE PERFECT ... will have stridden

PAST PASSIVE

Stride is never used in the passive voice.

COMPLEMENTS

stride *walk with long steps*

He doesn't walk, he strides.
The boys were pretending to stride like soldiers.
He was striding so fast that he was almost running.

stride _____ *walk briskly*

ADVERB OF PLACE TO/FROM

He strode **across the room** in two quick steps and jerked open the door.
They strode angrily **down the street and into the mayor's office**.
The delegation strode **past us**, grim faced, not looking to the left or right.

PHRASAL VERBS

stride along/away/down/in/out/ up/etc. *stride in a specified direction*

He was striding along, muttering to himself.
Leon glared at the boss, then strode away.
The captain strode up and shook my hand.

PRESENT

I strike	we strike
you strike	you strike
he/she/it strikes	they strike

• *The idea strikes us as promising.*

PRESENT PROGRESSIVE

I am striking	we are striking
you are striking	you are striking
he/she/it is striking	they are striking

• *The flu is striking everyone.*

PAST

I struck	we struck
you struck	you struck
he/she/it struck	they struck

• *She struck her foot on a chair.*

PAST PROGRESSIVE

I was striking	we were striking
you were striking	you were striking
he/she/it was striking	they were striking

• *The union was striking at midnight.*

PRESENT PERFECT ... have | has struck/stricken
PAST PERFECT ... had struck/stricken

FUTURE ... will strike
FUTURE PROGRESSIVE ... will be striking
FUTURE PERFECT ... will have struck/stricken

PAST PASSIVE

I was struck/stricken	we were struck/stricken
you were struck/stricken	you were struck/stricken
he/she/it was struck/stricken	they were struck/stricken

• *He was suddenly struck by a brilliant idea.*

COMPLEMENTS

strike *attack, cause sudden damage/injury*

An earthquake struck this morning in northern California.
Disaster struck when the ferry capsized in heavy seas.
The killer has struck again.
Many snakes hiss before they strike.

strike *refuse to work until one's demands are met*

The maintenance workers voted to strike.
We will strike if our demands are not met.
They are striking for better health benefits.

strike _____ *hit forcefully*

OBJECT

A falling tree limb struck **me** on the shoulder.
The van struck **several parked cars**.
He struck **the ball** with his head.
Sunshine struck **the mirror**, temporarily blinding me.

PASSIVE

The Pinkston family was struck by tragedy today.
We were all struck by the coincidence.

strike _____ *occur to*

OBJECT

A great idea just struck **me**.
The solution to the problem struck **him**.

it + strike + OBJECT + THAT-CLAUSE

It struck **us** *that our problem had been solved.*
It strikes **me** *that you are taking an unnecessary risk.*
It struck **everyone** *that it was getting very late.*

OBJECT + *as* PREDICATE NOUN

NOTE: The predicate noun refers to the subject, not the object.

The attack struck **the policeman** *as a suicide bombing.*
He struck **her** *as an honest man.*
His scheme struck **us** *as a stupid idea.*

OBJECT + *as* PREDICATE ADJECTIVE

NOTE: The predicate adjective refers to the subject, not the object.

Thomas struck **her** *as nice but a little strange.*
The proposal struck **me** *as promising.*
Their children struck **us** *as well-behaved.*

strike strike | strikes · struck · have struck
strike | strikes · struck · have stricken

☑ IRREGULAR
☑ IRREGULAR

strike _____ *reach/achieve [an agreement, compromise]*

OBJECT

The two sides finally struck **a deal**.
You must strike **the right balance between compassion and assertiveness**.

PASSIVE

A compromise on the budget was finally struck.

PHRASAL VERBS

strike back/down/out *attack in a specified direction*

The hero struck back with his mighty sword.

strike SEP **back/down/out** *hit in a specified direction*

Roger struck Steve down with a blow to the head.

strike SEP **down** *invalidate [a law]*

The Supreme Court struck down the gay marriage ban as unconstitutional.

strike SEP **off** *remove*

The secretary struck off the names of those who hadn't paid dues.

strike off/out (for _____) *set out (to [someplace])*

Thousands struck out for California in search of gold.

strike on _____ *realize suddenly*

The author struck on the idea of setting the novel in colonial America.

strike out *fail*

Brandy struck out trying to convince the boss to give her a raise.

strike SEP **up** *begin*

Ben struck up a conversation with the receptionist.
Sadie and Sally struck up a friendship at school.

EXPRESSIONS

strike a balance (between _____) *compromise (between [two things])*

She manages to strike a balance between her work and her family.

strike a bargain/deal *reach agreement*

The union and the company struck a bargain at the eleventh hour.

strike a chord (with _____) *sound familiar to [someone]*

Those words strike a chord with me; what song are they from?

strike a happy medium *find a satisfactory compromise*

She speaks French and I speak English, so we struck a happy medium and watched a French film with English subtitles.

strike a nerve *cause a strong negative reaction*

Your insensitive comment about immigration really struck a nerve.

strike _____ **funny** *seem humorous/odd to*

It strikes me funny that they dropped charges against the politician.

strike home *make sense*

His advice to save for a rainy day really strikes home.

strike it rich *become suddenly wealthy*

They struck it rich in the real estate business.

strike [one, two, ... twelve / midnight] *[OF A CLOCK] indicate the hour by a certain number of sounds*

The clock struck one, and the mouse ran down.
[NURSERY RHYME]

strike pay dirt *become suddenly successful*

The Mars rover has struck pay dirt: It has discovered evidence of water on the planet.

strike [someone's] fancy *appeal to [someone]*

Miss Elizabeth Bennet struck Mr. Darcy's fancy.

strike while the iron is hot *do something while one has the opportunity*

The economy is booming, and the board recommends that the company strike while the iron is hot.

top **30** verb

PRESENT

I string	we string
you string	you string
he/she/it strings	they string

• *He strings Christmas lights in the trees.*

PRESENT PROGRESSIVE

I am stringing	we are stringing
you are stringing	you are stringing
he/she/it is stringing	they are stringing

• *The kids are stringing beads.*

PAST

I strung	we strung
you strung	you strung
he/she/it strung	they strung

• *I strung the bows for the children.*

PAST PROGRESSIVE

I was stringing	we were stringing
you were stringing	you were stringing
he/she/it was stringing	they were stringing

• *We were stringing shells for a wall hanging.*

PRESENT PERFECT	... have | has strung
PAST PERFECT	... had strung

FUTURE	... will string
FUTURE PROGRESSIVE	... will be stringing
FUTURE PERFECT	... will have strung

PAST PASSIVE

I was strung	we were strung
you were strung	you were strung
he/she/it was strung	they were strung

• *My tennis racket was strung too tight.*

(COMPLEMENTS)

string ＿＿＿ *hang/stretch [in a line]*

OBJECT   We used to string **popcorn and cranberries** on our Christmas tree.
The fishermen strung **lines** in the channel.
The decorating committee wanted to string **lanterns** in the hall.

PASSIVE   A trip wire had been strung across the path.

string ＿＿＿ *thread (on a line/cord)*

OBJECT   Kids love to string **different shapes of uncooked pasta**.
When we catch fish, we string **them** on a line.

PASSIVE   The beads were strung to make simple necklaces.

string ＿＿＿ *put strings on [a racket, bow, musical instrument]*

OBJECT   You can't string **a tennis racket** by hand.
It takes a great deal of strength to string **a powerful bow**.

PASSIVE   The instruments were all strung by a professional musician.

(PHRASAL VERBS)

string <u>SEP</u> **along** *keep [someone] hoping for romance / a reward*   Jenny strung Reggie along for several months before telling him to get lost.
He strings employees along by promising raises that they never get.

string <u>SEP</u> **out** *prolong*   The professor was stringing out his lecture on quantum gravity.

string <u>SEP</u> **up** *hang by the neck*   An angry mob strung the cattle thieves up in the town square.

strive strive | strives · strove · have striven
strive | strives · strived · have strived

☑ IRREGULAR
☑ REGULAR

PRESENT

I strive	we strive
you strive	you strive
he/she/it strives	they strive

• *He strives to do his very best.*

PRESENT PROGRESSIVE

I am striving	we are striving
you are striving	you are striving
he/she/it is striving	they are striving

• *He is striving to succeed.*

PAST

I strove	we strove
you strove	you strove
he/she/it strove	they strove

• *We strove to get the job finished on time.*

PAST PROGRESSIVE

I was striving	we were striving
you were striving	you were striving
he/she/it was striving	they were striving

• *Everyone was striving to beat the deadline.*

PRESENT PERFECT ... have | has striven
PAST PERFECT   ... had striven

FUTURE   ... will strive
FUTURE PROGRESSIVE ... will be striving
FUTURE PERFECT   ... will have striven

PAST PASSIVE

Strive is never used in the passive voice.

(**COMPLEMENTS**)

strive _____ *make a great effort, try very hard*

INFINITIVE

You must always strive **to improve yourself.**
We always strove **to get the kids to school on time.**
Successful companies constantly strive **to make their products better.**
If you don't strive **to succeed**, you will surely fail in the long run.
The whole team was striving **to be the best in the league.**

strive _____ *fight, struggle*

for OBJECT

We strive **for peace and freedom.**

against OBJECT

The activists are striving **against poverty and injustice.**

PRESENT

I swear	we swear
you swear	you swear
he/she/it swears	they swear

 • *He swears that he knew nothing about it.*

PRESENT PROGRESSIVE

I am swearing	we are swearing
you are swearing	you are swearing
he/she/it is swearing	they are swearing

 • *They are swearing that they are innocent.*

PAST

I swore	we swore
you swore	you swore
he/she/it swore	they swore

 • *The witness swore to tell the truth.*

PAST PROGRESSIVE

I was swearing	we were swearing
you were swearing	you were swearing
he/she/it was swearing	they were swearing

 • *The soldiers were swearing and yelling at us.*

PRESENT PERFECT ... have | has sworn
PAST PERFECT   ... had sworn

FUTURE   ... will swear
FUTURE PROGRESSIVE ... will be swearing
FUTURE PERFECT   ... will have sworn

PAST PASSIVE

I was sworn	we were sworn
you were sworn	you were sworn
he/she/it was sworn	they were sworn

 • *The appropriate oaths were sworn during the ceremony.*

COMPLEMENTS

swear *use offensive language, usually in anger* | He swore under his breath.
Please don't swear around the children.
It was enough to make one swear!

swear _____ *promise, vow, pledge, state very seriously*

| OBJECT | I swore **a solemn promise.**
Peter swore **his undying love to Héloïse.**
The nobles all swore **their allegiance to the king.** |
| PASSIVE | The oath was sworn and witnessed. |
| INFINITIVE | I swear **to do it.**
Criminals always swear **to never commit another crime.**
He swears **to mend the error of his ways.**
"I swear **to tell the truth, the whole truth, and nothing but the truth.**" [COMMON COURTROOM OATH] |
| THAT-CLAUSE | I swear **that we were not the cause of the accident.**
The defendant swore **that he only shot in self-defense.**
The kids all swore **that they didn't let the dog out.**
"I do solemnly swear **that I will faithfully execute the office of President of the United States....**" [OATH OF OFFICE] |

PHRASAL VERBS

swear at _____ *curse at* | He swore at me when I told him to leave the room.

swear by _____ *have great faith in* | Trudy swears by yoga.

swear SEP **in** *administer an oath to* | The Chief Justice of the Supreme Court swears in the President of the United States.
The witness was sworn in by the bailiff.

swear off _____ *promise to quit* | Randi has sworn off dieting.

EXPRESSIONS

swear _____ **to secrecy** *cause to promise not to repeat a secret* | Annette swore me to secrecy about her background.

swear to it *be absolutely certain about something* [USUALLY NEGATIVE] | I wouldn't swear to it, but I think Elvis is still alive.

sweat

sweat | sweats · sweated · have sweated
sweat | sweats · sweat · have sweat

☑ REGULAR
☑ IRREGULAR

PRESENT

I sweat	we sweat
you sweat	you sweat
he/she/it sweats	they sweat

• He sweats heavily when he exercises.

PRESENT PROGRESSIVE

I am sweating	we are sweating
you are sweating	you are sweating
he/she/it is sweating	they are sweating

• I am really sweating tomorrow's exam.

PAST

I sweat	we sweat
you sweat	you sweat
he/she/it sweat	they sweat

• They sweat so much they felt faint.

PAST PROGRESSIVE

I was sweating	we were sweating
you were sweating	you were sweating
he/she/it was sweating	they were sweating

• We were all sweating by the time we finished.

PRESENT PERFECT ... have | has sweat
PAST PERFECT ... had sweat

FUTURE ... will sweat
FUTURE PROGRESSIVE ... will be sweating
FUTURE PERFECT ... will have sweat

PAST PASSIVE

I was sweat	we were sweat
you were sweat	you were sweat
he/she/it was sweat	they were sweat

• The wrestlers were sweat until they got down to 190 pounds.

COMPLEMENTS

sweat *perspire*	I always sweat when I work out.
	Everyone in the hot office was sweating like crazy.
	He sweats so much that he has to change his clothes after lunch.
sweat *form drops of water on its surface*	The bottles of water began to sweat.
	The plaster walls were actually sweating in the humid air.
	The cheese is sweating and needs to be refrigerated.
sweat *be worried/nervous*	The police let him sweat overnight.
	Don't sweat. Everything will be okay.
	They are going to make him sweat until he tells what happened.
sweat _____ *cause to perspire through exertion*	
OBJECT	The coach wants to sweat **the football players** at every practice.
	The training session had sweat **everybody**.
PASSIVE	The horses were sweat by the trainers and then allowed to slowly cool off.
sweat _____ *be worried/nervous about*	
OBJECT	Noel was sweating **the job interview**.
	Everyone sweats **the final exam**.
over OBJECT	Maureen sweat **over her English literature grade**.
	Ruth was sweating **over the upcoming conference in Montreal**.
sweat _____ *work very hard on*	
over OBJECT	The winner sweat **over the wording of his acceptance speech**.
	Jeffrey sweat all last week **over his essay**.

PHRASAL VERBS

sweat _SEP_ **off** *lose [an amount of weight] by exercising*	Angie sweat off 22 pounds in two months.

EXPRESSIONS

sweat blood *work very hard*	She was willing to sweat blood for a spot on the Olympic team.
sweat bullets *be extremely worried/nervous*	Poor Leroy was sweating bullets outside the principal's office.

PRESENT

I sweep	we sweep
you sweep	you sweep
he/she/it sweeps	they sweep

* He sweeps the leaves into the gutter.

PRESENT PROGRESSIVE

I am sweeping	we are sweeping
you are sweeping	you are sweeping
he/she/it is sweeping	they are sweeping

* She is sweeping the front porch.

PAST

I swept	we swept
you swept	you swept
he/she/it swept	they swept

* The Giants swept the three-game series.

PAST PROGRESSIVE

I was sweeping	we were sweeping
you were sweeping	you were sweeping
he/she/it was sweeping	they were sweeping

* The incoming tide was sweeping across the bay.

PRESENT PERFECT   ... have | has swept
PAST PERFECT   ... had swept

FUTURE   ... will sweep
FUTURE PROGRESSIVE   ... will be sweeping
FUTURE PERFECT   ... will have swept

PAST PASSIVE

I was swept	we were swept
you were swept	you were swept
he/she/it was swept	they were swept

* The room was swept this morning.

COMPLEMENTS

sweep _____ clean with a broom/brush

OBJECT
    You need to sweep **the kitchen floor**.
    I'll sweep **the carpet** in the entryway.

PASSIVE
    The garage has already been swept.

sweep _____ clear away

OBJECT + ADVERB OF PLACE TO/FROM
    The archaeologist carefully swept **dirt** *from the bones*.
    The waiter swept **the crumbs** *onto a tray*.

PASSIVE
    The trash had been swept *into a pile in the corner*.

sweep _____ carry along in a continuous motion

OBJECT + ADVERB OF PLACE TO/FROM
    The cook swept **a greasy cloth** *over the lunch counter*.
    The current swept **the boat** *onto the rocks*.
    The mud slide swept **the house** *off its foundation*.

PASSIVE
    We were swept *out to sea* by the offshore winds.

sweep _____ pass over in a continuous motion

OBJECT
    The guard's eyes swept **the room**.
    The politician's glance swept **the crowd**.

sweep _____ move quickly

ADVERB OF PLACE TO/FROM
    The rumor swept **through the crowd**.
    A gust of rain swept **down the empty street**.

sweep _____ search

OBJECT
    The volunteers swept **the woods**, looking for the lost children.
    Technicians swept **the office** for hidden electronic devices.

PASSIVE
    The crime scene has already been swept.

sweep _____ win all that can be won in

OBJECT
    Our party swept **the fall election**.

PHRASAL VERBS

sweep along/down/in/off/out/past/up/etc. *sweep in a specified direction*
    The queen swept in with all her attendants.
    The motorcade swept past.

sweep SEP **along/aside/away/back/in/off/out/past/up/etc.** *sweep [something] in a specified direction*
    The Russian revolution swept the old system away overnight.
    His election swept in a host of governmental reforms.
    The tornado swept up everything in its path.

swell

swell | swells · swelled · have swelled
swell | swells · swelled · have swollen

☑ REGULAR
☑ IRREGULAR

PRESENT

I swell	we swell
you swell	you swell
he/she/it swells	they swell

• *My ankles swell if I stand too long.*

PRESENT PROGRESSIVE

I am swelling	we are swelling
you are swelling	you are swelling
he/she/it is swelling	they are swelling

• *The wood is swelling from all the moisture.*

PAST

I swelled	we swelled
you swelled	you swelled
he/she/it swelled	they swelled

• *The sails swelled in the wind.*

PAST PROGRESSIVE

I was swelling	we were swelling
you were swelling	you were swelling
he/she/it was swelling	they were swelling

• *Naturally, her parents were swelling with pride.*

PRESENT PERFECT   ... have | has swollen
PAST PERFECT   ... had swollen

FUTURE   ... will swell
FUTURE PROGRESSIVE   ... will be swelling
FUTURE PERFECT   ... will have swollen

PAST PASSIVE

I was swollen	we were swollen
you were swollen	you were swollen
he/she/it was swollen	they were swollen

• *The river was swollen by weeks of rain.*

COMPLEMENTS

swell *become larger/stronger, expand*

My hands swelled from the heat.
The crowd in front of the gate was swelling by the minute.
The orchestra music was swelling and the lights dimmed.
The balloon swelled and began to lift.

swell _____ *cause to become larger/stronger, cause to expand*

OBJECT

The snowmelt had swollen **all the lakes.**
The bad news swelled **the rumors about layoffs.**
The pump quickly swelled **the balloons** to full size.

PASSIVE

My lymph nodes were swollen.

swell _____ *become filled [with an emotion]*

with OBJECT

Ebenezer's heart swelled **with the Christmas spirit.**
Tiny Tim swelled **with gratitude.**
The cyclist was swelling **with confidence** after winning
the Tour de France.

PRESENT		PRESENT PROGRESSIVE	
I swim	we swim	I am swimming	we are swimming
you swim	you swim	you are swimming	you are swimming
he/she/it swims	they swim	he/she/it is swimming	they are swimming

• He swims three times a week.

• The kids are swimming in the pool.

PAST		PAST PROGRESSIVE	
I swam	we swam	I was swimming	we were swimming
you swam	you swam	you were swimming	you were swimming
he/she/it swam	they swam	he/she/it was swimming	they were swimming

• I swam competitively in college.

• My head was swimming from her perfume.

PRESENT PERFECT ... have | has swum
PAST PERFECT   ... had swum

FUTURE   ... will swim
FUTURE PROGRESSIVE ... will be swimming
FUTURE PERFECT   ... will have swum

PAST PASSIVE

—   —
—   —
it was swum   they were swum

• The English Channel was first swum in 1875.

─────────────────────────────(COMPLEMENTS)───

swim *travel through water by moving one's arms and legs*

Look at me! I'm swimming.
Do you know how to swim?
I could swim before I could ride a bicycle.

swim *be dizzy*

The cocktails make my head swim.
After the accident, my head swam and my ears rang.
They gave me so many different directions that my head was swimming.

swim _____ *travel through water by moving one's arms and legs*
ADVERB OF PLACE TO/FROM

Let's swim **out to the reef.**
The fish swam **into the net.**
We had swum **clear across the lake.**
The kids like to swim **under the dock.**

swim _____ *cross by swimming*
OBJECT

Salmon can swim **most of the Columbia River.**
A few people have swum **the Strait of Messina.**
The kids are trying to swim **the length of the pool** under water.

swim _____ *seem to be whirling*
ADVERB OF PLACE

After he drank the punch, the room swam **before his eyes.**

swim _____ *be completely covered with* [USED ONLY IN THE PROGRESSIVE TENSES]
ADVERB OF PLACE

The lettuce was practically swimming **in salad dressing.**

─────────────────────────────(PHRASAL VERBS)───

swim along/around/away/in/off/out/ up/etc. *swim in a specified direction*

The kids were swimming around in the pond.
After we fed the dolphins, they swam off.

─────────────────────────────(EXPRESSIONS)───

sink or swim *fail or succeed*

Donna has a new job, and we are wondering if she will sink or swim.

swim against the current/tide *act in a way opposite to others*

I swam against the tide in high school—and often got punished for it.

PRESENT

I swing	we swing
you swing	you swing
he/she/it swings	they swing

• *Watch out—the door swings toward you.*

PRESENT PROGRESSIVE

I am swinging	we are swinging
you are swinging	you are swinging
he/she/it is swinging	they are swinging

• *You are swinging the bat too late.*

PAST

I swung	we swung
you swung	you swung
he/she/it swung	they swung

• *He swung his racket and missed.*

PAST PROGRESSIVE

I was swinging	we were swinging
you were swinging	you were swinging
he/she/it was swinging	they were swinging

• *The kids were swinging on vines.*

PRESENT PERFECT ... have | has swung
PAST PERFECT ... had swung

FUTURE ... will swing
FUTURE PROGRESSIVE ... will be swinging
FUTURE PERFECT ... will have swung

PAST PASSIVE

I was swung	we were swung
you were swung	you were swung
he/she/it was swung	they were swung

• *The heavy beam was swung into place.*

COMPLEMENTS

swing *sway/rock back and forth*	The gate was swinging in the wind.
	The earthquake caused the chandeliers to swing.
	The dancers were swinging in time to the music.
swing *change suddenly*	His moods were swinging more and more wildly.
	Opinion polls were swinging all over the map.
swing *strike at something in a sweeping motion*	The batter swings and misses.
	The tired boxers were swinging wildly.
	A good golfer swings with his hips, not just with his arms.
swing _____ *move ([something]) in a sweeping motion*	
ADVERB OF PLACE TO/FROM	The cowboy swung **into the saddle**.
	The children swung **onto the wagon**.
	I swung **into the driver's seat**.
OBJECT	He swung **the bat** and drove the ball into left field.
	Biff swung **a punch** when the referee wasn't looking.
	He swung **the golf club** and topped the ball.
OBJECT + ADVERB OF PLACE TO/FROM	I swung **my leg** *over the top rail* and jumped.
	Larry swung **his suitcase** *onto the bed*.
	She swung **her arm** *around my shoulder*.
	The kids swung **the rope** *over a limb*.
swing _____ *influence decisively*	
OBJECT	The senator thought his ad could swing **the election**.
	We hoped to swing **enough undecided voters** to win.

PHRASAL VERBS

swing around/down/in/off/out/etc. *swing in a specified direction*	The cowboy swung down from the saddle.
	The path swings off to the right at the top of the hill.
swing <u>SEP</u> **around/down/in/off/out**/etc. *swing [something] in a specified direction*	The knight swung his sword around, and everyone stepped back.
swing by/over *visit briefly*	Susan will swing by if she has a chance.
swing by/over _____ *visit briefly*	I'll swing by Grandma's on the way to the store.
	Can you swing over to the grocery and buy some milk?

PRESENT

I take	we take
you take	you take
he/she/it takes	they take

• *He always takes the bus to work.*

PRESENT PROGRESSIVE

I am taking	we are taking
you are taking	you are taking
he/she/it is taking	they are taking

• *He is taking a long time.*

PAST

I took	we took
you took	you took
he/she/it took	they took

• *Someone took the last cup of coffee.*

PAST PROGRESSIVE

I was taking	we were taking
you were taking	you were taking
he/she/it was taking	they were taking

• *We were taking the bus to New York.*

PRESENT PERFECT   ... have | has taken
PAST PERFECT   ... had taken

FUTURE   ... will take
FUTURE PROGRESSIVE   ... will be taking
FUTURE PERFECT   ... will have taken

PAST PASSIVE

I was taken	we were taken
you were taken	you were taken
he/she/it was taken	they were taken

• *All of the seats were already taken.*

COMPLEMENTS

take _____ *grasp, take possession of*

  OBJECT   He took **his daughter's hand.**

    PASSIVE   Our ID cards were taken by the police.

take _____ *get, obtain*

  OBJECT   Frank took **a job at the radio station.**
                Gerry took **a jar of olives** from the refrigerator.

take _____ *carry, transport*

  OBJECT   You should always take **your passport** when you travel.
                Take **an umbrella** in case it rains.
                Can you take **the kids** with you?
                I usually take **my lunch.**

  OBJECT + ADVERB OF PLACE TO/FROM   Would you take **these books** *to the library*?
                Amos took **the package** *to the post office.*
                This bus takes **riders** *to the stadium.*

take _____ *bring, lead*

  OBJECT + ADVERB OF PLACE TO/FROM   Bill is taking **Fran** *to the dance.*
                This path takes **you** *to the top of Buttimer Hill.*

take _____ *travel by [a vehicle, route]*

  OBJECT (+ ADVERB OF PLACE TO/FROM)   We can take **the elevator or the stairs**—you choose.
                My parents once took **the Queen Mary.**
                Let's take **the scenic route.**
                We took **Route 66** *from Chicago to Los Angeles.*
                The kids took **a shortcut** *through the woods.*
                They took **the bus** *home.*

take _____ *move to [a position]*

  OBJECT   Gentlemen, please take **your seats.**
                The two teams are taking **the field.**

take _____ *engage in [an activity]*

  OBJECT   Let's take **a 10-minute break.**
                Thomas always takes **an afternoon nap.**
                We took **a nice walk in the park.**
                I took **a class in income tax preparation.**

take _____	eat, drink, swallow	
OBJECT		I'll take **a black coffee and two donuts,** please.
		I took **an aspirin** for my headache.

take _____	capture, win	
OBJECT		After a brief fight, the soldiers took **the fort.**
		The Cards took **three out of four games** from the Mets.

take _____	subscribe to, rent	
OBJECT		They take **several newspapers and magazines.**
		We took **an apartment in the city.**

take _____	steal	
OBJECT		Somebody took **my wallet.**
		People often take **newspapers** without paying for them.

take _____	require, use up	
OBJECT + INFINITIVE		It took **a long time** *to repair the leak.*
		It takes **$50** *to fill the truck with gas.*
		They took **two days** *to drive to Dallas.*
		It takes **a lot of courage** *to go skydiving.*

take _____	endure, suffer	
OBJECT		Football players take **a lot of physical punishment.**
		I can't take **this heat and humidity.**

| take _____ | make by photography | |
| OBJECT | | Uncle Cecil took **pictures** during the family reunion. |

| take _____ | interpret | |
| OBJECT + ADVERB OF MANNER | | She took **my joke** *seriously.* |

⸨ **PHRASAL VERBS** ⸩

take _SEP_ **along/aside/away/down/in/ out/up/etc.** *bring/carry/lead/transport in a specified direction*
Grandmother took us along to the store.
The elevator takes you down to the parking garage.

take _SEP_ **down** *write down, record*
The officer took down his address and phone number.

take _SEP_ **down** *dismantle*
Volunteers took the political signs down afterwards.

take _SEP_ **for** *mistake for*
Betty took me for my older brother.

take in _____ *attend, visit*
We could eat at Lombardo's and take in a movie.
Today we'll take in the zoo and the art museum.

take _SEP_ **in** *give shelter to*
My husband takes in stray cats from the neighborhood.

take off *leave, depart*
Our plane will take off at 3:05 P.M.

take off *become very active/successful*
Sales of used cars have taken off like a rocket.

take _SEP_ **off** *remove [clothing, etc.]*
The players took off their helmets.

take _SEP_ **off** *deduct*
The dealer took 50% off because the table was scratched.

take _SEP_ **on** *hire*
My company took 30 new employees on in March.

take _SEP_ **on** *undertake*
Sorry, I just can't take on another project.

take _SEP_ **out** *remove*
The surgeon took Dad's gallbladder out.

take _SEP_ **over** *begin managing*
A recent college graduate took over the programming department.

take to _____ *become fond of*
Khalil has really taken to calligraphy.
Susan has taken to Leonard in a big way.

take up _____ *fill, occupy*
Your printing presses are taking up the whole basement!
Meetings took up the governor's entire afternoon.

take _SEP_ **up** *become interested in*
Stephanie has taken up knitting.

PRESENT

I teach	we teach
you teach	you teach
he/she/it teaches	they teach

· He teaches computer science.

PRESENT PROGRESSIVE

I am teaching	we are teaching
you are teaching	you are teaching
he/she/it is teaching	they are teaching

· I am teaching Introduction to Physics again.

PAST

I taught	we taught
you taught	you taught
he/she/it taught	they taught

· I taught in Spain for a year.

PAST PROGRESSIVE

I was teaching	we were teaching
you were teaching	you were teaching
he/she/it was teaching	they were teaching

· They were teaching him to play baseball.

PRESENT PERFECT ... have | has taught
PAST PERFECT ... had taught

FUTURE ... will teach
FUTURE PROGRESSIVE ... will be teaching
FUTURE PERFECT ... will have taught

PAST PASSIVE

I was taught	we were taught
you were taught	you were taught
he/she/it was taught	they were taught

· English was taught beginning in the earliest grades.

(**COMPLEMENTS**)

teach instruct professionally

I have been teaching for ten years.
Her sister teaches at Osaka University.
I would like to teach.

teach _____ provide training/instruction in [a skill, topic]

OBJECT

He teaches **martial arts.**
I would like to teach **English.**
Experience teaches **moderation in all things.**

INDIRECT OBJECT + DIRECT OBJECT

She taught _them_ **the names of the constellations.**
He taught _first-year students_ **world history.**
I taught _myself_ **the basics of geometry.**

to PARAPHRASE

She taught **the names of the constellations** _to them._
He taught **world history** _to first-year students._
I taught **the basics of geometry** _to myself._

teach _____ provide training/instruction to

OBJECT

Kathy teaches **seventh graders.**
She only teaches **graduate students.**
He teaches **management trainees.**

OBJECT + INFINITIVE

I taught **the kids** _to drive._
The army taught **them** _to be disciplined._

PASSIVE

We were taught _to think for ourselves._

(OBJECT +) WH-INFINITIVE

Their religion teaches **how to act.**
The class teaches _students_ **how to write a résumé.**
The book taught _investors_ **what to look for in a stock.**

teach _____ provide [a particular philosophy/knowledge] to

(OBJECT +) THAT-CLAUSE

History teaches **that the pen is mightier than the sword.**
My parents taught _us_ **that hard work never hurt anyone.**
The instructor taught _the class_ **that a 60-40 mixture of stocks and bonds is best.**

(**EXPRESSIONS**)

teach _____ **a lesson** show [someone]
the correct way to behave

His mother taught him a lesson on the
value of money by making him work for his allowance.

PRESENT

I tear	we tear
you tear	you tear
he/she/it tears	they tear

• *He tears stamps off envelopes.*

PRESENT PROGRESSIVE

I am tearing	we are tearing
you are tearing	you are tearing
he/she/it is tearing	they are tearing

• *Be careful—you're tearing your shirt.*

PAST

I tore	we tore
you tore	you tore
he/she/it tore	they tore

• *The ligament tore with a "popping" sound.*

PAST PROGRESSIVE

I was tearing	we were tearing
you were tearing	you were tearing
he/she/it was tearing	they were tearing

• *The kids were tearing into the chocolate brownies.*

PRESENT PERFECT ... have | has torn
PAST PERFECT ... had torn

FUTURE ... will tear
FUTURE PROGRESSIVE ... will be tearing
FUTURE PERFECT ... will have torn

PAST PASSIVE

I was torn	we were torn
you were torn	you were torn
he/she/it was torn	they were torn

• *A huge hole was torn in the building by the explosion.*

NOTE: The irregular verb *tear*, which rhymes with *care*, is presented here.
The regular verb *tear*, which rhymes with *deer*, means "cry."

──────────────────────────────────(COMPLEMENTS)──

tear *rip, come apart*	Darn it! My new jeans are tearing. The canvas will tear if there is a high wind.
tear _____ *cause to rip / come apart*	
OBJECT	I tore **the envelope** trying to open it. A big gust of wind tore **our only sail**.
PASSIVE	The documents had been torn in shipping.
tear _____ *make/punch [a hole, opening] in*	
OBJECT	The artillery fire tore **a huge gap** in our right flank.
PASSIVE	A hole was torn in his shield by a spear.
tear _____ *move with force/speed*	
ADVERB OF PLACE TO/FROM	The kids tore **out of the room**. The horses tore **around the last curve**.
tear _____ *damage [a muscle, ligament] by overstretching*	
OBJECT	Dirk tore **his rotator cuff** playing tennis. Soccer players often tear **muscles in their knees**.
PASSIVE	His shoulder was torn lifting weights.
tear _____ *damage greatly* [USED ONLY IN THE PASSIVE]	
OBJECT	The country was torn by war and famine.

──────────────────────────────────(PHRASAL VERBS)──

tear around/away/down/off/out/etc. *move with force/speed in a specified direction*	The limousine tore away from the curb. The neighbor's dog always tears out after moving cars.
tear _SEP_ **apart/away/down/off/out/up/** etc. *pull in a specified direction*	Tear the coupons apart and organize them. Carpenters tore up the old carpet.
tear into _____ *begin to do/eat/etc. forcefully*	Jackie is tearing into remodeling the kitchen. The girls really tore into the peanut butter.
tear into _____ *scold severely*	The boss tore into an employee who was late.
tear _SEP_ **up** *reject*	The manager tore up the singer's contract and offered her 10 times the money.

PRESENT

I telecast	we telecast
you telecast	you telecast
he/she/it telecasts	they telecast

- *They telecast in English and Spanish.*

PAST

I telecast	we telecast
you telecast	you telecast
he/she/it telecast	they telecast

- *The station first telecast in 1983.*

PRESENT PERFECT   ... have | has telecast
PAST PERFECT   ... had telecast

PRESENT PROGRESSIVE

I am telecasting	we are telecasting
you are telecasting	you are telecasting
he/she/it is telecasting	they are telecasting

- *We are now telecasting soccer games live.*

PAST PROGRESSIVE

I was telecasting	we were telecasting
you were telecasting	you were telecasting
he/she/it was telecasting	they were telecasting

- *The network was telecasting the World Series.*

FUTURE   ... will telecast
FUTURE PROGRESSIVE   ... will be telecasting
FUTURE PERFECT   ... will have telecast

PAST PASSIVE

—	—
it was telecast	they were telecast

- *The first TV programs were telecast before World War II.*

COMPLEMENTS

telecast *broadcast by television*

When did the station first telecast in color?
No station can telecast until it gets FCC approval.
The station is telecasting live from Civic Center.

telecast _____ *broadcast by television*

OBJECT

Many networks telecast **reality programs** because they are very inexpensive to produce.
Networks are required to telecast **a certain number of public service programs.**
A local station telecasts **a "To Your Health" feature** during the 10 o'clock news.

PASSIVE

The royal wedding was telecast live around the world.

PRESENT

I tell	we tell
you tell	you tell
he/she/it tells	they tell

• *He tells people what they want to hear.*

PRESENT PROGRESSIVE

I am telling	we are telling
you are telling	you are telling
he/she/it is telling	they are telling

• *I'm telling the whole world that I love you.*

PAST

I told	we told
you told	you told
he/she/it told	they told

• *I told the truth.*

PAST PROGRESSIVE

I was telling	we were telling
you were telling	you were telling
he/she/it was telling	they were telling

• *We were just telling them what happened.*

PRESENT PERFECT ... have | has told
PAST PERFECT ... had told

FUTURE ... will tell
FUTURE PROGRESSIVE ... will be telling
FUTURE PERFECT ... will have told

PAST PASSIVE

I was told	we were told
you were told	you were told
he/she/it was told	they were told

• *The children were told that they could stay up late.*

(**COMPLEMENTS**)

tell *reveal secret/confidential information*	Please don't tell. I will never tell.
tell *have a definite effect*	The long hours are beginning to tell. The constant battering by the artillery was starting to tell.
tell *know the outcome/result* [USED IN QUESTIONS AND NEGATIVE SENTENCES]	Who can tell? I certainly can't tell.
tell ____ *put into words, express*	
OBJECT	I told **the truth**, but he was telling **a flat-out lie**. He told **a story about growing up in Greece**.
INDIRECT OBJECT + DIRECT OBJECT	I told *the kids* **a ghost story**. Who wants to tell *them* **the bad news**?
to PARAPHRASE	I told **a ghost story** *to the kids*. Who wants to tell **the bad news** *to them*?
tell ____ *inform*	
OBJECT + THAT-CLAUSE	We need to tell **them** *that the trip has been canceled*. I told **everyone** *that we were engaged*.
PASSIVE	The press had been told *that the senator was ill*.
OBJECT + WH-CLAUSE	The consultant told **us** *what we should do*. I told **them** *how much it would cost*.
OBJECT + WH-INFINITIVE	The taxi driver told **us** *where to go*.
PASSIVE	The staff was told *what to expect*.
tell ____ *order, command*	
OBJECT + INFINITIVE	I told **her** *to return the book as soon as she could*.
PASSIVE	They had been told *to stay inside during the storm*.
tell ____ *recognize, determine with certainty* [USUALLY WITH *can* OR *could*]	
THAT-CLAUSE	I couldn't tell **that anything had happened**. Can you tell **that we remodeled the kitchen**?
WH-CLAUSE	Can you tell **who it is**? I can't tell **what went wrong**.

(**PHRASAL VERBS**)

tell ^{SEP} **off** *scold, criticize*	She told my brother off for not keeping his room clean.

PRESENT		PRESENT PROGRESSIVE	
I think	we think	I am thinking	we are thinking
you think	you think	you are thinking	you are thinking
he/she/it thinks	they think	he/she/it is thinking	they are thinking

• He thinks that the movie begins at 7:45.   • Don't rush me—I'm thinking.

PAST		PAST PROGRESSIVE	
I thought	we thought	I was thinking	we were thinking
you thought	you thought	you were thinking	you were thinking
he/she/it thought	they thought	he/she/it was thinking	they were thinking

• I thought long and hard about it.   • They were thinking that the worst had happened.

PRESENT PERFECT   ... have | has thought
PAST PERFECT   ... had thought

FUTURE   ... will think
FUTURE PROGRESSIVE   ... will be thinking
FUTURE PERFECT   ... will have thought

PAST PASSIVE	
I was thought	we were thought
you were thought	you were thought
he/she/it was thought	they were thought

• The accident was thought to have been caused by pilot error.

(COMPLEMENTS)

think   *use one's mind, reason*   Think twice before you do anything.
"I think, therefore I am." [RENÉ DESCARTES]

think _____ *believe, expect*
    THAT-CLAUSE   I thought **that dinner was good, but a little too heavy.**
Do they think **that the flight will leave on time?**

think _____ *consider, judge*
    OBJECT + (*to be*) PREDICATE NOUN   The reviewer thought **the book *(to be) a bit of a dud.***
The public thought **Clark *(to be) a dashing hero.***
       PASSIVE   At first, Truman was thought *(to be) a failed president.*
    OBJECT + (*to be*) PREDICATE ADJECTIVE   Everyone thought **Thomas *(to be) promising.***
They thought **the idea *(to be) ready to present to the board.***
       PASSIVE   The car was thought *(to be) quite overpriced.*
    OBJECT + INFINITIVE   I thought **him *to have more sense than that.***
       PASSIVE   He was thought *to own several Renoirs.*

think _____ *remember* [USED IN QUESTIONS AND NEGATIVE SENTENCES, OFTEN WITH *can* OR *could*]
    of OBJECT   I can't think **of the girl's name.**
    INFINITIVE   Did you think **to lock the back door?**
Who thought **to bring some insect repellent?**
    WH-CLAUSE   We couldn't think **what his name was.**
I couldn't think **where we were supposed to meet the group.**
    WH-INFINITIVE   I couldn't think **what to say.**
Aunt Polly couldn't think **where to turn next.**

think _____ *contemplate, consider*
    of/about OBJECT   The board was thinking **of Rex for secretary.**
She thinks **about him** all the time.
    of/about PRESENT PARTICIPLE   Anne was thinking **of asking Wentworth to the concert.**
We were thinking **about ordering Chinese for dinner.**

(PHRASAL VERBS)

think _SEP_ **over** *consider carefully*   I need to think your proposal over before making a decision.

think _SEP_ **up** *invent, plan*   We thought up a better way to manage inventory.
They thought up a clever way to trick Bart and Jacob.

thrive | thrives · thrived · have thrived
thrive | thrives · throve · have thriven

PRESENT

I thrive	we thrive
you thrive	you thrive
he/she/it thrives	they thrive

• *The senator thrives on controversy.*

PRESENT PROGRESSIVE

I am thriving	we are thriving
you are thriving	you are thriving
he/she/it is thriving	they are thriving

• *The children are thriving in their new school.*

PAST

I throve	we throve
you throve	you throve
he/she/it throve	they throve

• *The delicate plants throve through the winter.*

PAST PROGRESSIVE

I was thriving	we were thriving
you were thriving	you were thriving
he/she/it was thriving	they were thriving

• *Despite the economy, our business was thriving.*

PRESENT PERFECT ... have | has thriven
PAST PERFECT ... had thriven

FUTURE ... will thrive
FUTURE PROGRESSIVE ... will be thriving
FUTURE PERFECT ... will have thriven

PAST PASSIVE

Thrive is never used in the passive voice.

(**COMPLEMENTS**)

thrive *flourish, prosper*

These plants thrive in a warm, moist climate.
Children need stability to thrive.
A company needs capital to thrive.
The young lettuce plants throve in spite of the hard frost last week.

thrive _____ *flourish/prosper [because of]*

on OBJECT

People can thrive **on a vegetarian diet.**
I thrive **on hard work.**
Swindlers thrive **on people who want to make money without working.**

PRESENT

I throw	we throw
you throw	you throw
he/she/it throws	they throw

· *He throws great parties.*

PRESENT PROGRESSIVE

I am throwing	we are throwing
you are throwing	you are throwing
he/she/it is throwing	they are throwing

· *I am throwing an informal reception for them.*

PAST

I threw	we threw
you threw	you threw
he/she/it threw	they threw

· *I threw another log on the fire.*

PAST PROGRESSIVE

I was throwing	we were throwing
you were throwing	you were throwing
he/she/it was throwing	they were throwing

· *He was throwing rocks into the pond.*

PRESENT PERFECT	... have | has thrown
PAST PERFECT	... had thrown

FUTURE	... will throw
FUTURE PROGRESSIVE	... will be throwing
FUTURE PERFECT	... will have thrown

PAST PASSIVE

I was thrown	we were thrown
you were thrown	you were thrown
he/she/it was thrown	they were thrown

· *A rope was thrown to the people in the canoe.*

(COMPLEMENTS)

throw *toss/hurl a projectile*	He doesn't throw with much force. I couldn't throw because I had injured my shoulder. If you want to play baseball, you have to learn how to throw.
throw _____ *toss, hurl*	
OBJECT	Kids love to throw **rocks**. The mob started throwing **bricks**. The pitcher could throw **the ball** sidearm.
OBJECT + ADVERB OF PLACE TO/FROM	My sister threw **her coat** *on the sofa*. Josh threw **the report** *on my desk*.
throw _____ *propel suddenly and forcefully*	
OBJECT + ADVERB OF PLACE TO/FROM	The explosion threw **me** *to the ground*. Someone threw **a chair** *against the wall*. The cook threw **the pizza dough** *high into the air*.
PASSIVE	The driver was thrown *into the ditch*.
throw _____ *direct, cast*	
OBJECT + ADVERB OF PLACE TO/FROM	The actor threw **a dirty look** *at the people talking in the front row*. The lantern threw **light** *around the barn*.
PASSIVE	All of our resources were thrown *into the project*.
throw _____ *toss, give*	
INDIRECT OBJECT + DIRECT OBJECT	He threw *the dog* **a bone**. Throw *me* **that notebook**, will you?
to PARAPHRASE	He threw **a bone** *to the dog*. Throw **that notebook** *to me*, will you?
throw _____ *host [an event]*	
OBJECT	The church threw **a potluck dinner**.
INDIRECT OBJECT + DIRECT OBJECT	We threw *my sister* **an engagement party**. They are going to throw *us* **a going-away party**.
for PARAPHRASE	We threw **an engagement party** *for my sister*. They are going to throw **a going-away party** *for us*.

throw _____ *put suddenly [in a place, condition]*

OBJECT + *into* OBJECT

The sheriff threw **the suspects *into jail*.**
His remarks threw **the audience *into hysteria*.**

(**PHRASAL VERBS**)

throw <u>SEP</u> **around/aside/back/down/
in/off/out/up**/etc. *toss/hurl in a specified
direction*

The players were throwing a Frisbee around.
Would you throw the ball back?
He threw his head back and laughed.
He threw his book bag down.

throw <u>SEP</u> **around** *spend [money] freely*

He throws money around like it grows on trees.

throw <u>SEP</u> **away** *discard, get rid of*

Don't throw the lamp away; I'm going to fix it.

throw <u>SEP</u> **in** *interject*

Jan threw in the idea of working at a soup kitchen.

throw <u>SEP</u> **in** *add as an extra*

They will throw in a medium pizza for free.

throw <u>SEP</u> **off** *mislead, fool*

His foreign accent threw the police off.

throw <u>SEP</u> **on** *put on in haste*

I'll throw on a jacket and be ready to go.

throw <u>SEP</u> **out** *discard, get rid of*

We won't throw the plastic out; we'll recycle it instead.

throw <u>SEP</u> **out** *expel*

The teacher threw him out for using profanity.

throw <u>SEP</u> **out** *reject*

The judge will throw the convict's testimony out.

throw <u>SEP</u> **out** *offer*

Dave is always throwing out suggestions.

throw <u>SEP</u> **together** *put together in haste*

Let's throw together some pasta for supper.
We can throw a scale model together in a week.

throw **up** *vomit*

He threw up on the way home from the ballpark.

throw <u>SEP</u> **up** *build quickly*

A developer threw up a flimsy apartment building
on the corner.

(**EXPRESSIONS**)

throw _____ **a curve** *surprise [someone]*

The company threw us a curve
by switching medical insurance plans.

throw **a fit/tantrum** *display anger*

Johnny throws a fit when I ask him to wash his hands.

throw **[a lot of / some] light on** _____
clarify, give details about

Scientists threw some light on the human genome.

throw **cold water on** _____ *discourage*

The committee threw cold water on our ideas for
reducing waste.

throw _____ **for a loop** *shock/confuse
[someone]*

The program glitch threw the programmers for a loop.

throw **good money after bad** *waste even
more money on something*

Frank threw good money after bad by buying 100 more
shares of the worthless stock.

throw **in the sponge/towel** *quit, give up*

The firm is throwing in the towel after losing its three
biggest customers.

throw **[one's] hands up** *quit in despair*

After losing eight straight Solitaire games, Dad threw
his hands up and decided to read the newspaper.

throw **[one's] weight around** *use one's
power excessively*

Mid-level managers love to throw their weight around
when the boss is gone.

throw **[oneself] into**
_____ *involve oneself
in [something] eagerly*

Paul threw himself into basketweaving.

throw **the book at**
_____ *charge [someone]
with as many crimes
as possible*

The district attorney threw the book at the alleged
child molester.

top 30 verb

PRESENT

I thrust	we thrust
you thrust	you thrust
he/she/it thrusts	they thrust

• *He thrusts the note in his pocket and sighs.*

PRESENT PROGRESSIVE

I am thrusting	we are thrusting
you are thrusting	you are thrusting
he/she/it is thrusting	they are thrusting

• *Someone is always thrusting a petition at you.*

PAST

I thrust	we thrust
you thrust	you thrust
he/she/it thrust	they thrust

• *I thrust through the crowd frantically.*

PAST PROGRESSIVE

I was thrusting	we were thrusting
you were thrusting	you were thrusting
he/she/it was thrusting	they were thrusting

• *A rodent was thrusting through the undergrowth.*

PRESENT PERFECT ... have | has thrust
PAST PERFECT ... had thrust

FUTURE ... will thrust
FUTURE PROGRESSIVE ... will be thrusting
FUTURE PERFECT ... will have thrust

PAST PASSIVE

I was thrust	we were thrust
you were thrust	you were thrust
he/she/it was thrust	they were thrust

• *A gun was thrust into my hand.*

(**COMPLEMENTS**)

thrust _____ *push forward suddenly*
   OBJECT + ADVERB OF PLACE TO/FROM

The soldier thrust **a sword** *through his shield*.
Batman thrust **his elbow** *into the villain's stomach*.
The host thrust **the children** *into the limelight*.

   PASSIVE

My head was thrust *into a barrel of water*.
Fame had been thrust *on her* at an early age.

thrust _____ *move forward forcefully*
   ADVERB OF PLACE TO/FROM

A tugboat was thrusting **through the waves**.
Her scream thrust **through the still night air**.

thrust _____ *jut, extend out*
   ADVERB OF PLACE TO/FROM

A long wharf thrust **into the river**.
A diving board thrust **over the water**.

(**PHRASAL VERBS**)

thrust back/down/in/out/up/etc.
move forcefully in a specified direction

The boy's tongue thrust out as he
   sighted down the barrel.
Daffodils were thrusting up on the first warm day of spring.

thrust _SEP_ aside/away/back/down/
in/out/up/etc. *push suddenly in a
specified direction*

The police thrust the protesters aside.
He opened his briefcase and thrust the report in.

tread

tread | treads · treaded · have trod/trodden ☑ IRREGULAR
tread | treads · trod · have trod/trodden ☑ IRREGULAR

PRESENT

I tread	we tread
you tread	you tread
he/she/it treads	they tread

• *He treads lightly for such a big man.*

PRESENT PROGRESSIVE

I am treading	we are treading
you are treading	you are treading
he/she/it is treading	they are treading

• *The diplomat is treading lightly in negotiations.*

PAST

I trod	we trod
you trod	you trod
he/she/it trod	they trod

• *The soldiers trod along the muddy path.*

PAST PROGRESSIVE

I was treading	we were treading
you were treading	you were treading
he/she/it was treading	they were treading

• *The visitors were treading a path across our lawn.*

PRESENT PERFECT ... have | has trod/trodden
PAST PERFECT ... had trod/trodden

FUTURE ... will tread
FUTURE PROGRESSIVE ... will be treading
FUTURE PERFECT ... will have trod/trodden

PAST PASSIVE

— —
— —
it was trod/trodden   they were trod/trodden

• *The snow in town was trodden into a dirty slush.*

COMPLEMENTS

tread _____ *walk, go on foot*

ADVERB OF PLACE TO/FROM   The column of soldiers trod slowly **along the road**.
"Fools rush in **where Angels fear to tread**." [ALEXANDER POPE]
Dejectedly, he slowly trod **up the long staircase**.
Don't tread **on the new lawn**.

ADVERB OF MANNER   We trod **slowly** to keep from sinking into the soft ground.
The children are treading **carefully** past the sleeping dogs.
We need to tread **quietly** so as not to wake the children.
"I have spread my dreams beneath your feet;
   Tread **softly** because you tread on my dreams." [W.B. YEATS]

tread _____ *act cautiously*

ADVERB OF MANNER   The company has to tread **lightly** or risk legal action.
The judge warned the prosecutor to tread **carefully**.

tread _____ *wear (a path), trample*

OBJECT + ADVERB OF PLACE   We trod **a path** *out to the mailbox*.
The deer had trod **a route** *through the forest*.

PASSIVE   A muddy trail had been trod *across the tile floor*.

PRESENT

I understand	we understand
you understand	you understand
he/she/it understands	they understand

• *He understands the situation perfectly.*

PRESENT PROGRESSIVE

I am understanding	we are understanding
you are understanding	you are understanding
he/she/it is understanding	they are understanding

• *We are understanding each other better now.*

PAST

I understood	we understood
you understood	you understood
he/she/it understood	they understood

• *They understood only a few words.*

PAST PROGRESSIVE

I was understanding	we were understanding
you were understanding	you were understanding
he/she/it was understanding	they were understanding

• *They weren't understanding his Italian very well.*

PRESENT PERFECT ... have | has understood
PAST PERFECT ... had understood

FUTURE ... will understand
FUTURE PROGRESSIVE ... will be understanding
FUTURE PERFECT ... will have understood

PAST PASSIVE

I was understood	we were understood
you were understood	you were understood
he/she/it was understood	they were understood

• *The tour guide was easily understood.*

(COMPLEMENTS)

understand *know the meaning of something*

Do you understand?
He is too young to understand.

understand ＿＿ *comprehend, know the meaning of*

OBJECT

The doctor understood **the nature of the patient's symptoms.**
Do you understand **this equation?**
Nobody could understand **the cockney slang used in the movie.**

PASSIVE

The assembly instructions must not have been understood.

WH-CLAUSE

I understood **what he was trying to say.**
Did you understand **where we were going?**
We need to understand **how much this is going to cost.**

WH-INFINITIVE

Do you understand **whom to call if you have a problem?**
I understand **what to do.**
Do you understand **where to pick up your passengers?**

understand ＿＿ *know what makes [something] work/happen*

OBJECT

It takes students a long time to really understand **evolution.**
Does anyone understand **the stock market?**
Almost no one understands **credit and default swaps.**

PASSIVE

The role of washing hands to control disease was not understood
at the time.

WH-CLAUSE

Do you understand **what drives the global economy?**
Even third graders understand **why the sun seems to rise
in the east and set in the west.**

understand ＿＿ *know and be sympathetic to the feelings/attitudes of*

OBJECT

My boyfriend doesn't understand **me.**
I don't think the director understood **Lady Macbeth** very well.
Older people never understand **the younger generation.**

understand ＿＿ *get the idea/notion* [OFTEN AS A POLITE FORM OF IMPLIED QUESTION]

OBJECT + INFINITIVE

I understand **you** *to be a student at Santa Cruz.*
We understand **them** *to be having lunch with us.*
I understand **the apartment** *to be available.*

THAT-CLAUSE

I understand **that you are applying for a job with us.**
We understand **that the flight may be delayed.**
It is understood **that the parents will have joint custody.**

PRESENT

I uphold	we uphold
you uphold	you uphold
he/she/it upholds	they uphold

• *The firm upholds its tradition of service.*

PRESENT PROGRESSIVE

I am upholding	we are upholding
you are upholding	you are upholding
he/she/it is upholding	they are upholding

• *The Marines are upholding centuries of tradition.*

PAST

I upheld	we upheld
you upheld	you upheld
he/she/it upheld	they upheld

• *The court upheld the lower court ruling.*

PAST PROGRESSIVE

I was upholding	we were upholding
you were upholding	you were upholding
he/she/it was upholding	they were upholding

• *We were upholding our end of the bargain.*

PRESENT PERFECT ... have | has upheld
PAST PERFECT ... had upheld

FUTURE ... will uphold
FUTURE PROGRESSIVE ... will be upholding
FUTURE PERFECT ... will have upheld

PAST PASSIVE

—	—
—	—
it was upheld	they were upheld

• *The ruling was upheld by the appellate court.*

COMPLEMENTS

uphold _____ *confirm/support [a decision, opinion]*

OBJECT The courts will usually uphold **lower court rulings** unless there is a demonstrable error of fact or law.
The whole committee upheld **the ruling of the subcommittee**.
The Supreme Court upheld **the plaintiff** in *Brown v. Board of Education*.

PASSIVE The decision was upheld unanimously by the appeals court.

uphold _____ *maintain [a custom, practice]*

OBJECT John upheld **the family tradition** by joining the Navy.
Sadly, the school has not been able to uphold **its superior image**.
The new CEO vowed to uphold **the company's reputation for fiscal responsibility**.

PASSIVE The honor of the Corps had been upheld.

PRESENT

I upset	we upset
you upset	you upset
he/she/it upsets	they upset

• *The new development upsets all our plans.*

PRESENT PROGRESSIVE

I am upsetting	we are upsetting
you are upsetting	you are upsetting
he/she/it is upsetting	they are upsetting

• *I'm sorry that I'm upsetting you.*

PAST

I upset	we upset
you upset	you upset
he/she/it upset	they upset

• *The president's decision upset the voters.*

PAST PROGRESSIVE

I was upsetting	we were upsetting
you were upsetting	you were upsetting
he/she/it was upsetting	they were upsetting

• *The weather was upsetting our arrangements.*

PRESENT PERFECT ... have | has upset
PAST PERFECT ... had upset

FUTURE ... will upset
FUTURE PROGRESSIVE ... will be upsetting
FUTURE PERFECT ... will have upset

PAST PASSIVE

I was upset	we were upset
you were upset	you were upset
he/she/it was upset	they were upset

• *Naturally, we were quite upset by what happened.*

COMPLEMENTS

upset _____ *knock over*

OBJECT   The dogs upset **some potted plants** on the patio.
      The waiter upset **a bottle of wine** as he was clearing the table.

PASSIVE   A whole gallon of paint had been upset.

upset _____ *cause to be disturbed/worried/unhappy*

OBJECT   The hotel clerk's rudeness really upset **us**.
      Thunderstorms upset **the dogs** terribly.
      Spicy food always upsets **my stomach**.
      He delights in upsetting **the administrators**.

PASSIVE   The parents were upset at the news of the school's closure.

upset _____ *disturb the order/working of*

OBJECT   The kids are really good at upsetting **my daily routine**.
      The rain upset **our plans for a trip to the beach**.
      Global warming is upsetting **many delicate ecosystems**.
      The collapse of the credit market has upset **the normal balance of supply and demand for housing**.

PASSIVE   The orderly transfer of power was totally upset by the prince's unexpected death.

upset _____ *win a surprising victory over*

OBJECT   The Jets upset **the Colts** in Superbowl III.
      Harry Truman upset **Thomas Dewey** in the 1948 presidential election.

EXPRESSIONS

upset the apple cart *ruin something*   Grady upset the apple cart by telling Louise about the surprise party.

wake | wakes · waked · have waked
wake | wakes · woke · have woken
waken | wakens · wakened · have wakened

☑ REGULAR
☑ IRREGULAR
☑ REGULAR

PRESENT

I wake	we wake
you wake	you wake
he/she/it wakes	they wake

• *He usually wakes at seven.*

PRESENT PROGRESSIVE

I am waking	we are waking
you are waking	you are waking
he/she/it is waking	they are waking

• *He's waking the neighbors with his lawn mower.*

PAST

I woke	we woke
you woke	you woke
he/she/it woke	they woke

• *I woke just before the alarm went off.*

PAST PROGRESSIVE

I was waking	we were waking
you were waking	you were waking
he/she/it was waking	they were waking

• *The birds were always waking us at dawn.*

PRESENT PERFECT ... have | has woken
PAST PERFECT ... had woken

FUTURE ... will wake
FUTURE PROGRESSIVE ... will be waking
FUTURE PERFECT ... will have woken

PAST PASSIVE

I was woken	we were woken
you were woken	you were woken
he/she/it was woken	they were woken

• *We were woken in the middle of the night by a dog barking.*

(**COMPLEMENTS**)

NOTE: *Wake* and *waken* have the same meanings and the same general uses. They are similar to *awake/awaken* (verb No. 2), with this difference: *Wake* is used with *up* (*Jane woke up at 7 o'clock*), but *awake, awaken,* and *waken* are not.

wake *quit sleeping*

We need to be quiet because the children wake so easily.
The patient began wakening from the anesthetic.
In the springtime, I wake long before I need to get up.

wake _____ *arouse from sleeping*

OBJECT

Wake **the children** at eight if they are not up already.
Don't wake **me** unless it is an emergency.
His snoring would wake **the dead**.

PASSIVE

I was woken by the sound of dripping water.

WH-CLAUSE

The thunderstorm woke **whoever was sleeping**.

wake _____ *stir up*

OBJECT

Spring woke **the slumbering land**.
The injustice woke **a feeling of outrage in the entire community**.
His good fortune wakened **feelings of envy in the little village**.

(**PHRASAL VERBS**)

wake up *become aware of what is happening*

I hope he wakes up before it's too late.
Fritz woke up after the heart attack and started exercising and eating right.

wake _SEP_ **up** *cause to become aware of what is happening*

The advisor woke the mayor up to the danger of rising water.
This report will wake citizens up to the importance of alternative energy sources.

(**EXPRESSIONS**)

wake up and smell the coffee *become aware of what is happening*

The world has changed, and we must wake up and smell the coffee.

PRESENT

I wear	we wear
you wear	you wear
he/she/it wears	they wear

• He always wears a coat and tie.

PRESENT PROGRESSIVE

I am wearing	we are wearing
you are wearing	you are wearing
he/she/it is wearing	they are wearing

• I am wearing a skirt and sweater to the concert.

PAST

I wore	we wore
you wore	you wore
he/she/it wore	they wore

• She wore her little black dress to the party.

PAST PROGRESSIVE

I was wearing	we were wearing
you were wearing	you were wearing
he/she/it was wearing	they were wearing

• What were they wearing?

PRESENT PERFECT ... have | has worn
PAST PERFECT ... had worn

FUTURE ... will wear
FUTURE PROGRESSIVE ... will be wearing
FUTURE PERFECT ... will have worn

PAST PASSIVE

I was worn	we were worn
you were worn	you were worn
he/she/it was worn	they were worn

• In those days, white was never worn after Labor Day.

COMPLEMENTS

wear remain in good condition after much use	That fabric won't wear very well.
	The carpet in the hall will wear for years.
wear _____ have/carry on one's body	
OBJECT	The kids wear **jeans** most of the time.
	Politicians felt it necessary to wear **flag pins**.
	Men are required to wear **ties** when meeting with clients.
	Mary wears **bifocals** now.
PASSIVE	Casual clothing is worn nearly everywhere.
WH-CLAUSE	The tribe only wore **what they themselves produced**.
	I give up; wear **whatever you want to**.
wear _____ have [a certain hairstyle]	
OBJECT + ADVERB OF MANNER	She wore **her hair** *off the shoulder*.
	He wore **his hair** *in a ponytail*.
PASSIVE	Her hair was worn *in a huge Afro*.
wear _____ have [a certain facial expression]	
OBJECT	He was wearing **a silly grin** when he made the announcement.
	His face wears **a permanent scowl**.
	Why are you wearing **such a sad face**?
wear _____ damage/erode gradually, usually by friction	
OBJECT	Wagon wheels wore **ruts** along the Oregon Trail.
	The Mississippi River wore **a new channel** east of Kaskaskia.
PASSIVE	A path had been worn through the forest.

PHRASAL VERBS

wear _SEP_ **down** make weak/tired	The 12-hour days are wearing the staff down.
wear off go away gradually	The effects of the painkiller wore off after a few hours.
wear on continue, pass	The meeting wore on into the early hours of the morning.
	It got more cloudy as the day wore on.
wear out become exhausted/useless	The tires have worn out on my pickup truck.
wear _SEP_ **out** use until exhausted	Our son has worn out his winter coat.
wear _SEP_ **out** exhaust, tire out	Shopping all day with his wife wore him out.

weave

weave | weaves · wove · have woven
weave | weaves · weaved · have weaved

☑ IRREGULAR
☑ REGULAR

PRESENT

I weave / we weave
you weave / you weave
he/she/it weaves / they weave

* She weaves baskets from birch bark.

PRESENT PROGRESSIVE

I am weaving / we are weaving
you are weaving / you are weaving
he/she/it is weaving / they are weaving

* The children are weaving simple placemats.

PAST

I wove / we wove
you wove / you wove
he/she/it wove / they wove

* The spider wove a web across the doorway.

PAST PROGRESSIVE

I was weaving / we were weaving
you were weaving / you were weaving
he/she/it was weaving / they were weaving

* They were weaving a wool rug.

PRESENT PERFECT ... have | has woven
PAST PERFECT ... had woven

FUTURE ... will weave
FUTURE PROGRESSIVE ... will be weaving
FUTURE PERFECT ... will have woven

PAST PASSIVE

— / —
— / —
it was woven / they were woven

* These wall hangings were woven by hand.

—————————————————————————(**COMPLEMENTS**)—

NOTE: The regular past form *weaved* is used only in the sense "move in and out / side to side"; *wove* and *woven* are used in all other senses.

weave *pass threads/strips/etc. over and under one another to form something*

They are teaching the students how to weave.
Children learn by watching their mothers weave.
In some cultures, only men weave.

weave *move in and out / side to side*

A red SUV weaved through the bridge traffic.

weave _____ *pass [threads/strips/etc.] over and under one another [to form something]*
  OBJECT

They wove **palm fronds** to make a thatched roof.
I wove **my fingers** to make a step for her.
We wove **the reeds** into a simple boat.

weave _____ *form by passing threads/strips/etc. over and under one another*
  OBJECT

The mill wove **beautiful linen tablecloths**.
Every society on earth has woven **some kind of basket**.
The women wove **a crown from flowers they had picked**.

  PASSIVE

A crude filter was woven from plant stalks.

weave _____ *combine to make a whole*
  OBJECT

A good story weaves **a number of plot lines**.
The poem weaves **the themes of love and loss in 19th-century England**.

weave _____ *make by combining into a whole*
  OBJECT

"Oh! what **a tangled** web we weave
  When first we practice to deceive." [SIR WALTER SCOTT]

  PASSIVE

Wagner's operas are woven from many musical themes.

weave _____ *form [a web] [OF A SPIDER]*
  OBJECT

A spider wove **a beautiful web** between those two trees.

PRESENT

I wed	we wed
you wed	you wed
he/she/it weds	they wed

• *His opera weds two different traditions.*

PRESENT PROGRESSIVE

I am wedding	we are wedding
you are wedding	you are wedding
he/she/it is wedding	they are wedding

• *The composer is wedding folk and rock music.*

PAST

I wed	we wed
you wed	you wed
he/she/it wed	they wed

• *They wed as soon as they graduated.*

PAST PROGRESSIVE

I was wedding	we were wedding
you were wedding	you were wedding
he/she/it was wedding	they were wedding

• *He was wedding the design to other brochures.*

PRESENT PERFECT ... have | has wed
PAST PERFECT ... had wed

FUTURE ... will wed
FUTURE PROGRESSIVE ... will be wedding
FUTURE PERFECT ... will have wed

PAST PASSIVE

I was wed	we were wed
you were wed	you were wed
he/she/it was wed	they were wed

• *The couple was wed by her family's minister.*

COMPLEMENTS

wed *marry*

When did they wed?
John and Marcia wed after a tumultuous engagement.
My parents wed in Hawaii when Dad was in the Navy.

wed _____ *marry*

OBJECT

She wed **her childhood sweetheart.**
Whom did she finally wed?
My father wed **my mother** in 1982.

wed _____ *perform the marriage ceremony for*

OBJECT

I have wed **hundreds of people** over the years.
Reverend Gerry wed **your parents.**

PASSIVE

They were wed in the garden, if I remember correctly.

wed _____ *unite, join closely*

OBJECT

Fusion cuisine weds **cooking styles from all over the world.**
The building weds **Spanish and modernist styles.**
His art weds **realism and postmodernism.**

PRESENT

I weep	we weep
you weep	you weep
he/she/it weeps	they weep

* *He always weeps at weddings.*

PRESENT PROGRESSIVE

I am weeping	we are weeping
you are weeping	you are weeping
he/she/it is weeping	they are weeping

* *She is weeping uncontrollably.*

PAST

I wept	we wept
you wept	you wept
he/she/it wept	they wept

* *They wept when they heard the news.*

PAST PROGRESSIVE

I was weeping	we were weeping
you were weeping	you were weeping
he/she/it was weeping	they were weeping

* *The children were all weeping.*

PRESENT PERFECT   ... have | has wept
PAST PERFECT   ... had wept

FUTURE   ... will weep
FUTURE PROGRESSIVE   ... will be weeping
FUTURE PERFECT   ... will have wept

PAST PASSIVE

—	—
—	—
it was wept	they were wept

* *No tears were wept for him.*

COMPLEMENTS

weep *shed tears, cry*	You have to take time to weep.
	The whole family was weeping during the service.
	She wept every time she thought of the accident.
weep *give off drops of liquid*	The walls were weeping in the humid air.
	Aloe plants weep if you cut them.
	The damp air weeps when it comes into contact with the cold metal.
weep _____ *shed [tears]*	
OBJECT	Weep **no tears** for me.
	He wept **bitter tears** for what he had done.
PASSIVE	Endless tears were wept over such a senseless death.

PRESENT

I wet	we wet
you wet	you wet
he/she/it wets	they wet

* *She always wets her lips before she speaks.*

PRESENT PROGRESSIVE

I am wetting	we are wetting
you are wetting	you are wetting
he/she/it is wetting	they are wetting

* *She is wetting her hair to keep it from blowing.*

PAST

I wet	we wet
you wet	you wet
he/she/it wet	they wet

* *He wet his fingers before taking the ball.*

PAST PROGRESSIVE

I was wetting	we were wetting
you were wetting	you were wetting
he/she/it was wetting	they were wetting

* *They were wetting the tent to make it cooler.*

PRESENT PERFECT ... have | has wet
PAST PERFECT ... had wet

FUTURE ... will wet
FUTURE PROGRESSIVE ... will be wetting
FUTURE PERFECT ... will have wet

PAST PASSIVE

—	—
—	—
it was wet	they were wet

* *Once the insulation was wet by the storm, it was useless.*

COMPLEMENTS

wet _____ *moisten, dampen*

OBJECT

The barber always wets **my hair** before he cuts it.
You should wet **the cork** before putting it back in the bottle.
Lightly wet **the metal** with oil so the engine won't smoke.

PASSIVE

The oily pavement had been wet by the mist, making it slippery.

wet _____ *urinate in/on*

OBJECT

The baby always wets **his diaper** at the most inconvenient time.
We will need to change his pajamas; he wet **them** again.
One of the kids wet **the bed**.

PHRASAL VERBS

wet _SEP_ **down** *put water on*

After every game, they wet the infield down.

EXPRESSIONS

wet [one's] whistle *take a drink*

Thirsty? Here's some lemonade for you
to wet your whistle.

PRESENT

I win	we win
you win	you win
he/she/it wins	they win

• *He wins most card games he plays.*

PRESENT PROGRESSIVE

I am winning	we are winning
you are winning	you are winning
he/she/it is winning	they are winning

• *We're winning!*

PAST

I won	we won
you won	you won
he/she/it won	they won

• *I won first place in the math contest.*

PAST PROGRESSIVE

I was winning	we were winning
you were winning	you were winning
he/she/it was winning	they were winning

• *They were winning most of their games.*

PRESENT PERFECT ... have | has won
PAST PERFECT ... had won

FUTURE ... will win
FUTURE PROGRESSIVE ... will be winning
FUTURE PERFECT ... will have won

PAST PASSIVE

I was won	we were won
you were won	you were won
he/she/it was won	they were won

• *The election was won by superior organization.*

COMPLEMENTS

win *be victorious in a contest/competition*
I never win.
They could win if they played their very best.
Who's winning?

win ＿＿ *be victorious in [a contest, competition]*

OBJECT
Alice and Albert won **the dance competition.**
Barack Obama won **the 2008 presidential election.**
Heather always wins **the argument.**

PASSIVE
The game was won in the last minute.

win ＿＿ *receive as the result of a contest/conflict/bet*

OBJECT
We won **a week's vacation in Hawaii.**
After bitter fighting, they finally won **the fortress.**
They hope to win **the Rose Bowl** this year.
I almost won **the jackpot in last week's Lotto.**

INDIRECT OBJECT + DIRECT OBJECT
You could win *yourself* a prize.
The victory won *us* a little more time.
Excellent coaching won *them* the championship.

for PARAPHRASE
You could win **a prize** *for yourself.*
The victory won **a little more time** *for us.*
Excellent coaching won **the championship** *for them.*

win ＿＿ *gain [affection, support, admiration, etc.]*

OBJECT
Ministers have to win **a congregation's respect.**
The comedian won **the audience's applause.**
Their goal was to win **the hearts and minds of the people.**
Faint heart never won **fair lady.** [PROVERB]

PHRASAL VERBS

win out *be finally victorious*
It took six months, but our proposal won out.

win ＿SEP＿ **over** *convert, persuade*
The president won congressional leaders over to his point of view.

PRESENT

I wind	we wind
you wind	you wind
he/she/it winds	they wind

• *The path winds across the hills for miles.*

PRESENT PROGRESSIVE

I am winding	we are winding
you are winding	you are winding
he/she/it is winding	they are winding

• *The press conference is winding down.*

PAST

I wound	we wound
you wound	you wound
he/she/it wound	they wound

• *She wound the cloth around her head.*

PAST PROGRESSIVE

I was winding	we were winding
you were winding	you were winding
he/she/it was winding	they were winding

• *She was winding the clock with a key.*

PRESENT PERFECT ... have | has wound
PAST PERFECT ... had wound

FUTURE ... will wind
FUTURE PROGRESSIVE ... will be winding
FUTURE PERFECT ... will have wound

PAST PASSIVE

I was wound	we were wound
you were wound	you were wound
he/she/it was wound	they were wound

• *The rope was wound around a tree trunk.*

NOTE: The verb *wind*, which rhymes with *kind*, is presented here; its irregular past form *wound* rhymes with *sound*. The regular verb *wind*, which rhymes with *sinned* and means "make out of breath," is rarely used.

COMPLEMENTS

wind _____ coil, move in twists and turns

ADVERB OF PLACE TO/FROM
We wound **in and out through the trees.**
The path wound **around the hill.**
Vines wound **around the old oak tree.**
The river winds **through a maze of canyons.**
The wire wound **across the ceiling and out the window.**

wind _____ wrap, cover by circling

OBJECT + ADVERB OF PLACE TO/FROM
To make an electromagnet, wind **wire** *around an iron core.*
He wound **his shirt** *over his fist* and broke the window.
I wound **the rope** *around my waist* and began to climb down.
She wound **her arms** *around her daughter* and consoled her.

PASSIVE
Her long hair had been wound *into a coil on her head.*

wind _____ tighten the spring of

OBJECT
Did you remember to wind **the clock**?
Wind **the top** and put it on the floor.

PASSIVE
In old cars, the starter was wound by hand.

wind _____ wrap around a center/core

OBJECT + ADVERB OF PLACE TO/FROM
We wound **the videotape** *to where the game started.*
She is winding **the yarn** *into a center-pull ball.*

PASSIVE
The film had been wound *to the end of the reel.*

PHRASAL VERBS

wind along/around/down/up/etc.
twist in a specified direction
The creek winds along for several miles.

wind down *come slowly to an end*
The party was winding down by midnight.

wind down *relax*
Mike was beginning to wind down after a hectic day at work.

wind up *end*
The conference is scheduled to wind up at noon.
The acrobat wound up in the hospital with a broken leg.
They wound up living in Paris for the rest of their lives.

wind _SEP_ **up** *bring to an end*
Let's wind this meeting up, okay?

PRESENT

I wring	we wring
you wring	you wring
he/she/it wrings	they wring

• *He wrings his hands when he's nervous.*

PAST

I wrung	we wrung
you wrung	you wrung
he/she/it wrung	they wrung

• *Betty wrung Alice's hand excitedly.*

PRESENT PERFECT	... have | has wrung
PAST PERFECT	... had wrung

PRESENT PROGRESSIVE

I am wringing	we are wringing
you are wringing	you are wringing
he/she/it is wringing	they are wringing

• *I'm wringing out my soaked trousers.*

PAST PROGRESSIVE

I was wringing	we were wringing
you were wringing	you were wringing
he/she/it was wringing	they were wringing

• *The farmer was wringing the chickens' necks.*

FUTURE	... will wring
FUTURE PROGRESSIVE	... will be wringing
FUTURE PERFECT	... will have wrung

PAST PASSIVE

—	—
—	—
it was wrung	they were wrung

• *The towel was wrung out until it stopped dripping.*

COMPLEMENTS

wring *writhe*

His hands were wringing compulsively.
My hands wrung uncontrollably as we waited for the verdict.

wring _____ *break by twisting forcibly*

OBJECT

Many ancient societies executed criminals by wringing
their necks.
Every Saturday, my grandmother wrung **a chicken's neck**
for Sunday dinner.

PASSIVE

The dancer Isadora Duncan's neck was wrung by her own
scarf in a freak automobile accident.

wring _____ *obtain/extract by exerting pressure*

OBJECT + *from* OBJECT

The police wrung **a confession** *from the suspect.*
The union wrung **new contract terms** *from the company.*

PASSIVE

A few concessions were wrung *from the mayor's office.*

PHRASAL VERBS

wring <u>SEP</u> **out** *squeeze and twist*
to force liquid out of

I wrung the dishcloth out and
wiped the kitchen counter.
Wring out the clothes before you hang them up to dry.
The bathing suits were wrung out and spread on the
patio chairs.

EXPRESSIONS

wring [one's] hands *twist/squeeze*
one's hands in distress

The boss was wringing his hands as he
announced the layoffs.
The widow was wringing her hands and weeping.

PRESENT

I write	we write
you write	you write
he/she/it writes	they write

• He never writes anymore.

PAST

I wrote	we wrote
you wrote	you wrote
he/she/it wrote	they wrote

• Jane Austen wrote Emma before 1816.

PRESENT PERFECT ... have | has written
PAST PERFECT   ... had written

PRESENT PROGRESSIVE

I am writing	we are writing
you are writing	you are writing
he/she/it is writing	they are writing

• I am writing as fast as I can.

PAST PROGRESSIVE

I was writing	we were writing
you were writing	you were writing
he/she/it was writing	they were writing

• He was writing a letter to Georgiana.

FUTURE   ... will write
FUTURE PROGRESSIVE ... will be writing
FUTURE PERFECT   ... will have written

PAST PASSIVE

I was written	we were written
you were written	you were written
he/she/it was written	they were written

• The letter was written to a family friend.

COMPLEMENTS

write *form letters/words with a pen/pencil/etc.*

Please write neatly.
His arthritis made it hard for him to write.

write *compose and send a letter*

People don't write nearly as much as they used to.
I'll write when I have a chance.

write _____ *compose and send [a letter]*

  OBJECT

John and Abigail Adams wrote **each other** frequently.
Senator Blather wrote **his constituents** every three months.

  INDIRECT OBJECT + DIRECT OBJECT

George wrote *Marcia* **a touching letter**.

    tO PARAPHRASE

George wrote **a touching letter** *to Marcia*.

write _____ *compose [a text, work]*

  OBJECT

Donizetti apparently wrote *The Elixir of Love* in three weeks.
Mark Twain wrote **hilariously funny letters to the editor**.
Hilary wrote **poetry** in Ascona one summer.
We are writing **a rebuttal to the biased newspaper article**.

write _____ *put in writing*

  OBJECT

I wrote **a check for $40**.
The doctor wrote **a prescription for an antibiotic**.
Please write **your name and address** in the space provided.

write _____ *express/communicate in written form*

  (OBJECT +) THAT-CLAUSE

Darwin wrote **that species evolve over the course of generations through natural selection**.
He wrote *me* **that they might move back to California**.

  (OBJECT +) WH-CLAUSE

She wrote **how the product should be introduced**.
Sam wrote *his parents* **what he thought of the camp food**.

  DIRECT QUOTATION

"There was never a good war," wrote Benjamin Franklin, **"or a bad peace."**

write (away/off) for _____ *request in writing*

Andy wrote away for the new
seed catalogs.

write _SEP_ down *make a note/record of*

The secretary wrote down everything the boss said.
Gerry wrote the lyrics down while they were still
fresh in his mind.

write _SEP_ in *vote for [someone] by writing [his/her] name in a special place on a ballot*

Every election, someone writes Alfred E. Newman
in for president.

write _SEP_ off *give up on, cancel*

The bank wrote off the $8,000 loan.

write _SEP_ off *consider lost/hopeless/ etc.*

The hotel manager wrote off the missing towels.
Many fans write the Cubs off before September.
Our company had to write off several bad debts
last year.

write _SEP_ off *deduct from one's taxes*

We wrote the computer off as an itemized deduction.

write _SEP_ out *spell out [a number, abbreviation]*

Write out "621" as "six hundred twenty-one."
Be sure to write out all abbreviations.

write _SEP_ up *compose [a text, an article], often from notes*

It will take me two hours to write up the minutes
of the meeting.
Harper finally wrote up his review of the best pizza
restaurants in St. Louis.

write _SEP_ up *prepare a written/printed copy of*

The sales clerk will write your order up.

Irregular Verb Form Index

This index includes all irregular forms of the 188 irregular verbs in this book: the irregular past forms, as well as the irregular third-person singular present forms used by a few verbs.

A form followed by an asterisk (*) is a past form that is spelled like the base form of the verb; except for *read,* the past form is also pronounced like the base form.

am **be** 3
are **be** 3
arisen **arise** 1
arose **arise** 1
ate **eat** 49
awoke **awake** 2
awoken **awake** 2

bade **bid** 17
beat* **beat** 5
beaten **beat** 5
became **become** 6
become* **become** 6
been **be** 3
befallen **befall** 7
befell **befall** 7
began **begin** 9
begat **beget** 8
begot **beget** 8
begotten **beget** 8
begun **begin** 9
beheld **behold** 10
bent **bend** 11
bereft **bereave** 12
beset* **beset** 14
besought **beseech** 13
bestridden **bestride** 15
bestrode **bestride** 15
bet* **bet** 16
bid* **bid** 17
bidden **bid** 17
bit **bite** 19
bitten **bite** 19
bled **bleed** 20
blew **blow** 21
blown **blow** 21
bore **bear** 4
born **bear** 4
borne **bear** 4
bought **buy** 29
bound **bind** 18
bred **breed** 23
broadcast* **broadcast** 25

broke **break** 22
broken **break** 22
brought **bring** 24
built **build** 26
burnt **burn** 27
burst* **burst** 28

came **come** 37
cast* **cast** 30
caught **catch** 31
chid **chide** 32
chidden **chide** 32
chose **choose** 33
chosen **choose** 33
clad **clothe** 36
cleft **cleave** 34
clove **cleave** 34
cloven **cleave** 34
clung **cling** 35
come* **come** 37
cost* **cost** 38
crept **creep** 39
cut* **cut** 40

dealt **deal** 41
did **do** 44
does **do** 44
done **do** 44
dove **dive** 43
drank **drink** 47
drawn **draw** 45
dreamt **dream** 46
drew **draw** 45
driven **drive** 48
drove **drive** 48
drunk **drink** 47
dug **dig** 42

eaten **eat** 49

fallen **fall** 50
fed **feed** 51
fell **fall** 50

ABOUT THE AUTHORS

Mark Lester is an experienced grammarian, ESL expert, and professor emeritus of Eastern Washington University. He was the founding chairperson of the ESL department at the University of Hawaii, considered one of the best ESL programs in the United States. He is the author of more than a dozen books, including *Grammar and Usage in the Classroom,* one of the most widely used college grammar textbooks in the country. Mark obtained a B.A. in Philosophy and English Literature at Pomona College and a Ph.D. in Linguistics from the University of California–Berkeley. He also holds an M.B.A. from the University of Hawaii.

Daniel Franklin and **Terry Yokota** are the producers of McGraw-Hill's *Big Book of Verbs* series and are experts at creating effective language acquisition texts.

Daniel obtained a B.A. in Latin at Eastern Illinois University and did graduate work in linguistics at Harvard University. He is coauthor of four books in the *Big Book of Verbs* series (English, German, Italian, and Latin).

Terry obtained a B.A. and M.A. in Spanish Language and Literature at Washington University in St. Louis. She is coauthor, with Mark and Daniel, of *The Big Book of English Verbs.*

Together, Daniel and Terry have edited and produced references, grammars, and textbooks for learners of Chinese, English, French, Italian, Latin, German, Polish, Russian, and Spanish.